NETWORKING WITH NGOs FOR DEVELOPMENT –INDIAN PERSPECTIVE

NETWORKING WITH NGOs FOR DEVELOPMENT –INDIAN PERSPECTIVE

RAMESHWARI PANDYA

SERIALS PUBLICATIONS
NEW DELHI (INDIA)

First Published - 2006

ISBN: 81-8387-052-X

Published by
SERIALS PUBLICATIONS
4830/24, Prahlad Street, Ansari Road
Darya Ganj, New Delhi-110002 (India)
Phone : 23245225. Fax : 91-11-23272135
E-mail: serials@satyam.net.in

Dedicated

to

My Parents

Contents

Preface

This book has been prepared to serve as a reference book for students taking courses in extension education, adult education, community development programme in agricultural colleges and universities in India. This book is directed to the staff of the universities and trainers of field workers alike. Policy makers, planners, scholars and academicians and field level executors of development programmes, the professional workers in the field who have genuine interest in the task of sustainable development of the community will also be equally benefited from this book. This book is written primarily to meet the Indian situations.

This book has been written in the context of NGO's in present Indian scenario. It presents a critical review of the research work done on various aspects of NGO's through out India, as NGO's are playing very important role in all the conceivable aspects of Nation's Development.

The major development roles ascribed to NGOs are to act as planner, catalyst, mediater, supporter, facilitator of development education. NGO's are primarily preparing the people for a change which is basically an advocacy role.

This book is a result of the work done by different scholars, academicians research workers and change agents. Editor has knitted them together and given it its present form. Issues addressed in this book relates to NGO and women, children, elderly, income generation, disabled, adoption, consumer education, case studies as well as success stories.

NGO's are the ultimate answer to several problems this is clear from the above discussion. In recent years a number of research studies have taken place on the functioning of NGOs their contributions to environment, health, income generation and literacy. However there is still lack of reliable data on different aspects of NGOs.

Different topics are taught in the curriculum of the undergraduate college students who are getting trained as developmental practioners. The idea of writing a book on NGO's came to my mind while teaching these students the subjects like community Health and Recreation, Adult Education and Non–Formal Education. The students get first hand experience in the field during their field work in which they work in collaboration with different NGO's working with different target groups like children, women, aged, handicapped, etc.

We all agree that there is a growing body of knowledge in the social sciences that should have application in the real world. The material in this book is the result of an effort to bring together best information available in literature. However there is still great scope for improving both the selection and the treatment of the subject matter contained here in.

A special feature of this book is the inclusion of name and address of NGO's actively working in Baroda. The cited literature and the bibliography add to its usefulness.

It is sincerely hoped that this book will prove informative and useful both as a text and a reference material.

Here the author has edited several papers theoretical and empirical of eminent scholars from diverse themes so that one can clearly understand how NGOs are contributing to the development of the society.

These papers have been categorized into two groups.

(i) Perspectives

(ii) Empiricals

Rameshwari Pandya, the author of the book in her paper strongly argues about the problems in promotion of Adult Education. However the NGOs are well equipped to tackle these hurdles as over the years they have deviced their own mechanism. The problem of administration maintenance of records, training of functionaries and motivation are such issues which does not arise when NGOs take part in promotion of Adult Education. Leadership, commitment, rapport building, facilities and services, collaboration with other agencies and accountability has given an upper edge to NGO's in comparison to Government agencies. Networking of NGO's and University in promotion of Adult Education can bring the desired result. Reaching out to the community developing new models and varying alternatives have to be evolved having flexibility, diversification, newer techniques and widening of horizons. Important role can be played by Home Scientists in reducing obstacles in Adult Education. Multipurpose nature of Home Scientists is well established this helps them in successfully performing the role of change agents. Interlinking universities and NGOs can help in weaving the strands of Adult Education which will be dream come true.

D. Paul Chawdhry in his paper has presented comprehensive exposition of NGO's situation. The care of orphans, destitute, the handicapped and children with deviated behaviour received care and support from the community–based agencies as well as the government through its health, social welfare, education and child development departments. Post Independent India has observed a tremendous growth in the number of voluntary organizations under the leadership of the Central Social Welfare Board. Different child development programmes maternal and child health services are basic to survival. Realizing this the voluntary agencies were first to undertake on a very limited scale family planning programmes. Nutrition, pre–school child, education, Balwadis and crèches, child play activities, slow learners, gifted children.

With the combined initiative of the Central Social Welfare Board and Indian Council for Child Welfare SOS Children Village Agency set up cottage type new children homes. Thus there is a new turn in orientation of child welfare into a child development programme by the voluntary agencies.

S. Jaya has tried to analyze the situation of NGO's and disabled in India, the status of the girl child and women in general is low compared to the men and in the case of Girls with Disabilities (GWD). The sex ratio for the nation is 933 women per thousand males. The literacy rate of the country is 75.85% for males and 54.16% for females clearly indicating that a large number of women in India are illiterates. This situation only becomes bleaker when women and girls in general are subjected to physical and mental abuse. A few reasons for the dropout may be–child marriage, which is still practiced in few states of the country, child labour and occupation of girl child in domestic household work. In addition, practical problems including mobility, lack of suitable basic facilities such as toilets and perhaps exploitation are found to be contributing factors for this condition.

- Provision of Schemes for the GWDs
- Setting up of Employment–cum–Income Generation–cum–Production Units
- Indira Awaas Yojana (IAY)
- Short Stay Home for Women and Girls
- Mahalir Thittam

Other than these schemes, the Disabled People's International (India) has its own women wing. This wing addresses the issues of girl child with disabilities (GWD) providing them legal guidance and counseling. This wing provides a platform for GWDs to address their issues, needs and concerns. The GWDs encounter the same difficulties like other girl children regarding her basic rights to health service, education and employment. Different issues like Parent Attitude–(a) Over Protection & Neglect the GWD, Socio Cultural Mindset, Physical Abuse, Issues Regarding Marriage, Issues Related to the Maturity of GWDs, Issues Associated with the Type of Disability, Existence of Discrimination Among Siblings, Isolation from the Society–early health intervention, residential facilities in urban areas, specialized vocational training programme, counseling programmes, participation in organizations for persons with disabilities, women wings.

Author has listed–role of the mother, presence of working women's hostels and residential schools, presence of media regarding women's issues, education–the key process, some special efforts by the government and NGOs, light house for blind girls, family counseling centres (FCC). Awareness, support services and counseling programmes for GWDs exist at the macro level. It is recommended that this information, feedback and services be extended at the micro level and in the rural and inaccessible areas in the country.

Poonam Tiwari in her paper "Empowering Women and Bringing Social Change: Intervension by NGO's" has emphsised women are equal and important partners in the process of national development. NGO's have become professional helpers and change agents. NGO's are carrying out different activities of assessing, advocacy, mediating, expert knowledge, informing, suggesting alternative and helping in decision making thus theyhave become appropriate agencies to empower women. Employment and income generation through vocational training by activity networking, upgradition of interventions. Helping in formation of SHGs Orgainsing Health, medical relief and child care activities. Bringing wide spectrum of enlightened legislation and removing one social disability after another. Women in their groups can participate, discuss their collective needs. In doing so community will be sensitized leading to social change.

Asha Patil in her paper has tried to explain how good administration in NGO's can give excellent results. In various fields of national life, non governmental and economic, organizations have played a vital role in social progress. They are the means by which the nation makes full use of its human resources. Being close to the people, it gains confidence and trust of the people. Another important merit as change agents is that voluntary organizations have flexible and pragmatic approach, which help in better implementation of the programme. PVO's have to tackle hardcore development issues and sometimes change over to activities for which administration plays a pivotal role which they had not initially set out to do. Concept of administration, types of administration functions in administration will be planning, organizing, commanding, coordinating, controlling and budgeting.

Administrator must keep in mind to follow the principles of power, responsibility, span of supervision, communication, programme emphasis, organizational structure, investigation, planning and hierarchy. Effective process of administration–regular issues of memoranda by main administrators, continuously receiving support and care from long established relations and members of organizations, obtaining and holding internal organizational unity, quick decision making, rewards to sincere workers, effective coordinators, efficiency in work, maximum utilization of resources, profound proficiency, utility of feedback, accepting challenges for modern society. Administrative Machinery–planning in organization, members of board of an organization, supervisors, the system of programme evaluation, funding agency, management information system. Author further highlights the problems in administration.

Megha Sidhpura & Anuradha Mathu in their paper have highlighted the strength of NGO's in empowering women folk. "Voluntary Action" is an instrument for not only satisfying the needs of the community and solving its difficulties but also practicing in the affairs of the community whether it is social, economic or political and so on. The Five Year Plan that Panchyati Raj Institutions, cooperative societies, Self-Help Groups and VOs could play a paramount role in decentralized democracy and participatory development. VOs are expected to play different role models by executing planners' missions. These are: social mobilization, strengthening SHGs capacities,

Imparting Training for Entrepreneurial Abilities, Sharing managerial experiences with development bureaucracy, ensuring people's active involvement in development efforts, independent monitoring and evaluation. The concept of women empowerment took birth and shook the bureaucracy, political parties, legislature and judiciary. Thus women started with the result that women's issue and problems were debated at various forms of NGOs. This resulted into establishment of National and state commission for women.

Role of NGOs in Empowerment of Women–Involvement of Women in Income Generating Activities, Starting Women's Co–Operatives and Banks, Sensitize Women for Leadership, Promote Health, Promote Child Care Agencies, Providing Counseling Services, Open Functional Literacy Classes, Demystification of Technology and Strengths of Women include–Grass Root Presence, Motivation & Target Group Approach. Authors have made several recommendations. Voluntary agencies should further ensure the participation of poor women in the development process. Emphasis has been laid on important promotion of networking of NGO's and women empowerment.

Sujata Srivastava has given newer perspective of NGO's contribution in irradicting illiteracy. Education and development are closely related. Education is a vital input in human resource development and is an essential component for our country's growth and prosperity. Article 45 of the contribution stipulates that the 'state shall endeavor to provide, within a period of 10 years from the commencement of the constitution, for free and compulsory education for all children until they complete the age of 14 years.'

Since independence there have been number of policy recommendations to achieve universal elementary education. It has been universally accepted that the success of UEE is an important indicator of the social, economic, political and cultural development of any country. However the goals of UEE in India have remained elusive. Numerous factors like wastage and stagnation, problem in girl education, poor infrastructures, poor quality of teaching-learning process, problem of teachers etc have been responsible for this.

In the last decade there has been an increasing involvement of non-government organizations in education. NGOs have played a major role in creating innovation models of teaching, training of teachers, development of text-books and curricular materials, community participation etc. Different measures have been suggested facilitate their on-going work in the area of elementary education.

Sarjoo Patel in her paper has emphasized that Non governmental organizations have become the new hope of development cooperation. NGO's are increasingly assuming tasks which earlier were the domain of government sectors. Added by advances in information and communications technology, NGOs have helped to focus attention on the social and environmental externalities of business activity. NGOs are those organizations which pursue some sort of public interest or public good, rather than individual or commercial interests. One characteristic these diverse organizations share is that their non-profit status means they are not hindered by short-term financial objectives. Non-governmental organizations (NGO's) have played a major role in pushing for sustainable development at the national as well as international level. NGOs can be proud of their contribution to the consolidation of human rights in many Societies, and of their efforts for civil rights and for more efficient local organization with a greater capability to handle conflicts. NGOs also have won great credit by pointing out to government sector deficiencies and weak spots in developmental practice. Without the NGO's pressure and that of their lobby, the cross-sectorial topics of the environment, women and poverty–which are now firmly fixed in development cooperation–would not have entered the international political debate so quickly not have been implemented in projects and programmes. The role of NGOs should be to foster the emergence of a world wide civil Society, the first step towards making globalisation a more democractic affair (Narasaiah, 2003).

"A small body of determined spirits, fired by unquenchable faith in their mission, can alter the course of history". These were the words of Mahatma Gandhi for the committed Voluntary Organizations.

Arnold Toynbee, once commenting on the process of degeneration in our civilization, said that our civilization could be saved by means of proper guidance and commitment by the "creative minority" in which a "selective group" of leaders restrain themselves from corruptive influences, commune with God and return spiritually regenerated to inspire the masses. It is indeed these "Selective Group" of leaders from Voluntary Organizations, which have ever been making sterling contributions to bring about desired changes in society.

Sirimavo Nair has elaborated the importance of collaboration of NGO's in developmental programmes. Population and natural growth has increased to a great extent that it has started affecting the quality and standard of life. The long term impacts are reflected on the health of the general public. Thousands of people migrate to cities majority due to poverty and bad living conditions. Population in rural India grew by 18% whereas in urban it was 31%, during 1991–2004.

The 9th five year plan of India had estimated that urban population will be 605–618 million during 2021–2025. In the past, poverty was assumed to be mainly rural phenomena, owing to its relatively greater magnitude and visibility in comparison to the urban poverty which is largely camouflaged within its rich neighbourhoods. Although the majority of people, in absolute numbers, still live in the rural areas, a large and rapidly growing segment of the population lives in cities. Many of these do so in conditions of extreme poverty, without access to adequate shelther, other basic services and health services.

Various learning experiences from major cities of India like Bangalore, Delhi, Hyderabad, Indore, etc. contributed to varius urban health programs.

Bangalore–NGOs were involved in running UFWC under city cooperation with financial support from government of India and government of Karnataka. In Andhra Pradesh, the volunteers and women's health grouped linked activites which were interrelated and promoted them through NGOs. In Delhi, the NGOs like Mamta and Asha operated with partial support from government, thus enhancing partnership programs. In Indore, the world coordination model involving improving immunization services were made functional. The NGOs coordinated with Muncipal Corporation, health department, ICDS, local traders and community based organizations. In Gujarat, SEWA and SAATH focused on institutional capacities at slum level and created an effective build–up to manage all the development activities.

The following steps are to be born in mind while involving an NGO. They should be able to develop a standard contract. Specifications regarding administrative, technical and financial responsibilities should be defined. The outlines laid should be flexible and feasible. It should be tailor made as to particular requirements of the communities. Reporting should be systematic and accessible. If these guidelines are followed smooth functioning of partnerships between NGOs and government functionaries can be achieved.

Rameshwari Pandya, the author of the book in her empirical paper has examined the role of NGO's in today's changing world. Voluntary associations and community councils are structured groups in which numerous individuals work towards some common objectives. Inhabitants of urban centers may leave traditional patterns and learn to adopt new patterns. Voluntary organizations play an important role in the lives of modern men living and working in an urban environment. In the industrialized cities these associations have flourished without precedents. Self help has been the philosophy of these projects since the beginning. The success of the projects depends almost entirely upon the work of each individual community organizer who had to stimulate guide and sustain the whole process by working with individuals and groups and bring in outside help when needed. The loss of economic, educational, protective and recreational functions of family, neighbourhood community largely contribute to the growth of voluntary associations. Several functions of Voluntary Associations are performed. There are different voluntary agencies working in Baroda. More than 80 per cent of the agencies are involved in economic activities. A detailed analysis of activities, services and projects of the voluntary organizations reveal striking similarities which indicates that they share a common cultural pattern.

Megha Sidhpura & Rameshwari Pandya in their paper have made an attempt to study the different aspects of the NGOs and their problems. This study throws light on the most crucial aspects of the NGOs namely their functioning and beneficiaries. Hence, the findings of the present study will add to the knowledge about the NGOs and their role which they play for the welfare of women *leading to sustainable development.* Profile of the Beneficiaries; Opinions of the Beneficiaries regarding–Programmes, Staff

Members, Timings of the NGOs, Profile of the NGOs, Different Problems, Finance.

To conclude it can be said that NGOs have undertaken many programmes and services through different approaches for the welfare of women. Considering the findings reported by the administrators of the NGOs as well as beneficiaries it can be concluded that NGOs just do not have plans on papers only but in reality they want to improve the status of women. Opinions and improvement found by the beneficiaries suggested that they are very satisfied with the programme and services offered by the NGOs. Therefore, present study implies that NGOs' efforts towards welfare of women are of great success and should be appreciated.

Santosh Tikoo in her paper has given her view how NGO's can help in economic empowerment. Economic Development requires the utilization of wide range of resources that include the four factors of production-land, labour, capital and technology. The challenge before us today is to make the activities performed by women more productive. Availability of finance is an important and limiting factor. Women have to make fuller use of credit facility. So the present study was undertaken to find out the reasons for availing and not availing the credit facility and problems faced by women in obtaining the credit.

A combination of descriptive cum evaluator type of research design was used. A total sample size of 50 (25 borrowers and 25 non-borrowers) was taken. The results showed that all the borrower homemakers were engaged in independent business at small-scale level. Majority of the borrower homemakers were benefited by the loan scheme. The major reasons expressed for borrowing the credit was to purchase the raw material. Data also showed that 45% of the families did not take credit because of the fear of the complications associated with the credit. Majority of the borrower respondents felt that the whole procedure of getting loan was too long. This study shows that better publicity about bank credit facilities for women is needed as many of the women are not aware of these schemes. Orientation and training of bank personnel is also needed to enable them to respond positively to women's needs. NGO'S need the funds for making their functioning more effective.

G. Baradha in her research paper NGO and senior citizens describes the problems of aging like psycho–social problems, feeling of worthlessness, chronic diseases, feeling of tiredness, trouble in sleeping tension and dependency. However in the recent years Government has made different provisions to over come the problems of aging under National Policy on older persons. These provisions are made so that they get Financial Security, Health Care and Nutrition, Education, Shelter, Welfare and Media advocacy so that public is made aware of issues related to ageing. NGO's can play very important role of empowerment of aged both at the individual development (within the people) as well as at Area Development in relation to the living environment. Multiservices by NGO's for senior citizens has following strategies like Networking, Research, Direct Services to Senior

Citizens and Training. The multidisciplinary team approach consisting of the geriatrician, the demograph, the social worker, journalist along with people's participation and NGO's will go a long way to solve the problem of senior citizens.

Sarjoo Patel & Maneesha Shukul in their paper have presented clearly how the society has transformed to a "throw away culture" due to numerous disposable products available in the market which are convenient to handle and cheaper to replace than to repair. This is a great contributor to the increase in the solid waste generation. Much of the solid waste ends up in open dumps. Implications for public health and other problems have been linked to mismanagement of solid wastes. The rising waste is an alarming situation which calls for an effort to reduce the waste generation and to dispose waste in such a way that it facilitates recovery of resources by the way of recyling. There are two NGO's in Baroda city who provide solid waste collection and cleaning facilities in some colonies. They are Baroda Citizens Council and Beautiful Baroda Council. In Baroda most of the colonies appoint their own sweeper for solid waste cleaning. So three colonies were selected purposely, namely Shreenagar Society where Baroda Citizens Council was providing services, Adhyapak Kutir where Beautiful Baroda Council was providing such services and Harkashi Society where the sweeper was appointed by the colony itself. Considering all the above factors the study was designed to find out the solid waste disposal practices followed by the homemaker. The study was a descriptive research. The sample consisted of 120 homemakers 40 each from 3 selected housing societies of Baroda city by systematic random sampling method. Interview schedule was used as an instrument for gathering data. The study revealed that the homemakers from the colonies where solid waste collection and cleaning facilities were provided by outside agencies had good practices and opinion regarding disposal of solid waste as compared with the society which had its own solid waste collection facilities. So these non-government organizations should be encouraged to provide such services wherever the colony sweeper poses problems like irregularity. The colonies where there are no sweeper should be encouraged to approach such agencies which can provide waste collection facilities which is a major problem nowadays.

Nidhi Gupta & Rachel George in their research paper have presented findings how NGO's can be good tool of checking. Consumer is the focal point of all the activities, but they are unorganised. Therefore, the protection of their interest and rights is vital to the general welfare of the people, which is the major goal of the any modern welfare state. Despite development of consumerism, the common consumers feel prey to the exploitation at the hand of services/goods providers. Government has passed a plethora of laws and regulations to protect the interest of the consumers but the existing laws have created more scope for harassment and corruption without providing much relief to the consumers. In order to overcome various limitations in the legislation and implementation machinery, Consumer Protection Act, 1986 is an important piece of legislation in safeguarding the interest of consumers. Various consumer organisations have emerged to shield the interest of the consumers. The role of these consumer organizations is not only to educate and guide the consumers with respect to redressal of complaints, but also to make the consumer movement a reality, through co-ordinated efforts from all angles.

Hence, an attempt has been made in this paper to evaluate the activities of consumer organizations in view of the response of the consumers towards their various activities. The present effort aims at studying the opinion of the consumers about the voluntary consumer organisations. In order to achieve the objectives, both primary and secondary data have been utilized. To analyse the opinion of consumer towards various activities of consumer organisations for protecting their interest, Likert's method of Summated Rating was used to develop the attitude scale. A descriptive research design with survey method was adopted.

However, the distribution of the respondents when analysed by their observed score on the opinion scale classified as per the response categories revealed that none of them exhibited negative opinion about VCO. The opinion of the consumers about VCO was found to correlate positively with age and education. Self policing and collective action are the most important strategies that should be adopted to ensure better consumer protection.

Dipti Oza presents a phenomenological study which was conducted with 50 differently incapacitated adolescent girls who are associated with one or other voluntary organization in Baroda, she describes it is important to understand sex role identity formation as sex is biological determined, where as gender is socially and culturally constructed. Most of the time the term disability is used as a blanket term for impairment disability and handicapped. Notion of self in capacitated individuals is often low. The magnitude of the problem becomes all the more grave if the disabled are girls or women.

It was found that girls were going to different institution and special schools. These girls perceive that they possess certain special qualities. Inspite of perceiving their disability as their weakness and a hurdle in their development they feel that they have got many strengths as well which needs to be strengthened further for their development. These girls at times felt ashamed as they had to be dependent on others, when they could not express themselves properly. The most happy moments of the adolescent girls are winning prizes, praise by the teacher. The exposure "out of house" has helped them to have realistic picture of society and their place in this society.

Reena Bhatia & B. Balakrishnan in their empirical paper "Preservation and Promotion of Crafts: Role of NGOs in Gujarat Case Studies" have presented the empirical findings how different NGO's of Gujarat like SEWA, of Ahmedabad and SHRUJAN of Kutch are providing variety of services to crafts women and customers and helping in preservation and promotion of crafts of Gujarat.

The potential of crafts and craftspeople has brought them forward as skilled entrepreneurs and economic partners in the mainstream economy. Case study of two NGOs dealing with textile crafts in Kutch highlights their role in the promotion and preservation of these crafts.

D. Paul Chawdhry in his paper has given historical overview of development of NGOs in India. Availability of grants–in–aid, introduction of concept of training in social work and men and women from affluent middle class heading voluntary agencies brought in the practice of hiring social workers. Globalization and market economy with all its accompanying effect there is need to establish crèches, day care centres, juvenile delinquency etc.

NIPCCD should take a lead and evolve new methods of training and management of NGOs. Networking of NGOs with schools, aging NGOs is a theory which describes how some of the old NGOs have aged and are in the verge of dying. There was pioneering work done of different NGOs throughout India. Laws enacted for child welfare were made to safeguard children. At the central level different organization assist, guide and coordinate with the voluntary agencies. Gaps in services have been found to fill the lacuna innovative programmes are needed. The author has elaborately described and presented the case study of Nanhi Duniya, Dehradun.

Neerja Jaiswal & Ami Shah in their research paper have presented case studis of different NGOs of Mumbai which are actively engaged in helping people in distress. An attempt has been made in the present research to identify the existing voluntary consumer organizations in the metropolitan city of Mumbai, Maharashtra, and to collect information about their functioning pattern, the activities being carried and the educational programs undertaken by them to empower the consumers at Mumbai. The data were collected by personally interviewing the head of the voluntary consumer organizations on a pretested interview schedule. The in-depth information collected assisted in developing case studies for the selected non-governmental consumer organizations.

Acknowledgments

I am greatful to many people who have contributed significantly to the successful compilation of this book. My gratitude to them cannot be expressed in few lines.

I am also thankful to all the contributors for this edited version. Their quick response has made this work transformed in the shape of this book.

It is my pleasure to offer my sincere loving thanks to all my friends and well wishers who have extended their kind help, encouragement, unforgettable supporting attitude and cheerful company.

1 am thankful to all the administrators, programme officer's and instructors of NGOs for providing necessary information.

I would also like to express my gratitude to all the Faculty members of the Department of Home Science Extension and Communication, Faculty of Home Science, The M. S. University of Baroda, Vadodara. It was a pleasure working with the authors who contributed to this publication.

I cannot express in words, the moral support, inspiration, encouragement, love and never ending help given by my husband Dr. Mahesh Pandya without which this work would not have attained its present format. I would also wish to place in record my affection to my sons Siddharath and Shrikant who spared me from all parental obligations.

At this important moment of life, I wish to remember my parents who had always been an eternal source of inspiration and guidance to me.

Rameshwari Pandya
Baroda

Contributors

Dr. Rameshwari Pandya is Senior Lecturer in the Department of Home Science Extension and Communication, Faculty of Home Science, The M. S. University of Baroda. She is recipient of Leelaben Shah Gold Medal. Her areas of interests are Adult Education and Women Studies. She is the coordinator for Urban Extension Centre "PRAGATI" run by the department. She has published three books along with seven booklets and monographs and has several papers and articles in leading national and international journals. She has also presented papers in several international conferences.

Dr. (Prof.) Paul Chowdhry is former Director of NIPCID which is a premier institute of India. He has been associated with the UNDP/UNFPA/WHO/UNICEF/World Bank Special Programme of Research Development and Research Training. He is M.A., LL.B. and Ph.D. He has held various prestigious positions in the organizations at National and International levels. He has worked extensively in the area of women, children and health. Under his leadership NIPCID had sponsored several community development projects. He is responsible for the design, development and implementation of Training Modules for professionals engaged in self–help initiative. He has published 14 books and many research articles in reputed journals. He has to his credit various honorous and many awards. Residing in Delhi he has traveled almost whole world.

Ms. Poonam Tiwari is Research Associate in the All India Co-ordinated Research Project G.B. P.U. A & T Pantnagar. She has been actively involved in Field Action and outreach projects. She has been actively associated with the programme of community development and planning. She has also undertaken research for multilateral and bilateral donor agencies. Her special areas of focus have been rural, sector, gender, children's rights and education. She has made substantial contribution in the field of non–formal education by developing booklets for rural women. She has given visibility to the rural women of Utaranchal by sharing information about them at number of national and international conferences. Ms. Tiwari has written several articles, in the field of regional development and resource management published in national and international journals.

Dr. Asha S. Patil is a Reader in the Department of Home Science Extension and Communication, Faculty of Home Science, The M.S. University of Baroda, Vadodara. She obtained her M.Sc. and Ph.D. Degree from the same department. She is having 30 years of experience in teaching and research as well as in rural and urban extension for Community Development. She mainly works in the area of Extension Education and Rural Development. She has guided many projects in the Community Development independently, and in collaboration with Government Agencies as well as Voluntary Organisation. She also works with various voluntary and government agencies for the various activities under different projects.

Dr. Anuradha Mathu is a Lecturer in the Department of Home Science Extension and Communication, Faculty of Home Science, The M.S. University of Baroda. She has taught various subjects at U.G. and P.G. level and guided number of projects. Her area of interests are women studies, extension education and women entrepreneurs. She has contributed in several reputed journals. She has written and edited number of books, monographs and booklets. She has conducted several national and state level seminars and workshops.

Dr. Sujata Srivastava is a Sr. lecturer in the Centre of Advanced Study in Education, Department of Education, Faculty of Education and Psychology, The M. S. University of Baroda, Vadodara. She has a doctorate in the area of Educational Administration and Management. Her areas of interest include, Educational Administration and Management, Teacher Education, organizational communication, primary education, Value Education etc. She is presently involved in different projects related to these areas. She is a visiting faculty for 'Faculty of management Studies, M.S.U, where she teaches a course in Business Communication in the MBA regular and MBA evening programmes.

Dr. Sarjoo Patel is Lecturer in The Department of Home Management, Faculty of Home Science, The Maharaja Sayajirao University of Baroda, Vadodara. She has been teaching in the Department since past five years. She has presented papers at National and International level and has published several articles in books and journals. She has completed her M.Sc. and Ph.D. from the same University. She has authored a book "Housing for Family Living".

Dr. Sirimavo Nair graduated from Kerala University with a B.Sc. degree. In 1984, she joined the M.Sc. program offered by M.S. University in Department of Zoology. Her research stints took her to pursue Ph.D. in Human Physiology in 1993. She was a teaching faculty from 1991–94 in the same department. She joined her services in Home Science faculty, Department of Foods and Nutrition in 1999 and is still continuing. During this tenure, she meted out her research stints into public health aspects (Iodine Deficiency Disorders). To her credentials she completed a project from Indian Council of Medical Research in 2004. Further, she went abroad to China for an year to implement a biotechnology program in one of the institutes. She has been a consultant for Iodine Deficiency Disorder programs with UNICEF. To add further, she had good administration skills and served the faculty as teacher supervisor for a period of three years towards benefit of the students, teachers, class III and class IV staffs. In China, she had the opportunity to train 15 Indian staffs and 20 Chinese staffs as per their requirements.

Ms. Megha Sidhpura did her M.Sc. Home Science (Dissertation) under the supervision of Dr. R. Pandya, she received "Prof P.S. Chari" Scholarship for securing 1st position (A Grade) in Jr. M.Sc. Class. She is currently working with "Samvardhan" project of Centre for Environment Education (CEE) Ahmedabad, a national institute, engaged in developing programmes and materials to increase awareness about the environment. She is incharge of material development and documentation. She has actively participated in several National and state level seminars and conferences. She possess a rich experience of field work in the discipline of extension education.

Dr. Santosh Tikoo is currently working as Senior Lecturer at Arya P.G. College, Panipat, Haryana where she teaches Community Resource Management. She has published a couple of papers in the referred journal. She has participated in several national and international seminars and conferences, workshops. She is very actively associated with number of professional organisations in India.

Dr. (Major) G. Baradha is a senior faculty at the Department of Human Development, Avinashilingam Deemed University. She has more then 30 years of experience as a teacher, development practioner planner and researcher. Her areas of specialization are rural development, women in development, women and law and girls education. She has taught and conducted research on a variety of issues. Baradha has several awards to her credit. Best project paper by Tamil Nadu council for science and Technology and India Development Education award in World children summit in 2002. She has published extensively on Child Development, Women and Violence and Reproductive Health.

Prof. Maneesha Shukul is the Head of the Department of Home Management, Faculty of Home Science, The Maharaja Sayajirao University of Baroda, Vadodara. She has been teaching for more than 20 years. Her areas of interest are environment, management, communication etc. She has been guiding several masters and doctoral students. She has been invited as resource person for various workshops and seminars. She has presented papers at National and International level and has published several articles in reputed books and journals. She has authored many books. She has been invited by reputed colleges, schools, voluntary organizations for delivering lectures and giving demonstrations thus has a great contribution in extension work. She has been invited as examiner and as expert on Board of Studies by various universities all over India.

Dr. Nidhi Gupta received her M.Sc in Family Resource Management (FRM) from S.N.D.T. Women's University, Bombay, in 1994. She obtained her Ph.D degree from M.S.University of Baroda, Vadodara, in Jan. 2003. Presently she is working as a senior lecturer in FRM Dept. of Home Science College, Sardar Patel University, Vallabh Vidyanagar, Gujarat. Her research interest includes consumer behaviour studies, environmental studies and ergonomic designing. Many of her papers have been published in national journals. She has successfully completed one research project funded by University Grant Commission (UGC) on generating consumer awareness among rural masses. Presently handling one major project funded by World Bank to generate data base about awareness, attitude and practices of street food handlers and consumers.

Prof. Rachel George is Ex. Dean, College of Home Science, G.B. Pant University of Agriculture and Technology Pant Nagar, Uttranchal. She has an impeccable academic record. She has worked as Extension specialist and coordinated technology transfer project. She has conducted several research projects funded by UGC/DST/ICAR/ICSSR. She is the author or co–author of approximately hundred articles, review papers and book chapters. She has presented papers and chaired several sessions as expert at international conferences in India and Abroad.

Dr. Dipti J. Oza, Reader in Department of Education, Faculty of Education & Pscyhology, The M.S. University of Baroda, Vadodara. She is M.A. (Clinical Psychology), B.Ed., M.Ed. (Guidance & Counselling), Ph.D. (Education), M.B.A. (Human Resource Management) PGDHE. She has designed and successfully launched the course on guidance and counseling in CASE. She has more than 20 years of experience as a teacher, guidance and counselor, researcher and research guide. She has completed eleven major projects, mainly foucssing on primary education, adolescence education, gender, disability and value education. She has contributed on module writing on gender. Presently she is guide to Government of Gujarat for Adolescence Education project.

Dr. Reena Bhatia, Lecturer in the Department of Clothing and Textile in the Faculty of Home Science, The M.S. University of Baroda, Vadodara. She has participated in several national and international seminars / conferences/workshops. She has also published number of research papers and her recent book is "Introduction to Clothing and Textile". She is member of several professional organizations.

Prof. B. Balakrishnaiah is an eminent Home Scientist having a rich teaching and research experience of over 35 years and retired as the head of the Department of Clothing and Textile. He has held various positions in the Home Science Association as well as in the Faculty like Examination Incharge, Dean of Students, Inchrage Dean of Faculty. He has to his credit many presentations and publications.

Dr. Neerja Jaiswal, Lecturer in the Department of Home Management, Faculty of Home Science, did her Graduation in Home Science (Hon) from G.B. Pant University of Agriculture and Technology, Pantnagar, and was conferred with the V.C. Bronze Medal for being one of the best students of the College. Dr. Jaiswal has an overall 17 years of teaching experience to her credit at the Under Graduate and Post Graduate level. Eight students have completed their P.G. Dissertation under her guidance. She has co-edited a monograph on research papers and has co-authored books. She has many research papers to her credit. Dr. Jaiswal has participated as resource person and presented papers in several workshops, seminars and conferences at National and International level. She has been associated as member with various prestigious professional bodies.

Miss Ami Shah a research scholar from the Department of Home Management, Faculty of Home Science, The Maharaja Sayajirao University of Baroda, Vadodara, completed her Post Graduation Degree from the same University. She is presently working with the private sector Industrial Undertaking in the United States of America. She has research work experience of around 5 years.

PART – I
Perspectives

RAMESHWARI PANDYA

1 NGO's: Weaving The Strands of Adult Education

The World Bank's Operational Directive on NGOs defines them as, 'Groups and institutes that are entirely or largely independent of government and characterized primarily by humanitarian or cooperative, rather than commercial objectives'. In the Bank's operational directive, the term NGO is used to refer principally to those private organizations that presents activities to relieve suffering, promote the interest of the poor, protect the environment or undertake community development.

NGOs have certain advantages and disadvantages. Some of them are small, flexible, close to people with good local roots and contacts. They work at grassroot levels in underdeveloped areas. Their sense of purpose and voluntarism along with high values for the development of people enable them to work with the people with their support and participation. Innovation and creativity along with humanness help the NGOs to achieve their social purpose. Many NGOs work to develop people by helping them to become self reliant using the available resources and developing their own competencies. Team work, high quality leadership and committed people who work in rural areas are some of the strengths of NGOs.

In the changing scenario a good number of responsibilities have been handed over to the Non–Government Organizations by the government and by the people to protect the society from the adverse effects that follow the changes to ensure welfare needs and to enable to grow and to develop. Earlier the NGOs were established with the purpose of solving the problems of health, economy, literacy, etc. and to develop the society for national development. In the changing scenario the Non Government Organizations have also started working on the major issue of "Adult Education".

Adult Literacy aims at enabling an individual to read and write short simple sentences and workout sums or calculations. It helps the adult learner to improve the standard of living through participation in various development programmes. Many such programmes have been specially designed to improve the poor and the deprived sections of the society. Due to illiteracy, born ignorance and lack of appropriate skills, they cannot take advantage of these developmental programmes.

The following are some of the most commonly observed inadequacies in the implementation of the programme in the context of development strategy and process:

1. The literacy percentage of the target group is particularly low and the disadvantaged groups were large scale exploitation is prevalent do not effectively participate.
2. There is inadequate motivation among the learners and there is insufficient emphasis on post literacy and follow–up activities.
3. The financial resources for most of the programmes are restricted, therefore, low cost strategies needed to be devised but no effort is taken in that direction.
4. No effort has been made to mobilize technical resources and provide right type of its decentralization.
5. Open learning systems cannot be judged in isolation and inter–departmental and inter–sectoral cooperation and linkage, with other systems are virtually non–existent.
6. There is no feedback or arrangements for monitoring and evaluation.
7. No attention has been paid to the quality and quantity of the instructional material.

The problems in promotion of Adult Education are many but for easy understanding they have been divided into problems related to:

(a) Administrator
(b) Personnel
(c) Facilities and Services

(a) ADMINISTRATOR

1. Lack of Management

Adult Education is a process through which people can attain abilities, skills, knowledge, etc. besides changing their attitude towards life and community. This should not be secured through a rigid system of formalities but through flexible approaches. It is an organized educational activity carried on outside the formal institutions and at convenient times conducive to the participants. The venue, timing, approach, personal, aims and objectives, etc. they are not been fixed in consultation with the participants and community. Programs are not life oriented and they do not create enthusiasm and ensure constructive and whole hearted participation.

The reason being literacy is not merely reading and writing but it should focus on certain skills for improving productivity and citizenship, which is always being lacking in Adult Education programme. It was found that just teaching how to read and write did not arouse motivations for the adults, who became literate could not make use of their literacy skills meaningfully and successfully. Government is allotting money but adult education functionaries are not clear how to use that money to achieve objectives of adult education programme. This requires a kind of orientation for the members towards the aims and objectives of the programme, the strategies of implementation, aspects of monitoring and evaluation, methods and materials, etc.

This important factor in Adult Education Programme is well handled by NGO's as over the years they have deviced their own management structure.

2. Organising Agency

There should be some machinery to co–ordinate and effectively run the Adult Education programme. Instead of different departments and units organizing and supervising the programme, there is no collaboration between these departments. Adult education programme should embrace all kind of educational programme ranging from preschool stage to up and over the aged. So various governmental, semi–governmental, voluntary, etc. organizations should go hand in hand for the development of the people.

Adult education programme can be best run by voluntary agencies because the strength of voluntary agencies lies in their approach and method for motivating people to participate in development process. So their should be proper and thorough check up on the effective utilization of the money sanctioned and personnel appointed.

Various organizing and funding agencies should work in collaboration with each other for the success of Adult Education programme. Schools, colleges, co–operation, municipality, socioeconomic organization, like libraries, sports and arts club, debating societies, women's club, they should be equally vital links in organization of Adult Education Programme.

3. Supervision

There are rare continuous supervisory units for management staff and various functionaries involved in the implementation of the programme by the higher authorities. Continuous supervision of the problem helps to find out various loop holes in the programme and reduces the chances of failure, Supervisors are just a friend and a guide, thus to help whenever necessary, demonstrate occasionally and discuss with worker whole heartedly on various aspects of the programme. There are very few get–togethers of instructors/workers and organizers or project officers which is very important aspect of plan implementation strategy. This will highlight difficulties experienced by the personnel involved in the programme, how they overcome the same, whether the steps are generalisable, what are the steps still left, how best they can be tackled etc. Also the innovations by way of methods, preparation and use of teaching aids, securing public support etc. can be discussed and exchanged.

Supervision is the simplest method of knowing the position in relation to the programme. It is a process which helps in detecting the flaws, assist in decision making and in giving decision to the programme. Obviously, it will be necessary to identity monitoring features and contents. It could take the form of receipt of status information from operating and implementing levels, status appraisal of financial and physical performance as compared to targets, schedules and standards, identification of shortfall, bottlenecks, lagging areas, causes for shortfalls, problems and difficulties and impending shortfalls as well as problem areas. Supervision in NGO's is more open and democratic in nature resulting into healthier organizational climate thus can act as a catalyst in promotion of Adult Education.

4. Maintenance of Records

In order to evaluate the programme, and to improve the planning of future programmes it is important to know what actually happens at the field level. It is the instructor who has the first hand knowledge and experience of what actually happens in the community where the programme is implemented.

The instructor should keep a systematic record, in the form of a daily diary, of what he /she observes in the field, the problems he / she faces, the success the learners achieve, the changes which take place as a result of the adult education programme.

Maintenance of registers and records is very important for any programme. Reports on the activities of the centres have to be sent up to higher authorities of the centres for consolidation and verification. This helps in proper implementation of the projects at national and state levels. Necessary forms have to be prepared in workshops of experts and practitioners so that there is not much waste of energy and funds. The field workers have to be oriented to the filling and maintenance of records and registers. The NGOs do not have red tapism to follow so it becomes very easy for the functionaries to keep the records.

5. Lack of Trained Functionaries

It needs to be recognized, that the performance of the instructor will depend a great deal on the kind of training they are given before and during their work. The training programmes for the instructors would provide them the necessary information, knowledge and skills, but this is completely lacking in Adult Education Programme. Also there are no monthly meetings for mutual learning and sharing of experiences between instructors, supervisors and the project director.

The instructors should however not depend entirely on the training programmes organized by the project. Government functionaries do not take any initiative to get information from the supervisors and from any other source like other educated people in the area, newspapers, radio, government offices, voluntary organizations etc. Training is to be treated as an ongoing activity. The best training one gets is while performing one's job. The instructors should make use of new opportunity to improve their own knowledge and resource. In fact the whole period of instructorship should be seen as a training ground for the young men and women (instructors) to become effective agents of change.

Training situation should be as close as possible to the field and to the realities. Training in Adult Education programme should equip the functionaries with necessary knowledge and skills required for purposeful planning and effective implementation of the programme. It should equip the participants to face possible difficulties in the implementation of the programme. Good training requires effective learning situations which include five major elements viz., teacher, learner, subject matter, teaching aids and facilities or environment and it should provide effective learning experience to the trainees. All the things are lacking in present training situation due to which there is lack of trained functionaries in Adult Education Programme.

Voluntary organizations are special educational institutions working in the field of adult education are encouraged to develop curricula and provide financial assistance for the purpose. The University Colleges and the State Resource Centres can provide useful service in this regard. At the national level, the Directorate of Adult Education, the Indian Adult Education Association and other national specialized agencies can organize workshops for key personnel engaged in curriculum construction with a view to provide general guidelines and orientations.

8. Lack of Motivation

There is no actual willingness and desire among the administrators to attain the objectives of the programme. Training should be imparted among the administrators to educate them so that they are fitted, qualified, proficient in doing their job. It is a known fact that people working in different NGO's are like minded people who are highly motivated and feel for a cause, so they will be able to solve the problem of Adult Education.

9. Corruption

Since long literacy programmes has been run by the government and still number of illiterates are increasing in India. The major reason for this is corruption at every stage of the programme. For literacy programmes funds are allotted by the central government and then it goes to each state, zillah and taluka level. At every level people take up some amount from it and when it comes to real beneficiaries it is very less and because of which illiteracy remains as it is. This is not true in case of NGO's.

10. Centralization of the Programme

India is land of diversities and people in every state have diversified needs and interests. Programmes are planned by higher authorities without considering the needs and interest of the people at the grass roots thus leading to the failure of the programme e.g. if you plan same literacy programme for Kerala and Bihar then obviously programme would be a failure because in Kerala in literacy level is much high in comparison to Bihar where it is very low. NGO's are local and work at grass root level, so this problem is very well taken care by them.

(b) PERSONNEL

Instructor is a key person in Adult Education Programme. He should be asked to bring behavioural changes among the beneficiaries, by evolving the programmes according to various needs, interests and priorities of the learners. There should be supervision at every step of the programme because it may happen that programme is planned successfully but it fails if the instructor fails to play his/her role.

1. Lack of Motivation

The function of a (motivator) Prerak should not be viewed narrowly. He/she is viewed as a leader of a team of Adult Education Programme. He is the person responsible for organization of diverse kinds of post–literacy and continuing education programme. Such a role may often lead him/her to play a mobilizing role in the community–enabling local community to reflect a social, cultural, economic and environmental situation, encouraging them to work together for their betterment and assisting them to establish rapport with person and agencies who can assist in this respect. With this overall perspective the specific functions of a prerak would include:

(a) To run the various activities of Adult Education Programme with the help of volunteers.

(b) Organizing various inter village sports and cultural completion for increasing the motivation among learners.

(c) Willing and interested persons from other village for interactors with development functionaries etc.

(d) To supervise adult education centres.

Major problem lies here is:

1. Functionaries of adult education programme are not well paid for their efforts.
2. Functionaries of adult education programme are not provided with proper training for planning and implementation of the programme.
3. There are no proper transport facilities for the personnels.
4. Lack of education facility for the children of functionaries of Adult Education Programme.
5. Lack of supervision of the Adult Education Programme.
6. Lack of condusive teaching learning environment.
7. Lack of proper course guidelines for the functionaries.
8. Lack of orientation for functionaries.
9. No promotional activities and opportunities for personnel.
10. Lack of professional achievement.
11. No provision of a set incentives such as recognition at public functions, meetings with programme planners/higher authorities etc.

These are some of the major demotivating factors in the functionaries of Adult Education Programme.

2. Lack of Participatory Approach by Personnel

Participatory approach should be used in each and every step of adult education programme right from planning till evaluation. According to modernization theory, participation refers to citizen's involvement in the process of self governance, and is enacted through voting and association with political party mechanisms.

Participation of the beneficiaries in the development process is very necessary for protecting them from deprivation, subjugation and their exploitation by others.

In Adult Education Programme, there is Authoritarionism procedure followed by personnels. They presumed to know better than the others. Due to which they do not take into consideration the needs and interests, of their beneficiaries. Participation would help the beneficiaries to open up and express their needs and interests. Until and unless people feel the program is for them and participate in the program, the program will not be successful.

Due to lack of participation of beneficiaries there is lack of resources both in terms of human and non–human. When people participate in development programs it results into emergence of cooperatives, associations or communities which encourage people to contribute to development of nation.

Due to lack of participation in the programme beneficiaries are not able to develop their skills and abilities to solve their problems by themselves.

Active participation of the committee helps in the preparation and execution of effective development action plans by making assessment of felt needs and constraints of people easier. Besides this it helps in mobilizing resources for effective plan implementation and also reduces the cost of implementation of programme.

3. Lack of Training and Orientation

There is lack of training for functionaries of Adult Education programme towards:

1. Aims and objectives of the programme
2. Strategies of implementation
3. Aspects of monitoring
4. Evaluation of the programme
5. Methods and materials used for teaching the adults
6. Maintaining of records, etc.

4. Lack of Training on How to Organize

The training may be for 4 to 5 weeks with emphasis on theoretical and practical aspects. If the same is arranged at the state level, use of mother tongue as medium of instruction may be preferred. Diverse modern techniques of training have to be used. The trainers, properly selected, need some orientation as to the objectives of the training programme. The Course (Training) Director should arrange a seminar or discussion with all the resource persons to be involved in the training programme. The venue, physical arrangements, facilities for reference material, fieldwork, tabulation and analysis etc. have to be fixed up. If possible, they may be made available to the selected participants so that they come prepared for discussions and are aware of their role in the training process.

5. Lack of Leadership Qualities Among Functionaries

In adult education the learners should inculcate with leadership qualities and should be involved in decision making and develop the ability to form organizations. They should be involved in community welfare programmes. The most important element in adult education programme is leader: He is a key factor in determining whether the learning experience is effective, entertaining, educator and satisfying. His leadership style, what he does, and how he acts, should vary from programme to programme. The materials, physical surroundings, the group members, the programme sponsors, and the particular topic or content will all have their effect. But leader is the key upon his skills and abilities depends the extent to which the members of the group becomes involved, continue in and benefit by the programme.

6. Lack of Training for Preparing Teaching Learning Material

For making any programme successful teaching learning material plays very important role so training should be provided to functionaries on how to carefully identify the factors responsible for increasing the cost of programme and serious efforts made to play the existing wastages e.g. If functionaries are working in health and agriculture area simultaneously then there should be proper management of money in both the areas. It should not happen that one of the programmes fails due to constraints of funds.

7. Language Problem

As we know India is a land of diversified culture and languages. Sometimes in adult education programmes communication gap occurs between functionaries and beneficiaries due to language problem which leads to failure of the programme. Functionaries are not provided with adequate training for local language due to which they are not able to put forth their point in front of beneficiary and so it hinders smooth functioning of the programme. Also due to frequent transfer of functionaries, language is a big problem of Adult Education Programme. This problem does not arise as NGO's have local nature so rapport building is excellent and they do not face this problem at all.

(c) FACILTIIES AND SERVICES

The capacity of the government to meet development needs of their citizen is reduced considerably by the economic constraints arising from the new economic compulsion. Because of large majority being poor an under poverty line the rural development can not be activated by government alone.

1. Road and Transport Facility

The learners have to come from far off distance to attend the programmes. The project officer normally visit the centres in jeep provided under the project. But the poor learners have to come from far off distance for education, where they are not getting proper transport facility. As the villages are not motorable, so it is obvious that they may be left out from regular monitoring by the project and District Offices, unless they make special efforts. NGO's are stationed in the heart of community whether it is urban or rural so it is very convenient to be approached and thus help in promotion of Adult Education.

2. Village Library

In village proper libraries are not available for the learners. The people who have the motivation to learn something they are deprived of that opportunity because of lack of library facility from where they can get the proper learning material. Government and voluntary organization should emphaise on follow up material which beneficiaries can get in the library. Documentation of successful project should be kept in libraries for easy accessibility.

3. Non Availability of Teaching Learning Material

Mostly the centres of adult education do not have enough teaching learning material for educating the beneficiaries. Several handicaps relating to non–availability of many infrastructure facilities can somehow be taken care by if the instructor is a little enterprising and the community is a little interested. However it is difficult to run Adult Education Centres without adequate, relevant and set learning materials available at the centres. To some centres there is a delay in supply of learning materials. Some centres receive the material after the programme has already been conducted. Even though some centres get the learning material they are not adequate.

Recently this trend has been observed that the NGO's, even if they are not very big in structure but they have started developing their own documentation and resource center for promotion of Adult Education.

4. Collaboration with Agencies

Adult education organizations should be well managed by government and non government organization in collaboration with each other. Organization refers to organisation of channel, means, the organisation of male, female, youth and adult according to their interest. This interest could be occupational, recreational and skill related. If the work of adult education undertaken through such organization the participation and involvement of community members increases. People without its organization cannot think or plan to work as a single unit. Voluntary organization used as a link between government bureaucracy. For overall development of population voluntary organization can take up lead in this area and work along with other agencies for promoting adult education programme.

NETWORKING OF NGO'S AND UNVERSITY IN PROMOTION OF ADULT EDUCATION

The widely accepted function of the university is communication of existing and creative activity. If the university succeeds in achieving its basic obligations–communication and extension of knowledge–it creates in the wake of its success two problems; a large number demanding access to the privileges of such education; and a tremendous increase in disciplines creating a stress in the educational activities of the university.

Under the impact of the first, university became 'Massversity' and with the second it became 'Multiversity'. Such a situation created a dilemma for universities and the challenge was met by the new structural type of a university, the Open University and with the curricular process for inter–disciplinary approach.

With the exponential growth of knowledge, specifically in social, physical and biological sciences, synchronizing with increase in the rate of obsolescence of the prevalent knowledge, it has become necessary for the institutions of higher education to ring out the old and ring in the new in their curricular offerings.

Due to the acceptance of democracy as our way of life, educational opportunities are no longer limited to a few urban elite but have to be planned for larger groups of persons of different strata of society and for different regions of the country. In order to reduce inequalities existing in our society, our universities will have to reorganize their structure, content and strategies. They have to reach out to the community and hence new models and varying alternatives have to be evolved with stress on flexibility, diversification, newer techniques and widening of horizons.

Under this conflicting impact, the university will have to perform an evolutionary character. The university has continuously to satisfy the needs of social environment in which it is placed and yet it must not throw away its innate characters as a catalyst of social change. This tight rope progress required adjustment to the society's needs while being an active agent of social change.

The main issues arising out of this new situation require examination of the needs of modern society, whether our education system is capable of meting these needs and in the light of this analysis plan our future strategy and what role university can play in removing obstacles and issues in our Adult Education system.

Universities are the creation of the society and must serve the community of which they are part. Educational system cannot now afford too remain a closed circuit. The function of the university according to modern thinking is to help the social, economic, educational and cultural growth of the community which it serves. That the universities should be closely involved in the life of the society is imperative both for the society and for the universities themselves. The aim of the University Education should not be only to produce mere specialists, rather cultivated men and women needed for the development of the country this can be best done by networking with NGO's and thus helping in weaving the strands of Adult Education.

ROLE OF HOME SCIENTISTS IN REDUCING OBSTACLES IN ADULT EDUCATION

Home scientists are the back bone of all home science extension programmes, since the success of planning and execution of the programmes depend on the quality, excellence and dedication of its workers. Since they perform the role of change agents, it is essential that they have certain required qualities, besides being aware of their role as change agents. Due to multipurpose nature of a home scientists, she can perform various roles in removing obstacles in Adult Education Programme.

1. Home scientists can help to seek the attention of the beneficiaries by establishing rapport with the group, attention of people can be sought through identification of their needs approaching leaders, or conducting bench mark surveys.
2. Home scientists can help by developing interest of beneficiaries towards adult education programme. Interest can be developed by making people aware of their unfelt needs and their solutions.
3. Home scientists can make continuous efforts to bring the group to the level of motivation so that the desire to adopt a new idea on practice is finally expressed.
4. Home scientist can make the people convinced to adopt knowledge of adult education programme.
5. Home scientist can help the people to convert conviction into action. That is, people want to make efforts to adopt a new practice. Here, home scientists job is to make it possible and easy for the group to act.
6. Home scientists can make use of participatory approach for making adult education programme successful by using various teaching learning methods.

7. Home scientists can help in orientation of the beneficiaries which help them to know the importance of adult education programme for them.
8. Home scientists can help in building up confidence level of the learners by making them participate in each and every steps of the programme from planning till implementation and supervision.

BIBLIOGRAPHY

Bhatia, A. (2000), Women's Development and NGO's. Rawat Publication Jaipur and New Delhi.

Singh, M.R. (2000), NGO Snap Shot Janodaya Social Welfare Vol. 47 (6) Sept.

Vadasam K.P. (1997-98), Adult Education Challenges of 21st Century Newsletter of Indian Adult Education Associations Vol. 19 (9–10) Dec–Jan.

The Mission for All: National Literacy Mission. Directorate of Adult Education, GOI, Department of Education, MHRD, New Delhi, 1994.

Mohanty D. (1992), Current Issues in Education New Delhi, Cosmo Publications.

Mishra, N. (1983), "Adult Education Programme: Some Problems", Indian Journal of Adult Education, 44 (12).

Sodhi, T.S. "Adult Education, A Multidisciplinary Approach ed. Bhatia K.K. Katson Publishing House, Ludhiana.

Chathley, Y.P. (1993), Educational Development and Socio–Economic Conditions–A Case Study of Border Areas of Punjab, Man and Development.

Joshi S.T. (1999), Women and Development. The Changing Scenario, Mittal Publications, New Delhi.

V. Rajagopala Rao (1995), First Generation Learner's The Hindu, August.

D. PAUL CHOWDHRY

2 Voluntary Action For Child Development

Child bearing and rearing has been the mother's pride but its care, growth and development has been the responsibility of its family, as the child depends upon the family, particularly the mother for physical, social and emotional support. On the other hand is a source of emotional wellbeing to its family. In this process of child–care, welfare and development outside resources of government, and the community are utilized. This became necessary because of growth of child–care related knowledge through medical and social sciences. Moreover, the care of the orphans, destitute, the handicapped and children with deviant behaviour received care and support from the community–based agencies as well as the government through its health, social welfare, education and child development departments. Thus, whereas the primary responsibility for child development has been that of family, secondary institutions have over the years, taken more and more responsibility in this field.

COMMUNITY ACTION

The concept of community action in the fields of social welfare and development has undergone several changes in terms of their objectives, focus, methods, organization, etc. The quality and quantum of their contribution has been related to social motivation, dedication, state attitude and resources. Thus, several persons and organizations have been contributing for education, health, recreation, and care of vulnerable sections of children with social, physical, mental and emotional handicaps. There are several phrases connected with community action such as 'public cooperation', 'community participation', 'voluntary agencies', 'non–governmental organizations' (NGOs) 'social activits' etc. It is neither possible nor necessary to go into the scope, form, objectives, methods and structure related specifically to child welfare and development agencies.

Although, voluntary action is spontaneous and motivated by dedication, it generally takes a form of an organization for dealing with problems and meeting social needs on a long–term basis. This brings in the elements, like constitution, rules and regulations, registration, financial discipline organizational and administrative structure and sometimes a code of conduct. It will however, not be correct to brand all people's or community based social organizations as NGOs. Strictly speaking in India an NGO really means an organization outside government structure, but may be funded and controlled by the government. In this context the so called autonomous bodies like NIPCCD, NCF and CSWB can be termed as NGOs, as these are neither voluntary nor governmental organizations.

PROMOTION OF VOLUNTARY AGENCIES

After independence, Nehru's government did not deliberately set up a department at the national level for looking after social welfare in general and child welfare in particular. The first five–year plan made a provision for establishment of the Central Social Welfare Board as an autonomous body to guide and promote voluntary agencies. Up to the end of the first plan the Board could identify around 3000 voluntary agencies working for women, children and the handicapped. This number went up to 6000 in the third five–year plan and today their list of aided agencies has stabilized at more than 10,000 voluntary agencies. It was only after 11 years of independence that in 1964 for the first time a department of social security was set up at the centre by Shri Lal Bahadur Shastri's government. Since then departments have not only changed and expanded their area of operation and programmes but also changed their nomenclature to 'social welfare' and then coming down to Social Justice and Women and Child Development.

NATIONAL CHILDREN POLICY

Paragraph 6 of the National Children Policy of 1974 lays down government policy towards voluntary organizations as under:

"The government shall endeavour that adequate resources are provided for child welfare programmes and appropriate schemes are undertaken. At the same time, voluntary organizations engaged in the field of child welfare will continue to have the opportunities to develop either on their own or with state assistance in the field of education, health, recreation and social welfare services. India has a tradition of voluntary action. It shall be the endeavour of the state to encourage and strengthen voluntary action so that state and voluntary effort complement each other. The resources of voluntary organizations, trust charities and religious and other endowments would have to be tapped to the extent possible for promoting and developing child welfare programmes."

HISTORICAL GROWTH OF VOLUNTARY CHILD–CARE AGENCIES

Before independence India had voluntary agencies which could be counted on finger tips. A beginning was made in the nineteenth century by Christian missionaries and ladies of English and Indian affluent families to provide, educational, medical, maternity and welfare services to the destitute and the disabled in several parts of India, particularly in southern states. Another group of agencies were those sponsored and guided by Gandhi. The Kasturba Gandhi National Memorial Trust established a net–work of rural balwadis. Then there were agencies which worked for the welfare of tribal and scheduled caste children like the Harijan Sewak Sangh and the Bhartiya Adimjati Sewak Sangha. The post–independent era saw the rapid growth of voluntary agencies under the leadership of the Central Social Welfare Board. However, official organizations concerned with public cooperation contributed precious little towards promotion of voluntary action.

VIRTUES OF VOLUNTARY AGENCIES

The policy statement in the National Children Policy about the role of voluntary agencies in the fields of child welfare and development was based on a clear understanding of virtues and their contribution over the years. Voluntary agencies being a part of community have nearness to the people needing their support. They are able to take quick decisions at the time of need as they do not suffer from any bureaucratic tangles like the government red tapism. They have the virtues of dedication and human–touch essential for handling children's problems and meeting their needs. However, over the years, these virtues of voluntary agencies have eroded. Their weaknesses are that:

(i) They cannot spread their work in a larger area and fields.

(ii) They have limited resources.

(iii) Grant–in–aid rules have tied their hands and jeopardized their freedom of work and accordingly innovation.

(iv) Appointment of qualified and trained professionals to make the place of voluntary workers has to some extent eroded their human–touch quality.

(v) They have copied government style of functioning of which they are proud.

(vi) Local community is unable to distinguish between government and voluntary agencies work.

SOCPE OF CHILD DEVELOPMENT

Without going into the services of child development, we will limit ourselves to its scope which broadly cover the following major areas:

1. **Child Survival** through family welfare and small family size, MCH services immunization, prevention of respiratory diseases, dehydration, breast–feeding, etc.
2. **Child Growth** refers to quantitative development indicated through weight and height with particular reference to care of low–weight birth babies, food and nutrition.
3. **Child Development** refers to overall and integrated development–physical, mental, social and emotional through food, nutrition, play, education, purposeful interaction with family and the community.
4. **Child Welfare** in providing special services to the destitute disabled, delinquent, working and street children's.
5. **Special Services** for and community awareness towards gifted children and girl child.

MATERNAL AND CHILD HEALTH

Effective MCH services are basic to child survival. In the early days, realizing complete dearth of MCH services affluent, urban ladies made some sporadic efforts in setting up maternity centres in urban areas some of which were later aided by the Central Social Welfare Board. The Kasturba Gandhi, National Memorial Trust helped rural women through *Arogya Kendras* which provides elementary medical and maternity services in rural areas.

This programme was further strengthened and aided by the Central Social Welfare Board, as part of their work in rural areas. In addition, there are good examples of individuals setting up maternity centres. Smt. Kamala Bai Hospet–a child widow initiated a chain of maternity centres in Maharashtra and Madhya Pradesh and is parent body known as Sitabaldi Maternity Hospital at Nagpur. The Andhra Mahila Sabha established bigger centres at Madras and Hyderabad. Late Dr. B.L. Kapoor set up maternity hospitals at Lahore, Ludhiana and Delhi. Dr. Arole's Comprehensive Health project at Jamkhed (Maharashtra), United Planter's Association of India, Voluntary Health Services / Association, CINI, Calcutta and many other substantial contribution in this field apart from useful work done by the Christian missionaries. Thus the voluntary agencies were pioneers in this field too. The Government took sometime to develop their infrastructure, particularly in rural areas.

FAMILY WELFARE

The size of a family has a direct bearing on the survival of mothers and children and their growth and development. Realizing this, the voluntary agencies were the first to undertake on a very limited scale family planning programmes in the fiftees. The Planned Parenthood Association of Bombay under the leadership of late lady Rama Rao took initiative in this direction. This was followed by Family Planning Association of India with branches in states and districts. Col Raina was appointed as the first advisor in the Ministry of Health on Family Planning. Being a dedicated person, he worked very closely with voluntary agencies. Thus the government on one hand linked family planning with their MCH Services and hospitals and on the other provided for funding for promoting voluntary action in family planning, some of whom also trained family planning workers. Unfortunately, Late Sanjay Gandhi's special interest in 1975 in this movement having been politicized, family planning received a set back thereafter.

NUTRITION

Malnutrition coupled with insanitary conditions, early weaning of breast fed–babies, low–weight birth babies, lack of knowledge of nutritional needs and poverty conditions have led to very high rate of infant mortality. Although, the governmental agencies in collaboration with medical colleges took initiative to combat mal–nutrition among mothers and children, yet in the delivery of nutrition services voluntary agencies played equally an important role. Some of these efforts are listed below:

1. **Applied Nutrition Programme** of the Ministry of Community Development through Mahila Mandals.
2. **Mid–day Meals** programme for primary school children.
3. **Balwadi Nutrition** programme implemented through the Indian Council for Child Welfare and the Adamjati Sewak Sangha.
4. **Special Nutrition Programme** for children below six years through local workers.
5. **ICDS** through Mahila Mandals and local honorary Anganwadi Worker with input of nutrition education and community support.
6. **Technical** support of Medical and Home Science Colleges.

PRE–SCHOOL CHILD

Based on the model of rural balwadis of the Kasturba Gandhi National Memorial Trust, the Central Social Welfare Board under the leadership of Dr. (Smt.) Durgabai Deshmukh initiated in 1954 what was then called the scheme of Welfare Extension Projects through Project Implementation Committees consisting of non–official workers in rural and later in urban–slum areas. The focus of these inter–alia was on balwadis for children below five years. In 1961–62 these rural child–care centres were handed over to local Mahila Mandals with partial funding. Most of these centers were either closed or are now struggling to exist.

In the early sixtees, the Indian council for child welfare under the leadership of late Smt. Indira Gandhi initiated with government assistance a programme of limited coverage known as the Demonstrated Projects for Child Welfare Services covering children up to the age of 16 years with focus on Balwadis.

Again, around 1964, the Central Social Welfare Board experimented on development of preschool rural children with the support of their mothers. This scheme known as the Family and Child Welfare run by locally promoted women's organizations covered a limited number of community development blocks. There was a strong input of trained *Bal Sevikas* and *Graha Sevikas*. The Ministry of community Development initiated but did not provide any meaningful support to promote rural balwadis through *Mahila Mandals*.

Thus, by the end of 1972, there was some sprinkling of voluntary effort for the development of pre–school child in rural and urban areas. In the mid seventees the erstwhile Ministry of Social Welfare started a programme of the Integrated Child Development Services (ICDS) through state governments. One of the salient features of this programme was the *Anganwadi Worker* and *Mahila Mandal* who were expected to contribute voluntary effort. *Anganwadi Worker* was conceived as a honorary local women functionary. There was no premium on her educational background. Thus, it was a good beginning of voluntary effort component in a government sponsored and funded programme till the local bureaucracy because of lack of understanding of this very important concept saw Anganwadi Worker as yet another government functionary. This was reflected in their recruitment procedure (through employment exchanges) even from outside the village and project area laying emphasis on educational qualifications, breaking their chain of relationship with Panchayats and Mahila Mandals. This change of image of Anganwadi Worker resulted in promotion of unionism and petering out of their interest in their work, and of discontentment. It is still believed that ICDS had some element of voluntary action but it is unfortunate that lack of appreciation of this concept has taken out its spirit. On the other hand, efforts to entrust some of the ICDS project to NGOs have not been successful.

Another features of ICDS is the cooperation of a large number of academic institutions mostly in the voluntary section. Medical, Home Science and Social Work Colleges who provide support in the areas of health, nutrition, child development, community participation and training. This contribution has not only raised the level of child care intervention, but also reduced to some extent financial burden on ICDS and as its by–product has helped in field–oriented training inputs to their own students at the post–graduate level. The Indian Council for

Child Welfare and many other voluntary agencies gave their full support for training of Anganwadi Workers and Supervisors.

EDUCATION

Traditionally, right from the British period, voluntary agencies have been playing a major role in sharing state responsibility in school education. Thus, preschool education particularly in metropolitan and smaller urban centres has been one of their major contribution. These are called aided and public schools as distinct from government and municipal schools. Admission in pre–school sections of these private schools ensures, by and large, children's admission in primary and higher classes. Several private schools have now sprung up in cities to prepare 2–3 years olds for admission into the so called prestigious public schools.

Thus pre–school child education and development has all along been in the voluntary sector. This has educational developmental, emotional, health and welfare angles. Because of competition in education and vocational system, unfortunately pre–school child is being pushed and pressurized to become part of formal education at a very tender age. Long travels in the bus, heavy school bag, note books, home work, classroom, examination etc. sometimes prove counter–productive and adversely affect child's mental, physical and emotional development. A close look at and study of modern pre–school education called KG will indicate that this system results in cruelty to a growing child. It is pity that we have not realized this. Voluntary agencies are equal partners in this malady.

BALWADIS AND CRECHES

The concept of balwadis is a combination of services under one roof for children up two years called a crèche and a nursery school of kindergarten meant for children from three to five years. This innovation was necessary and useful in Indian rural context where older children took care of young ones particularly in the case of working mothers and where me could not afford to set up two different institutions for 2–3 years and 3–5 years old children.

In the initial stages, a crèche was part of industries which employed women workers but over the years it became part of Balwadis under different schemes. Thus there are very few voluntary agencies in India who run only crèche. Even the reputed organization called the Mobile Creches run a programme similar to a Balwadi.

Voluntary agencies running pre–school programme of different colours and hues are in thousands spread all over the country. It would be difficult to mention their names in the limited space here. Some of the agencies which have worked for a long time for pre–school children and made valuable contribution are the Mobile Creches, Nanhi Dunya, Dehradun, Kishore Dal, Patna, Bal Niketan Sangha, Indore Nutan Bal Shikshan Sangha, Kosbad (Maharashtra) a large number of Bal Mandirs sprung up in almost all cities of Gujarat and parts of Maharashtra. The State Councils for Child Welfare, Lady Irwin College, Delhi, National Institute of Public Cooperation and Child Development, NCERT, Indo–Dutch Project, Hyderabad, CIE Delhi, state branches of Kasturba Gandhi National Memorial Trust, Adimjati Sewak Sangha, Mahila Mandals in some rural development blocks and many others.

Some of the local bodies in metropolitans and public schools run by voluntary agencies have over the years given more attention to their pre–school sections as their catchment area for admission to primary or elementary sections. The primary school teachers have appreciated the contribution of pre–school centres/sections as they prepare them in 3Rs, which traditionally is the responsibility of primary sections.

CHILD PLAY ACTIVITIES

Recreation is an essential activity in the life of a child. It helps in physical, creative and emotional development of a child. It is basically a leisure–time activity which provides education and opportunities of social interaction. In the fiftees one could see a large number of voluntary agencies particularly in Madras (Chennai), Hyderbad, Bangalore and Rajkot organizing play centres, library and cultural activates for children of different age groups. Some agencies started play parks in collaboration with local bodies. However, lack of guidance and space in schools have created problems of children recreation. In urban areas, lack of open space near their homes and high–rise buildings created the need for local agencies giving attention to children recreation as this will also to some extent wean away children from TV addiction. Absence of play area, impact of TV and heavy home work cause great tension both for children and their parents.

The voluntary agencies like Balkanji Bari, the Indian Council for Child Welfare, Bharat Scouts and Guides, YMCA, YWCA and several local organizations like Kishore Dal, Patna, Nanhi Dunya, Dehradun have contributed for children's recreation. Some of them took up innovative projects like holiday homes, Bal Bhawans, reading rooms and libraries, children's theatre and museums. The Central Social Welfare Board assisted several agencies for organizing holiday camps for children during holidays at places not far from their homes like hill stations, sea–side resorts, wild life parks, etc. school buildings were used for this purpose. Bal Bhawans were set up at Delhi, Chandigarh, Digboi Rajkot, Hyderabad and several other places by voluntary agencies. However, it is a pity that voluntary agencies having lost interest in this programme have left a vacuum in child's recreation who are suffering from ill–effects of TV and engaging themselves in such activities which manifest their frustration and tension.

SLOW LEARNERS

The present education system on the one hand, caters to the so called normal (average) children, on the other there are children with some disabilities. Between these two ends of the spectrum are gifted children slow learners or those with scholastic backwardiness. Both these groups are completely outside the education system. The competitive school education system throws out those with normal or average children in a class. There are voluntary agencies handling education of educable mentally retarded children but none for those who may not be toppers but can very well take advantage of education system with some special support and care.

GIFTED CHILDREN

Without going into definition, criteria and methods related to gifted children suffice it to say that families and educational institutions have to take initiative for working with gifted children. Already, a beginning has been made by some voluntary institutions such as Rotary Public School, Gurgaon, Bhartiya Vidya Bhawan, New Delhi, Shanti Niketan, Bolpur, SKH Public School, Mehrauli, Navyug School, NCERT, NIPCCD. There are some known educationists, who have also taken initiative in this regard.

CHILD WELFARE SERVICES

Voluntary agencies run by philanthropists particularly those sponsored by the Christian missions have been providing welfare services to the destitute, orphans and neglected children, primarily providing food and shelter. With the increase in child population almost three times and unemployment, it has not been possible for voluntary agencies to keep pace with growing needs of such children. The State had therefore, to step in, particularly through funding by the CSWB and the departments of Social Welfare (now Women and Child Developments) in setting up children's home also as part of their statutory responsibility. However, the provision of fit–person/institution in the Children's Act (now Juvenile Justice Act) was hardly used to entrust care of destitute, neglected and street children to voluntary agencies who could take care of such children with state assistance. Thus several unfortunate children have languished in state–run institutions without proper development inputs.

This shift of welfare to development approach brought on the fore neo voluntary groups to give proper direction to child welfare programmes. These are:

1. Sponsorship programme of CASP Plan for poor families particularly in slums who are given financial assistance by foreign organizations for meeting not only their children developmental needs but also to strengthen their family's capacity.
2. The Central Social Welfare Board and the Ministry of Social Welfare sponsored schemes of conversion of dormitory types of children's institutions run by voluntary agencies into small family type units with emphasis on home–care, education, recreation and health care of children.
3. With the combined initiative of the Central Social Welfare Board and the Indian Council for Child Welfare in the mid–sixtees SOS Children Villages agency set up cottage type new children homes under the care of house mothers. Although some of younger children found families in India and abroad through adoption, yet older children even in their adulthood could not be properly rehabilitated and continued to cling to SOS Children homes. This created the need for starting youth hostels for some of them. The same situation now exist in the homes run by state governments. Therefore, there is a need for closer look at the role of children institutions run by voluntary and state agencies.
4. The author as consultant to the Home Ministry assisted in establishment of the National Foundation for Communal Harmony–an NGO under the Home Ministry. While preparing the first scheme of the Foundation for rehabilitation of children of victims of communal riots who had suffered from trauma of seeing killing of their parents and siblings and burning of their homes apart from being without any means of subsistence, the author, in view of his experience of child welfare provided for financial assistance to children in families or their kith and kin, rather than being placed in institutions.

Thus, this new approach to the development of destitute children resulted in the following:

(i) Conversion of existing institutions from dormitory structures to family units,

(ii) Financial aid to children in families through sponsorship programme,

(iii) Foster care programme,

(iv) Guardianship placement,

(v) Adoption of children by Indian and foreign parents,

(vi) Restoring neglected children to their families through Child Welfare Boards,

(vii) Strengthening and supporting families to look after their children and to arrange their employment.

Voluntary groups dealing with destitute children have also not made much progress in enlarging the scope of their work because of lack of space, drying up of community resources, lack of trained social workers and inadequate or no state assistance.

Over the years, efforts were made to have a closer look at the development aspects of such unfortunate children most of whom were pushed into institutions because of poverty conditions. Social science researchers both in India and abroad realized that this approach to children was merely charity–oriented with emphasis on efforts to meet their physical needs only if at all possible within the available resources but emotional deprivation created more problems and mental blocks among these children in becoming self–reliant adults with confidence. It was therefore, felt that:

(i) As far as possible institutionalization of poor and destitute children be avoided.

(ii) Efforts should be made to keep children in family environments by strengthening the family.

(iii) If not, family like atmosphere be created in institutions.

(iv) Children be placed in families through, guardianship, foster care, sponsorship and adoption.

ADOPTION

The Hindu Adoptions and Maintenance Act 1956 provides for legal sanction for adoption of children among Hindus but traditionally these provisions related to children within the extended family and adoption was more a parent or father–oriented, rather than as a child welfare measure. Absence of adoption laws concerning other communities has been source of handicap in placing destitute children in families. However, on hearing a public interest petition, the Supreme Court of India laid down guidelines governing adoption of children in India and abroad from institutions. This has resulted in methods of giving recognition or licensing to several types of voluntary agencies in India and abroad concerned with adoption. These are:

(i) Placement agencies in guardianship ultimately leading to adoption in India or aboard through their local adoption laws–around 100 in India and 300 abroad.

(ii) Voluntary Coordinating Agencies consisting of local placement agencies to guide and supervise in adoption, particularly inter–country adoption.

(iii) Scrutinising agencies–Indian Council for Child Welfare and the Indian Council or Social Work.

(iv) Central Adoption Resource Agency (CARA) set up by the Department of Women and Child Development as a registered society for over–seeing the work of voluntary agencies engaged in adoption.

This programme has to some extent reduced the burden on children's institutions apart from placing such children in families in India and abroad. Common civil code at least in the area of adoption may perhaps give further strength to the concept of placing neglected and orphan children in families. This is yet another landmark in the development of children without families. However, there is a need for evaluation and surveillance of these agencies work, particularly those abroad. However, one cannot deny a new turn in orientation of child welfare into a child development programme by the voluntary agencies with the support of Supreme Court of India. Thus though voluntary agencies alone have pioneered and managed programme of adoption, yet there is a feeling around that all agencies are not doing clean job.

DELINQUENT CHILDREN

The State has the responsibility for care, protection, education, training and rehabilitation of delinquent and neglected children under the provisions of the Juvenile Justice Act 1986, which has replaced the Children Act 1960. The neglected children are now looked after by Juvenile Welfare Boards consisting of non–official social workers. The Act also provides that care of such children be entrusted to voluntary agencies. In Maharashtra and Delhi Children Aid Societies shared this responsibility but over the years, the state social welfare departments have completely ignored this with the result that neglected children are deprived of human touch and family type care. The tendency of Juvenile Welfare Board and their probation officers not try to locate and restore such children to their families. This has resulted in juvenile injustice. Lack of efforts to place younger children in adoption is yet another area of further neglect.

DISABLED CHILDREN

Disability among children is of four types–visual, hearing, mental and orthopaedic. In the earlier days treating this as a curse of God, children with mental and physical handicaps were dumped into institutions–some times even with the adults. Moreover, lack of knowledge about causes and treatment of disabilities, children with different types of disabilities were put together. As part of compassion and charitable instinct, they were given only some food sometimes under insanitary conditions. However, over the years, medical and social science research have enabled us to have better understanding of these problems and to deal with children with different disabilities in different surroundings.

The government of India's contribution was only through an appointment of an Education Officer in the Ministry of Education–Shri Lal Advani who himself was visually handicapped to look after disabled children. Thus, till the creation of the Department of Social Welfare the handicapped persons were looked after by voluntary agencies only to the extent of availability of resources, space and technical knowledge, if any. The establishment of the Central Social Welfare Board helped these agencies in their growth and development and gradually improving their services. The Ministry of Social Welfare, through a separate division established for this purpose gave further impetus to welfare services for the disabled. National institutes were established for the visually handicapped at Dehradun, hearing impairment at Bombay, orthopaedics at Calcutta and mentally retarded at Hyderabad apart from the National Institute of Mental and Neuro Sciences of Bangalore. Thakur Hari Prasad Institute of Rehabilitation of Mentally Handicapped, Hyderabad (a voluntary agency at the national level) has done considerable useful work particularly in motivating the government to establish the National Council for Mentally Handicapped, initiating legislation for establishment of National Trust for funding the care of mentally retarded.

Even with all the efforts and funding welfare services for disabled children by the State and the Central Government, the entire field has been in the care of voluntary agencies. Their numbers runs into thousands, spread in different parts of the country, particularly in metropolitans. Some progressive state governments, however, have established institutions of their own, particularly in areas where these services were not available. Several seminars and workshops were organized where experts from the fields of medicine, education, social work, social sciences, Braille code, hearing aids, orthopaedic limbs and appliances, physiotherapy, etc. interacted with voluntary agencies. This helped a great deal in improving their services for the disabled children. The national level voluntary agencies for the blind, deaf, mental retardation and physical handicaps had in the earlier years also contributed for the development in this field but their contribution has become insignifant in the light of the government efforts in recent years.

WORKING CHILD

Working child is a phenomenon in India that on the one hand helps in promoting family arts and crafts on the other it is a product of poverty conditions in larger families in rural areas. In our society, a large number of people earn their living from arts and crafts and children supplement their family income back home in the village. Working children in rural areas are forced to join the ranks of bonded labour and in urban areas those of street children. Despite protests and adverse comments of the international community on child labour, it appears to be difficult, if not impossible, to get rid of this problem immediately. However, a beginning has been made by some voluntary agencies to supplement inputs of education, health and recreation in the life of working child, apart from preventing employment of children under 14 years in hazardous and dangerous occupations through the provisions of Child Labour Act 1986.

Children are employed in glass and bangle factories in Ferozabad (UP), lock manufacturing establishments in Aligarh, brass–ware industry in Muradabad, carpet weaving in Kashmir and Mirzapur, bidi making, cloth printing, match making, crockery industries, rag–picking, etc. Long–term measures would include eradication of poverty and creation of employment for adults, primary education, prevention of rural–urban migration, family planning programmes and implementation of anti child labour laws. A beginning has been made by the Ministry of Labour in assisting selected voluntary agencies for organizing programmes of education, recreation and welfare in addition to providing alternative source of income to families of working children through centres established in Delhi, Bangalore, Ferozabad, Aligarh, Muradabad, Mirzapur, Sivakasi and bidi industry in MP. Names of organizations like NGO Forum for Street Children, Indian Council for Child Welfare, Delhi, Tamil Nadu and Karnataka state councils for child welfare, National Union of Working Women, Chennai, Butterflies and Prayas in Delhi St. Cathedral School Bombay may be mentioned in this connection.

GIRL CHILD

Traditionally a female child was not welcome in a family. Custom of dowry and possible abuse of young girls in their homes and outside, particularly under foreign rule, some of whom were even kidnapped created a gender bias since ages. Custom of Sati, ban on widow–remarriage, keeping the girl children away from education system, Dev Dasi system etc. are some of the deep–rooted maladies which manifest gender discrimination. Health nutrition and recreational needs of girls were completely neglected. The questions of ban on their participation in work outside their home arose out of this bias and over–protection. Purdah system which has been a part of Muslim culture was also adopted by Hindu families. Despite the role of social reformers like Ishwar Chander Vidya Sagar, Raja Ram Mohan Roy, Sir Syed Ahmed Khan, Swami Dayanand Saraswati and Mahatama Gandhi in raising the status of women, family attitude towards girl child did not change.

In the recent times Dr. Muthulakshmi Reddy of Avai Home, Chennai as an MLC in Madras Council Smt. Sarojini Naidu, Maharishi Karve of Poona, Dr. (Mrs.) Durgabai Deshmukh and several others worked as crusader for the cause of women.

Recently research studies have shown that important indicators such as educational, health and social status of women have helped in child survival, and development, International and UN agencies have strongly advocated and suggested measures for raising educational, health, nutritional, recreational and social status of women. Such measures as undertaken in Kerala have helped in maintaining the small size of family.

Establishment of Divisions for Women Development in the Department Women and Child Development and the National Institute of Public Cooperation and Child Development have greatly helped in creating awareness about the needs and problems of girl children through a number of seminars and workshops and brought interested voluntary agencies engaged in women and child development on a common forum in advocacy in favour of girl child. The deliberation of SAARC and UN bodies worldwide have further helped voluntary agencies to initiate special programmes for girl child. Thus even in this field, some of the enlightened voluntary agencies have done pioneering work.

BIBLIOGRAPHY

Chowdhry, D. Paul (4th ed.) (1995), Child Welfare and Development, Atma Ram & Sons, Delhi.

Chowdhry, D. Paul (1988), Inter–country Adoption. ICCW, New Delhi.

Chowdhry, D. Paul (1993), Handbook of Social Welfare, Atma Ram & Sons, Delhi.

Chowdhry, D. Paul (1990), Voluntary Effort in Social Welfare and Development, Siddharth Publishers, New Delhi.

GOI–Indian Constitution.

GOI–Ministry of Social Welfare–National Children Policy–1974.

UN–Convention on the Rights of Child.

GOI–Child related Laws.

a. Juvenile Justice Act 1986.

b. Child Labour Act 1986.

c. Hindu Adoptions and Maintenance Act 1956.

Orphanages and other Institutions Supervisions and Control Act 1962.

d. Foreign Contributions Regulation Act.

NIPCCD – Reports and Publications.

CSWB–Annual Report 1998–99.

Pradip Kumar (1984), Bhowmick 'People's Participation; a conceptual reality. Kurukshetra April.

Mishra (1991), 'Rural Development–the Indian Experience', Kurukshetra March.

Imtiyaz (1997), IRDP "The Review of Contemporary News and Views Vol. II No. A, April.

Dwarkanath (1995), 'Rural Development Policy and Programme Implementation: An Evaluation' Social Action, Oct–Dec. Vol. 45, No. 4.

Dhillon and B.S. Hanssa (1995), 'People's Participation in Rural Development Programme' Kurukshetra, January.

Sanjit (Bumker) Roy (1987), Voluntary Agencies in Development–Their Role Policy and Programme: The Indian Journal of Public Administrative, July–Sept. Vol. XXXII No. 3 New Delhi.

Udaya Bhaskers Reddy (1987), 'Role of voluntary Agencies in Rural Development' The Indian journal of Public Administration, July–Sept, Vol. XXXIII, No. 3 New Delhi.

S. JAYA

3 Efforts to Improve the Educational Status of Girl Child with Disabilities

In India the status of the girl child and women in general is low compared to the men and in the case of Girls with Disabilities (GWD) attainment of any kind of status is an unending process. Due to the cultural setup and the psyche of the nation, women in general are still struggling for their rights. Thus to improve the status of the disabled girls and women, their issues need to be integrated with women's movements that are already working towards the goal of women empowerment. The role of women in the nation plays an important role but is not balanced. To compensate this; it is necessary that they should be placed at the policy planning, decision-making and through implementation levels. Though the status of the girls with disability (GWD) may not be satisfactory, there is a slow and steady progress towards their empowerment.

POPULATION OF FEMALE CHILDREN IN INDIA

The population ratio for men and women clearly indicated that there was less disparity between women (48.26%) and men (51.72%). But these figures are not up to the international standard where the number of women should be more than men. It indicates that the male-female population in the country is almost equal, implicating that the rate of female population is steadily increasing. The sex ratio for the nation is 933 women per thousand males.

LITERACY

The literacy rate of the country is 75.85% for males and 54.16% for females clearly indicating that a large number of women in India are illiterates. In the state wise distribution it was noted that in the states of Uttar Pradesh, Rajasthan and Bihar the literacy rates were low with Bihar accounting for the least with only 33.57% of the female population as literates.

EDUCATIONAL STATUS OF GIRLS WITH DISABILITIES

In the rural areas factors like poverty and illiteracy lead to a lot of misconceptions. Lack of basic medical facilities brings a fear to the minds of the parents who are not aware of the aspects of rehabilitation for persons with disabilities. The kind of less or no provision in the rural areas automatically when linked with the mindset of people, who believe that girls are a burden, only results in bringing the needs of the GWDs as one of the most neglected priorities of the family. Girls' enrollment in secondary education is significantly lower than primary education. This situation only becomes bleaker when women and girls in general are subjected to physical and mental abuse. The disabled girls are also no exception for this kind of abuse. To provide a better understanding about the status of the GWDs, the report highlights basic indicators like health provisions, educational and employment services for the disabled girls and women in comparison with general population.

HEALTH INDICATORS

Integral demographic indicators are the health services for the girl child in the country. India is a country well known for its warmth towards its guests. But this same warmth is not extended for the birth of a girl child. Child infanticide still exists in the country with girl children being a high-risk group. The sex ratio in the country for the total population has improved from 927 in 1991 to 933 in 2001. But the ratio for the age group 0-6 is continuously sliding downwards. According to the National Family and Health Survey (NFHS) the mortality rate was 67.6% (1993-1999). From the infant mortality rate it may be inferred that the medical services require improvement.

EDUCATIONAL INDICATORS

There has been a change in the trend of the education pattern. In recent years, more number of girls are enrolled in schools. Female literacy has improved by 11% compared to 9% increase in case of males during 1991-97 (NSSO). This increase in enrolment is equally disheartening when the dropout figures are noted.

A few Reasons for the Dropout may be:

- Child marriage, which is still practiced in few states of the country.
- Child labour.
- Occupation of girl child in domestic household work.

The literacy rate of the girls in general is low in the country may be because of the belief that a woman is the homemaker and her place is in the home. In 1991 the female literacy rate in the country was 39% and in the year 2001 it was 54%. These figures further fall in the case of tribal population and population residing in rural areas. The

Government of India started the following programmes to educate the female population in the country.

(a) National Literacy Mission for Imparting Functional Literacy.

(b) Universalisation of Elementary Education.

(c) Non-Formal Education.

(d) Total Literacy Campaigns.

These programmes not only cover the rural population but also reach out to the disabled girls residing in rural areas. Initiatives have also been taken by the UGC for improving the higher educational status of women. Gender wise percentage of Children with Disabilities enrolled in schools clearly indicates that the number of disabled boys attending school is 23%, more than the disabled girls. This trend is the same for the general population also. The only noteworthy fact is the disparity in the figures i.e. 61.66% of boys and 38.34% of girls enrolled. Technical and vocational training programmes for persons with disabilities are ample, but these programmes and services are not utilized by even 50% of the disabled girls. This may be due to the cultural setup of the country where the marriage of the girl is the highest priority compared to any kind of vocational or technical training. 35.85% of disabled girls have undergone some form of vocational training. (Source: NCPEDP Survey on Services for the Disabled by NGOs in India.) This low figure may be attributed to two factors. Firstly the socio-cultural setup of the country especially in the rural areas and secondly, women have been mostly employed in cottage industries that do not require any kind of technical training. Disabled women working in cottage industries may have become independent, but they do not utilize their full potential with regard to their empowerment.

Another aspect found during the study was the lack of residential facilities as one important barrier for availing any educational services, as most of the population in India reside in rural areas and most of the schools are located in urban or semi urban areas. Many teachers and volunteers in special schools agree that parents reluctant to send girls, as they are worried that the girls will face problems while commuting from home to school. The need for residential facilities was identified as one of the reasons for low enrolment of girls.

Most of the people in the country belong to rural areas. Therefore mainstreaming of the girls with disabilities has been one of the most welcomed concepts as it appeals to a person's logic. Government of India started the IEDC Programme in 1974. Over the years there has been an increase in the number of disabled students studying in the integrated setup. In the gender wise distribution it was found that enrolment was low among girls compared to boys corresponding with the general trend in education. The participation of girls has considerably improved. 'The share of girls' enrolment has increased from 45.55 per cent in 1995-96 to 46.32 per cent in 1997-98. The gender equity is more than 95 for 21 of the 42 districts and between 85 and 95 in another 16 districts. Alternative schooling is expected to overcome related inequities even in the most educationally backward tribal-dominated districts (Agarwal, 1999). Among the school going girl children, those with disabilities are very low in number. Socio cultural factors may be one of the reasons for this trend. In addition, practical problems including mobility, lack of suitable basic facilities such as toilets and perhaps exploitation are found to be contributing factors for this condition.

PROVISION OF SCHEMES FOR THE GWDS

As far as the provisions and schemes for the GWDs are concerned there are no special schemes. The schemes available for the schedule castes, schedule tribes and for the girl child and those with disabilities in general are extended to GWDs. Socio Economic Programme for the needy destitute and physically handicapped women. The Department of Women and Child Development (DWCD), Ministry of Human Resource Development (MHRD), Government of India sponsors this scheme. Central Social Welfare Board through NGOs implements the scheme. The scheme aims at providing assistance to NGOs to organize vocational training programmes and provides financial assistance to set up income generating activities and provides opportunities to destitute, deserted women, widows and physically handicapped women.

SETTING UP OF EMPLOYMENT-CUM-INCOME GENERATION-CUM-PRODUCTION UNITS

The scheme aims to improve the status of women providing them avenues for training and self-employment opportunities in industrial units. Also proposes to train school dropouts and semi literates, mainly in non-traditional trades like electronics, computer training, garment making, secretarial practice and community health work and assist to set up income generation production units. This scheme is for poor adult women above 18 years residing in rural areas. Women from weaker sections like war widows and physically handicapped women are also eligible to utilize the scheme. This scheme is sponsored by the MHRD under DWCD. The scheme sponsors Balwadi Programmes, Maternity Services, Craft Training Centres, organizing Women's Groups for different activities. The scheme is supported and implemented by DWCD.

INDIRA AWAAS YOJANA (IAY)

This scheme is sponsored and implemented by the Ministry of Rural Areas and Employment. The scheme endeavors to construct dwelling units free of cost, and the allotment of these units is done in the name of the female member or in joint custody of both the husband and wife. This scheme is for the women victims of atrocities, freed bonded laborers, widows, SC/ST households affected by natural calamities, bereaved families of paramilitary servicemen and disabled women.

SHORT STAY HOME FOR WOMEN AND GIRLS

The DWCD, Voluntary Organizations, and Government of National Capital Territory of Delhi implement this scheme. The scheme aspires to provide short-term temporary shelter and care to women/girls in distress. Vocational training is also provided during the short stay with medical and counseling services to help them gain confidence and get back on their feet. This scheme is for girls/women who are victims of mental stress and disturbance, women victimized for dowry, women suffering from incurable diseases and women with physical disabilities.

MAHALIR THITTAM

A programme for the disabled women in the state of Tamil Nadu is called Mahalir Thittam. In this programme women with disabilities are trained. The first phase is aptitude training for the clients. In this stage the client's vocational interest is found out through assessment by an occupational therapist. Arrangements are made to collect the clients medical Certificates. This process goes on for a week. Skill level training is imparted to the clients in the second phase. The total programme is for one month and the clients are given TA and DA Rs. 30 per day. After the training 5 persons are clustered in a group in near proximity. Among them one representative and one catalyst are selected and savings account is opened in their name. Quotation is prepared and the application is given to the District Collector to get Rs. 10,000/- for the whole team under this programme.

Other than these schemes, the Disabled People's International (India) has its own women wing. This wing addresses the issues of girl child with disabilities (GWD) providing them legal guidance and counseling. This wing provides a platform for GWDs to address their issues, needs and concerns.

DIFFICULTIES ENCOUNTERED BY GWDS

Women much more than men carry society's cross on their backs but the cross that disabled women are burdened with all through their lives is much more heavier because of their gender, their disability and their being the most deprived group. The ugliest expressions of gender discrimination are found in the field of disability, frequently cutting across social, economic, political and cultural dimensions. The status of the GWDs is in sync with the status of the girl child in general. The

GWDs encounter the same difficulties like other girl children regarding her basic rights to:

- health service
- education and
- employment

Other than these the disability of the girl child in itself is viewed as a difficulty. Universal response when inquiring about the specific difficulties encountered by the GWDs, was firstly the child is a girl and above that she is disabled. This kind of stereotypical thinking has laid the foundation to a major mental barrier regarding any kind of improvement for the status of GWDs. The three indictors stated above clearly reveal that the status of GWDs is not up to the mark. Interviews with various officials, NGO representatives, parents, teachers and the GWDs themselves shed light on the specific issues concerning the status of GWDs.

ISSUES

Parental Attitude

The first reaction of every parent at the birth of a child with disability is disbelief. Once the reality sinks in, the parents start accepting the situation. If the child is a girl, then in most cases parents react in two typical behavior patterns.

(a) Over Protection

If the parents have some kind of awareness regarding disability and the disability movement, they tend to become over protective about the GWD. This kind of an attitude from the parents leads to the child becoming isolated from the society and at times overly dependent.

(b) Neglect the GWD

Another behavior pattern noted is neglect. The reason for this kind of neglect is the lack of awareness and/or lack of appropriate facilities especially in the rural area adding to helplessness of the parents.

Socio Cultural Mindset

One very significant factor that leads to the negative attitude of parents towards GWDs is the socio cultural mindset in the country. Statistically speaking, India still remains a country with a high preference for male children which is a reason for gender discrimination in the society. This kind of typical attitude and gender preferences when comes face to face with the birth of GWD, the issue is treated as a curse form God. Lack of awareness plays a catalyst role for parents to take drastic measures.

Physical Abuse

Women in general are subjected to some kind of physical abuse. Most of the parents are very strongly concerned regarding the safety of their daughters. Especially, daughters who are mentally retarded are the most vulnerable. They need to be protected and taken care of all the time. The issue of abuse is very sensitive and needs to be handled carefully.

Issues regarding Marriage

One of the chief concerns of the parent is the marriage of their GWD. Most of the parents are of the opinion that once they get their daughter married, they have done their duty. This kind of belief clearly indicates that the parents are more worried about the marriage of the GWD, than any kind of education, rehabilitation or vocational training.

Issues Related to the Maturity of GWDs

Most of the NGO representatives stressed that the Daily Living Skills training was imperative for all GWDs. Once the girls grow up they should take care of their needs by themselves or with least assistance. During the period of puberty the GWD requires counseling and training due to physical changes in the body and psychological changes in their thinking and behavior. As far as the GWDs are concerned, depending on the type of disability, the training programme and counseling are required. i.e. if the girl is visually impaired her skills in daily living should be strong and she can be prepared in advance regarding the changes in her body, whereas the approach for a mentally retarded child will be totally different and should be taught as the need arises.

Issues Associated with the Type of Disability

Other than issues of gender discrimination, poverty, illiteracy and malnutrition, GWDs have certain issues regarding the kind of disability and its rehabilitation. For instance, a visually impaired girl was noted that only after a lot of persuasion her parents sent her to school. She reported that after her Orientation and Mobility training she felt less hesitant to venture out of the house and was more confident regarding her moves and communication with people. Training to move about for a mentally retarded child is different from that of a child with visual impairment.

Existence of Discrimination Among Siblings

Other than gender discrimination GWDs are also subject to sibling discrimination. Many a time, if there is a disabled boy and disabled girl in the same house the education and rehabilitation of the disabled boy is given due importance. Whereas like any women in the country the disabled girl should learn to sacrifice her needs for the betterment of the family. This is because of the attitude of the parents, that the girl is going to get married and go away. It is the boy who is going to earn and take care of the parents in their old age and so his education and rehabilitation is more important.

Isolation from the Society

Due to sibling discrimination from the family and relatives, the GWDs feel isolated from the society too. Most of them feel that if they are not able to be a part of the family, they are also not welcomed by the society.

Due to this, they become hesitant and do not venture out much. It is of prime importance that the parents include the child in family gatherings and make the inclusion of the child smooth in their society. Isolation will lead to problems like depression and loneliness, making the child lose interest in her education.

Early Health Intervention

Most of the times the health and rehabilitation requirements of GWDs are neglected. This is not only due to the cultural mindset but also due to lack of facilities especially in the rural areas. Practically, it may not be possible to have a centre in every block but the placement of the centre may be accessible to most of the local areas and may provide outreach programmes to cover the interior blocks. The need for rehabilitation and health intervention should be placed in the priority list in the case of a GWD.

Residential Facilities in Urban Areas

Most of the GWDs felt that they had to put in a lot of efforts to convince their parents regarding their education. Parents were not happy if the child had to commute from the village to the school in urban areas everyday. To avoid this everyday commuting, the parents did not encourage education of the GWD. Awareness regarding opportunities provided by NIOS, IGNOU and UGC etc., is very less. The presence of residential facilities with the schools or special hostels in the urban areas of the city is indicated as the vital need of the GWDs. Most of the NGOs do provide residential facilities but are always full and over burdened. Thus a need for residential facility is a priority.

Specialized Vocational Training Programme

Most of the vocational courses provided are not very practical for GWDs. A considerable number of vocational programmes for GWDs have been identified but are not available due to lack of facilities or technical support. Some unique programmes like baking and food technology and computer courses are available with NGOs and institutes in urban areas. There is a need to extend such programmes to the rural areas and create awareness about the benefits of such programmes to GWDs.

Counseling Programs

Most of the GWDs were totally unaware of training. There is a need for a vocational counseller to guide them regarding self-employment programmes, government schemes and referral services for placement officers. Other than these services, GWDs expressed that they did not have anyone to talk about problems regarding their puberty. Regarding issues of their marriage, many GWDs said they require guidance and also felt that they will be well prepared to adjust and be integrated with the society if they are able to express themselves. Abuse of girls with disabilities leading to unwanted pregnancies, attempted abortions resulting in health hazards to the girls for no fault of theirs are issues to be addressed. Support of P.D. Act (1995) to get justice to girls and protection to girls under such circumstances through National Trust Act are vital to protect victimized girls with disabilities.

Participation in Organizations for Persons with Disabilities

Women with disabilities felt that they were not given much opportunity to participate in the decision making process of the organizations to which they belonged. This view is more personalized as all the organizations are not alike and all of them have their own protocols and policies. Most of the NGOs agreed that GWDs are marginalized but very clearly made their stand that there is no discrimination in the provision of services. It is up to the beneficiaries and the people in general who are to make optimum use of the services provided.

Women Wings

Most of the GWDs, Volunteers and Social workers felt that there is no platform for GWDs to raise their issues and concerns. They agreed on one aspect that there should be women wings working specifically to know, understand and help in the implementation of rights, address issues and carry out programmes of the GWDs.

POINTS TO PONDER

The status of GWDs in the country may not be very satisfactory. But genuine endeavours are being taken by various NGOs and the government itself. The support from United Nations, the Xth five year plan focusing the female child, and the last Women's World Conference in Beijing have made the GWDs as a highlighted focus group. This attention given to the GWDs reflects the global level efforts being to improve their status. A few issues regarding the GWDs may be looked into and given more thought as to gain a better understanding of their life style and the forces that control them.

ROLE OF THE MOTHER

A mother plays a vital role in her child's life. If the child is disabled, the mother becomes the source of constant support and motivation. In the case of a GWD, the child depends on the mother and thereby makes the mother a very important factor in the rehabilitation of the GWD. The GWD needs her mother's support during her adolescence. In all counseling programmes for GWDs the support and encouragement from the mother is always stressed upon. Therefore it is very important to make the mother of GWDs aware of the responsibilities towards their daughters.

PRESENCE OF WORKING WOMEN'S HOSTELS AND RESIDENTIAL SCHOOLS

Most of the GWDs dropout from school, as they are not able to commute from the rural areas to schools everyday. Many schools do provide residential facilities but most of the times are over crowded and not able to accommodate many students. In some cases the school does provide facilities but the enrolment itself is low.

PRESENCE OF MEDIA REGARDING WOMEN'S ISSUES

Media for ages has been the platform to question various issues. The media has also covered women's issues. But the issues of GWDs have not been highlighted adequately and their achievements also have not been brought to light.

EDUCATION, THE KEY PROCESS

Most of the special schools and general schools agree that along with academics the child should also be encouraged to participate in cultural activities. Participation in such activities with other children helps the CWDs socialize within informal settings. Many GWDs felt that participating in cultural programmes made them feel aesthetically more appealing as a women is always associated with beauty.

SOME SPECIAL EFFORTS BY THE GOVERNMENT AND NGOS

As mentioned earlier, the Janshala Programme started with 80 blocks in eight states. Now it has been expanded to 139 blocks in nine states of the country. This programme was started in collaboration with United Nations and the Government of India by the Ministry of Human Resource Development under the Department of Elementary Education.

LIGHT HOUSE FOR BLIND GIRLS

A girl is noted for physical beauty, bear and rear children, a homemaker and also serve as link for an entire household. When the girl is disabled, her ability to fulfill these roles are questioned. The lighthouse provides her with education and rehabilitation to be successfully included in the society. NGO runs a marriage bureau for persons with disabilities; girls are married from light house. The institute provides training for girls in house keeping and cooking. They are also assisted to gain employment or start their own self-employment units. A GWD walks into the institute as a child and leaves with full confidence of being a good wife, mother and above all a woman.

FAMILY COUNSELING CENTRES (FCC)

The FCCs are sponsored and implemented by the Social Welfare Board and Social Defense Department of Women and Child Development under the Ministry of Human Resource Development. This centre initiates to strengthen social ties thereby promoting a harmonious life for women, men and other members of the family to live together. FCC aims to provide services like crisis intervention, counseling in cases of maladjusted families and referral services to short stay homes.

SCOPE FOR UPSCALLING

- The Anganwadi and ICDs workers in the rural areas need to be made aware of preventive measures regarding disability. An orientation programme in their training module regarding various disabilities and preventive measures is recommended.
- As both Anganwadi and ICDs workers are working in the rural areas inter-linking between them and the disability representing non-governmental and governmental bodies is recommended.
- Parents of GWDs play an integral role in their empowerment of GWDs. Special counseling and awareness programmes regarding education, Rehabilitation and specific issues of GWDs is to be provided. Introducing successful GWDs as role models to parents is a highly recommended approach.
- The case of physical abuse of GWDs being a delicate issue, it is recommended that legal officers who deal with such cases are women.
- The need for residential facilities for GWDs is very clearly highlighted in the study. But on a practical vein it is not possible to have such facilities everywhere. Schools with hostels as in regular education can be initiated to increase enrolment of GWD in schools. Therefore it is recommended that the schools already existing in the rural areas be provided with technical support for the education of GWDs. This may be done with interlinkages of the local NGOs and government programmes working for persons with disabilities at the state level.

- Separate posters, pamphlets and brochures regarding the schemes for GWDs, their issues and rights be produced and circulated.
- Awareness, support services and counseling programmes for GWDs exist at the macro level. It is recommended that this information, feedback and services be extended at the micro level and in the rural and inaccessible areas in the country.

POONAM TIWARI

4 Empowering Women and Bringing Social Change: Interventions By NGO's

It has been realized by all that if we are to compete, develop and survive the most critical resources to rely on are people's talent and energies. For overall development of the society NGOs have been doing lot of good work but still much more needs to be done in India.

Local bodies to be given adequate orientation about the implementation of the whole programme through a number of orientation and training programmes for functionaries. In the modern world which is characterized by a vast array of human achievements in diverse fields of knowledge and action, the instrumentality of NGO as the prime mover of change and development has been established. This assumes significance in view of the redefined goals of development "as widening of people's choices" and consequently the initiation of concrete efforts to bring back "people" at the center of development" to build a new people's world order" (Human Development Report, 1990). Successive Human Development Report (HDR) addressed and examined different human development issues but the HDR, 1995 cautioned the world in a simple far reaching message...

"Human Development, if not engendered is endangered" (HDR, 1995).

This highlights the important and special role the NGOs are expected to play in the next millennium as equal partners in the process of national development.

NGOs assumes significance for two reasons. It is not only a means to achieve development and fulfill other development goals, but also an important aspect for social development itself. NGOs as an instrument of social change and transformation leads to the empowerment of people. These facts therefore, compel a special focus on NGO.

A review of the efforts made so far in policy formulation and planning on training in India indicates that though meticulous planning has been made but some how there is lot of wastage and duplication of efforts of

Government because of lack of co–ordination and networking among the different agencies.

One of the key components to community projects is the active involvement of the local partners and community. The need to reflect on the extent to which local partners and beneficiaries can genuinely participate in determining the direction of development projects has been highlighted by Craig and Porter (1997).

The aims and structure of a submission for funding necessarily outline the activities and enable monitoring against pre–set outcomes. However, if defined too rigidly, these can be restricting when it comes to fostering local initiatives and control which are important in ensuring that a project is responsive to the changing priorities of local people.

NGO's use different methods and materials in bringing about social change. Many case studies and researches have reported that key feature of the method was that all the information which local people required about the perceived problems and its solutions was contained in the "story" and given to the "local people" by NGO staff. The people are usually passive listeners, although drama, role play or songs were sometimes used to reinforce a point. Where questioning technique was used it was as a means of reinforcing a point already made.

Many of these awareness raising sessions were entertaining and enjoyable. The way in which trainers from different NGOs have developed different techniques and adapted it to a variety of different situations indicates that it is becoming embedded in their methodology and will continue to be used beyond one particular project.

The way in which local NGO trainers, especially have adopted different methods and materials at the micro–level of participatory approach leading to local initiatives which extend beyond the scope of a single development project. It has been observed that the use of locally generated case studies have provided an opportunity for NGO trainers to see the benefits of placing the experiences of target group at the center of a training session and using them in a positive manner to bring out the strengths within the group.

The NGO trainers have demonstrated the advantages of active participation by local group, this teaching method can be controlled as it is adaptable and flexible. NGOs have very active role in different programmes of development which are basically participatory, because of this there is increase in confidence, sharing of ideas and example of "good practice" and an increased motivation to develop new methods of working individually and supporting each other.

The importance of NGO as an instrument of change cannot be over emphasized. It has received recognition the world over, both in developing and underdeveloped countries. NGO's act as an tool for social change as they know the needs of the people, both felt and unfelt as well as the local environment where one lives. NGO's because of their strategic position they are able keep abreast themselves of the technologies and non–technological changes that is taking place everyday in the world around. They are easily able to disseminate technology, information about new political decisions regarding any dimension of development it may be health, agriculture, education economic and social problems with a view to involving them fully in solving these problems. This is why in India great importance is being placed on the role of NGO's in development, because we believe that one cannot develop man, but can only help him to develop himself and change. Hence the importance of making man aware of the potential and his role in bringing about the desired development.

Countries from where this term NGO has been imported through UN and international agencies there are either NGOs or public or government agencies. In India over the years, the government has sponsored the establishment of autonomous agencies and these are registered as societies or companies with government control and substantial funding. They are neither government nor voluntary nor autonomous.

Traditional social welfare services covered the needs of widows, destitute and old women through homes, condensed courses, literacy classes, maternity and medical services for women in need. As a matter of fact this effort helped a limited number of women. In the seventies and eighties a movement led by women activists resulted in several legal, economic and organizational steps for women's development. The concept of women empowerment took birth and shook the bureaucracy, political parties, legislature and judiciary. Thus a movement started with the result that women's issues and problems were debated at various forums of NGOs. This resulted in establishment of:

1. National and State Commissions for women.
2. A Division of women's development in the Ministry of HRD.
3. A division for research and training in the National Institute of Public Co–operation and Child Development.
4. Women's studies centres.
5. Women cells as part of police infrastructure.
6. Women legal aids cells in district courts.

A large number of voluntary agencies have in the past worked in the field of women's welfare. In fact this was the only input in women's welfare. Some of these and many new organizations have come up and have taken up various aspects of women development and empowerment. Their areas of work include creation of awareness about women's affairs and problems, reorganizing voluntary effort towards new approach to women's issues.

Voluntary organizations are the most appropriate agencies to empower women. By promoting literacy among rural women and organizing self help groups they are contributing greatly towards empowerment of women. Also some voluntary agencies are exclusively taking up only women's issues.

Role of NGO is preparing the people for a change, which is basically an advocacy role. As a development agency, role of NGOs turns controversial when it assumes that poverty is basically political and people have to be empowered to overcome the riddles of inequality power relations.

NGOs can perform their role effectively only if they collaborate and innovate. An NGO is only an enabler and as and when a society is made self–reliant, role of NGO is shifted to another place where NGO service is required. NGOs are not expected to play the role as political opposition.

No government can build a society. But voluntary action can. They raise consciousness, motivate, articulate and prioritise needs and mobilize social action. Participation and self–reliance provide positive philosophy for development model. NGO has to observe different roles such NGO's covers the entire community development. It combines all the activities related to the promotion of all sided development of communities political, social, cultural and moral improvement. This is because NGO's have their unique properties.

In India, especially from the Seventh Five Year Plan during the mid 1980s, the government not only accepted the NGOs role in social change, but also provided them a substantial funding or economic support. It is well known fact that due to globalization world has become very small and it is changing very rapidly. It is important that people of deprived world too must change and acquire the facility of change. To maintain a healthy balance with the world around people must be ready to accept change.

There is a new trend of change agents who help in facilitating the process of change. This help is now being given by professional helpers or change agents. There is a great problem of soliciting people's participation. In such a situation it is expected that voluntary or non governmental organisations can play a great role in development process and in getting cooperation and participation of the beneficiaries as well.

NGO'S ROLE AS THE CHANGE AGENTS

The NGO's as a change agents play the following activities:

1. **Diagnosing the Value of the Client System's Problems:** The NGO's can easily diagnose the extent of trouble and cause of trouble.

This they can easily do because of their strategic position in the community.

2. **Assessing the Client System's Motivation and Capacity to Change:** NGOs as change agent are able to assess the client's readiness to enter into a helping relationship.
3. **Choosing an Approach type of Helping Role:** The NGO's play multiple helping role in solving problems and bringing social change. They may be:
   1. Mediating and stimulating new connections within the society.
   2. NGO's presents expert knowledge.
   3. NGO's provide strength from within as they have very good rapport with the people.
   4. Providing and creating a special environment.
   5. Giving support during the process of change.

   The "social change" is a long term phenomenon and NGO's have been quite successful in attaining this objective of change and development as they have been working as catalytic agents. The process of change can be well understood by the following details:

1. NGO's help in the process of informing people.
2. They motivate people to adopt innovations.
3. They suggest alternative fields for the needs and resources of the people.
4. They are involved in the decision making ability of the people.
5. They help in bringing permanent improvement in the conditions of the people.
6. NGO's help in developing people's own programme.
7. They help in creating appropriate learning new things.
8. NGO's help in building confidence through action and conviction.

It is much observed phenomena that villagers, particularly resent people from outside, directing them. They argue that they know what is good or bad for their progress. To solve important delicate and sensitive issues we encourage the local leaders to take up the issues in their own hand and design solution to the problems and implement them. This methodology has been adopted very successful by NGOs. NGOs conduct in door to door survey or mass contact. Different educational programmes are conducted like population education, health education, income generation activities, environment education, reproductive health, food and water storage, poverty, lack of understanding and practice of democracy, etc.

It is our observation that there is a need for intensifying local participation and representation in making the programme a success. The NGO functionaries are trained in different techniques of mass contact, rapport building, persuading people and identifying the problems in the local areas and designing solution effectively. For this purpose, there is a need to streamline the programmes of university as well as programmes of NGOs. This helps both the volunteers as well as local people to build up confidence in themselves in realizing their potentialities and use the same for the betterment of the society.

Economic and social development is too complex a sphere to be left to government departments. It is increasingly realized that in the sphere of development, government efforts need to be supplemented with voluntary initiatives. The strength of voluntary agencies lies in their proximity to the people and their sensitivity to the needs of the community.

Economic development demands skilled labourers. But most of the rural women labourer are unskilled and therefore they do not know how to use the assets they get. Social and psychological barriers affecting the participation of work have been torn down. And yet despite the entry of women into male–dominated professions, their status has undergone little real change. Women have changed, the world has not.

As society changes so do the hopes and aspirations of women. A paradigm shift in policy has taken place, women are now seen as main actors in bringing social change whereas earlier they were viewed as mere beneficiaries. The new women's movement should examine the reality of women's lives and the path that they desire. Different strategies can be adopted by NGO's to empower women and bring social change.

Employment and Income Generation

In order to bring about the empowerment of women the NGOs can have awareness generation and vocational training with the objective of making those women self reliant. Awareness camps can be conducted in the villages or slums. Different self–employment, schemes for women, can be promoted by NGO's.

Traditionally, our history and also as depicted in our mythology, women have been the moral force of the society. They have held prime positions in the families and have developed the culture and soul of our Indian civilization. In recent years, the percentage of women beneficiaries in development programmes are increasing. Thus, in self–employing women, the need to train them is also increasing. Women can be successful entrepreneurs and self employed, as women get a higher economic status through self employment. This is the basic requirement for raising their status, otherwise women in labour force, inspite of their contribution to the family income are undervalued. Only women themselves can change this situation. For those women, who would like to remain at home and earn, having self employment opportunities in the home premises will serve the purpose. This self employment promotes the idea of flexible working hours, helping them to work in hours suitable to them and giving them a chance to do something other than household work, which can make the lives of many women pleasant and satisfying.

Since the past three or four decades, employment of women is becoming an important issue at national level in India. This trend has made it more essential for women with potential to develop certain skills, get the right kind of training to join the work–force with full confidence and faith. So only with the help of training, women's earning power can be increased. Training programmes provide training in selected vocations to women with skills which would enable them to earn through self employment.

Major tenents of empowerment can be:

1. Collectivisation
2. Capacity Building
3. Ownership and Control
4. Mediation.

Types of Intervention by NGO's for Empowerment of Women

Initiating, supporting and strengthening economic activities of various kinds is one way which has helped in influencing the socio–economic realities of poor women. There are many types of interventions in this direction which can be initiated to increase income.

1. Activity Networking
2. Upgradation Interventions
3. Generating Better Returns
4. Initiating New Activities

The link between banks and SHGs will bring formal credit within the reach of illiterate and disadvantaged rural women. Such women ordinarily would never have the courage or motivation to approach the portals of a bank.

The success of any empowerment programme depends on the perception of the concerned women folk. Deliverance from poverty and self sufficiency will naturally lead to social empowerment.

SHGs and support from NGOs will inculcate the habit of savings in the minds of women. The credit linkage programmes with the banks have to be expanded still further. The rural women hither to a stranger in the field of decision making, feels the power of decision making in the household and at the community level. The efforts taken by NGO's is yet another mile stone on the path of women's empowerment.

Health, Medical Relief and Child Care

NGO's have been providing health, medical relief and child care programmes in rural and urban slums. They cater to community health programme by providing simple, safe and low cost health kits both preventive and curative. They disseminate information on health, reproductive health and helps in obtaining government health services such as immunization and family welfare services. A major component can be educating mothers in child and health care. Local women should be trained to become community health workers.

The woman, especially the mother, is still the pivot around which the family revolves and it is the family around which the society revolves. Though women's social and economic status is far better today than ever before, we have to trudge the wary way, for miles ahead before we can say that the goal is in sight. We have brought into being a wide spectrum of enlightened legislation in our efforts to remove one social disability after another.

The greatest plus factors are the growing importance given to women's empowerment by increasing awareness among women of their own rights and a great social awakening that women can no longer be treated as second rate citizens. The result has been phenomenal in almost every avenue of employment, what with women vying with men in many vital sectors on equal terms. The momentum of the battle for equality will go on especially through the media of education, social welfare, social awareness, legislation, economic self reliance and on top of all, impelled by the basic reasoning that no society could forge ahead by neglecting half of its population.

In todays society a new type of organisation has emerged in which women are beginning to take an active role to bring about social change within the community. Most of the women at the village level usually have no "economic activity in the formal sense, but work on small income generation projects to supplement their meager resources. Small groups of women can participate in their organizations where they can discuss their collective needs. There will be impact on the community due to this type of groups in many ways. In daily many members in the community will be sentizied and mobilized in such a way that the families will become responsible to bring about social change.

Social services could no longer be provided in a fragmented form. All these services had to be fused together in order to achieve the total welfare of the human person.

REFERENCES

Neera Desai (1985), Indian Women, Changes and Challenges in the International Decade, Popular Prakashan Pvt. Ltd., Bombay.

Maithreyi, K. (1986), "Women's Studies in India", Popular Prakashan Pvt. Ltd., Bombay.

Sharma, A. Chatterji (1986), "The Indian Women's Search for an Identity" Vikas Publishing House, New Delhi.

Dash, I.N. (1993), Women, Family Life and Rural Welfare, Monak Publications, Delhi.

Sinha, A.M. (1993), Women in a Changing Society, Published by Ashish Publishing House, New Delhi.

Govindeppa G.T. (1999), "Rural Women Entrepreneurship Constraints and Strategies" Kurushetra Vol. 48, No. 2, p. 12.

Gopalan, S. (1995), Fourth World Conference on Women–Country Report Department of Women and Child Development, Ministry of Human Resources Development.

Jose Paul and Ajith Kumar (1999), Entrepreneurship Development, Himalaya Publishing House.

Lalitha Rani (1996), Women Entrepreneurs, A.P.H. Publishing Corporation, New Delhi.

K.A. Suresh (1998), "Role of Non–Governmental Organizations in Development" Kurukshetra, Oct. p. 59.

Planning Commission, Government of India. Ninth Five Year Plan, 1997–2000, Vol. II, p. 123.

ASHA PATIL

5 Administration in Voluntary Organizations

INTRODUCTION

In India, today there is a very strong emphasis on the appropriate development of the both urban and rural sectors. Many consider the speedier development of both sectors is the single most important factor, which will contribute to the development and growth of the Indian economy. Even though development is being conducted by a number of organizations like the state, central governments and financial institutions, industrial house and voluntary organizations; yet success has remained uneven and limited. This is largely because of the magnitude of the tasks involved in development. Each organization, whether government of non-government involved in the country's development, is making concentrated efforts through different activities.

In various fields of national life, non governmental and economic organizations have played a vital part in social progress. They are the means by which the nation makes full use of its human resources. They secure the active participation of far more people than the government alone would ever do and should ask for which they are better fitted than statutory bodies. They provide opportunity to individual citizens who cannot fully utilize their potential in their day-to-day life.

THE NON-GOVERNMENT ORGANIZATION

Non-Governmental Organization (NGO) is an organization that is not a part of a government and was not founded by states. NGOs are therefore, typically independent of governments. Although the definition can technically include for-profit corporations, the term is generally restricted to social, cultural, legal, and environmental advocacy groups having goals that are primarily noncommercial. NGO's are usually non-profit organizations that gain at least a portion of their funding from private sources. Because the label "NGO" is considered too broad by some, as it might cover anything that is non-governmental, many NGO's now prefer the term private voluntary organization (PVO).

It is believed that voluntary organizations are those organizations who provides honorary services with the help of their volunteers to the users who mainly belong to the neglected strata of the society and help at the time of natural calamities like drought, flood, famine, epidemic etc. But now a days meaning of voluntary organiztion has significantly changed. Many of the voluntary organizations now have paid workers who are well trained.

Private voluntary organization exist for a variety of purposes, usually to further the economic or social goals of societies. Examples include improving the state of the natural environment, encouraging the observance of human rights, improving the welfare of the disadvantaged, or representing a corporate agenda. However, there is a huge number of such organizations and their goals cover a broad range of PVO and development . Today there is not a single field in which the PVO's have not expanded their arms. They are working in each and every sector with each and every target group. The most common areas in which the PVO's are working are health, education, employment, empowerment, women's issues etc. PVO's are satisfying the need of their clientele by fulfilling the need of present time. The development services as of now are operated largely in the Government and other sectors have remained at the periphery without clear policy enunciation or institutional support. The system so far operated largely on inter-personal mode without planned and optimum utilization of human resource development and information support and with low level of involvement of beneficiaries in the efforts at technology development and dissemination. Therefore, private service in the process of transfer of technology is found to be inescapable to provide and alternate and at the same complimentary strategy.

EXISTENCE OF PRIVATE VOLUNTARY ORGANIZATION

The Seventh Five Year Plan recognized the limitation of Government functionaries as change-agents and invited voluntary organization to play an important part in national development. The voluntary organizations working in rural areas also have the advantages of better knowledge of the areas and its problems; felt needs of the local people. Being close to the people, it gains confidence and trust of the people. Another important merit as change agents is that voluntary organizations have flexible and pragmatic approach, which help in better implementation of the programme. PVO's have limited areas of operation, limited infrastructure and staff strength, paucity of funds and sometimes they have fallen apart the departure of dynamic leader/ founder. In the recent years its role is increasingly being recognized in the process of generation, verification, validation, refinement and promotion of technology, especially for areas with harsher environments and anthropological constraints. Normally, the PVO's adopt a multifunctional approach, which arises form a deeper understanding of their clients because of a close physical proximity to the people they intend to serve. In their area of operation, dedicated and disciplined personnel with a missionary zeal are some of the facets, which have been responsible for their success.

Thus, voluntary bodies have role in creating a welfare state. Their continued action is vitally necessary for their survival and growth. Large numbers of people have to take an active part in shaping their administration their affairs for development of the society. The more widespread voluntary activity is, the better it is for society as a whole, because progress in one aspect of national life affects and is affected by others.

The present day scenario of the PVO's can be identified with three major streams the 'grass root groups' with occupational similarity, e.g. tribal, harijans, the socially outcaste; and the well established 'professionalized groups' dealing with complex social processes using specialized technical knowledge. The third recent emergence of category known as 'consulting and support PVO's, which provide consultation and support service to the PVO.

Earlier PVO arose as an answer to the problems posed by development in the post-independent era, but now they are more need–based. To be able to survive in the mainstream, PVO's have to tackle hardcore development issues and sometimes change over to activities for which administration plays a pivotal role which they had not initially set out to do. Thus several PVO's have achieved sectorial successes through proper and perfect administration practices. Success stories in each state and region are interface with problems of survival, stagnation and sustainability.

CONCEPT OF ADMINISTRATION

The word Administration means management of affairs or taking care of the people of the unit to good performance and duties with responsibilities.

Administration was defined by William Newman (1956) as guidance leadership and control of the efforts of a group of individuals towards some common goals.

According to Dahama (1985), the essence of administration is the ability of the administrator to plan large projects. He further adds that administration is to keep the organization functioning smoothly and efficiently to achieve the agreed upon objectives well within the allotment of personnel time and resources available without doing all the work himself.

Administration concerns with What, How and When of the affairs. The 'What' is the content, the technical knowledge of the field which enables the administrators to perform their duties regarding the programme the 'How' is the technique of management, the principle according to which the programme are implemented successfully. The 'When' plays the important role in administrations. It is the time and duration which begins and complete the work so all three are necessary for administration.

The administration also includes the actions from head down to that of the lowest person in the unit. Getzel (1960) from Midwest administration centres claims that administration may be conceived of "structurally as the hierarchy of subordinate-superordinate relationship within a social system. This relationship is the focus for allocating and integrating roles and facilities in order to achieve goals".

TYPES OF ADMINISTRATION

The administration may be categorized into public administration and private administration. When the affairs of the people are managed by private individuals, it is called private administration and when it is done by the government it is called public administration. According Luther Gullick (1997), public administration is that part of the science of administration which has to do with Government and thus concern itself primarily with the executive branch where the work of Government is done. Simons says that public administration in common usage is the activities of the executive provides of the Nation, State of Local Government.

In the private administration the functions and responsibilities to get work done remains with a group of individuals who have organized the unit through their own efforts. These individuals are responsible for taking decisions, making policies, accordingly with other units as and when necessary, planning, controlling the actions required for execution and evaluating for checking the development undertaken by them.

Private organization is non political. The rules and precedents as well as financial aspects decision taken as per the boards of directors and trustee which will be less bothering about the uniformity to particular category. But it is observed that since past few years the budgetary practices of PVO have increasingly influenced the public administration.

The voluntary organization has been becoming more creative and active in the efforts to match themselves with current changing conditions of the societies. Voluntary organization is more of the social sciences. It concerns mainly with human development and thus it relates the behaviour of human beings.

Administration in voluntary organizations is a normative science as it deals with, what is and what should be. The present conditions may be lacking which needs to be changed and improved into better condition. It is the administration of certain achiever which brings the desired and positive changes. Thus, it is normative science.

Dahama has mentioned the differences between private administration and public administration. (a) Public administration is bureaucratic and private administration is business-like. (b) Public administration is political while private administration is non-political. (c) Public administration is characterized by red-tape while private administration is free from it. (d) In conformity with rules and precedents, public administration must be uniform in its application to individuals and classes and must not show preference for, or discrimination against them. (e) In public administration, finance is in the hands of the legislature while in private administration finance is in the hands of few individuals. (f) Public administration is more closely regulated by law and rules than private administration.

FUNCTIONS IN ADMINISTRATION

The Administration authorities have these functions: Executive, Legislative and Judicial. Every function has its own department of section running the department involves various functions. These functions become the administration in the organizations. The principal functions of Administration will be planning, organizing, commanding, coordinating, controlling and budgeting.

PLATFORM FOR ADMINISTRATION

It is believed that administration will be effective only when the principles of administration are followed. These principles assist the administration in guiding the administrative affairs. Thus, administrator is able to perform his tasks successfully. Therefore, an administrator must keep in mind to follow the principles given below.

Principle of Power

Effective administration will occur only when a person or individual who undertakes the responsibility of administration may receive adequate power to administer the work. The power and the responsibility should be clearly defined and understood by all those who have been involved in the work.

Principle of Responsibility

Only responsibility given to the individual will not serve the purpose of the administration. It requires in proportion the authority to take the required decisions and actions in administration. Therefore, it is very essential that the persons in-charge of an administration are given the responsibilities with authority which helps and supports them to take the decisions and actions as per the situations exist and it helps in effective administration. Responsibility without authority is just like asking individual to climb up stiff hill without any instrument or support.

Principle of Span of Supervision

It relates with the control one needs to supervise the number of the subordinates. It differs in administration in various organizations and agencies as the span of control is influenced by various factors such as leadership qualities, experience of an administrator and the types of activities related to problems undertaken.

Dahama has expressed the following factors influencing the span of control.

(a) The intensity and frequency of the need to see the chief.

(b) The magnitude of their problem.

(c) The age of the agency.

(d) The professional competence and length of service of the staff.

(e) The size of the agency.

(f) The size of the geographic area in which the supervisor must operate.

(g) The importance of the decisions which the supervisor must make.

(h) The degree of control that must be exercised.

(i) The degree of repetitiveness of the work to be done.

The span of supervision also allows decentralization of decision making as is required. The decision taken allows the proper smooth flow of work which helps achieving objectives set by an organization. The efficiency and effectiveness through initiation of the efforts is maintained for successful results.

Principle of Communication

The reactions and opinions of the subordinate help an administrator in decision making process. It also helps in designing, planning and modifying the plans of work and structures in institution. Communication helps in interactions and in deciding the strategies of work and there by in smooth functioning of organization.

In organization there is vertical and horizontal ways of communication. Thus, communication helps in understanding and accepting goals and responsibilities assigned with the power and function to each individual in an organization. With proper communication it becomes easier to follow the work. Without communication it is difficult for individuals to work, as they always remain with confusion and their morale and commitments towards the function remain low.

Principle of Programme Emphasis

Organizations plan various programmes for various groups of clientele. Every programme differs in the content and nature and thus activities planned also varies.The programmes can no longer remain fixed or static. As per needs of the clientele and situations, the programmes need to be altered and modified. Therefore, the emphasis in programme also changes and they differ from group to group. The staff need to be oriented as per programmes and emphasis on certain areas/issues.

Principle of Organizational Structure

Changes in organization occur as and when it is required by the organization itself. The demands and needs expressed by society always being noticed by organizations. The same is reflected in terms of changing objectives and areas of focus. Thus, there are changes in the objectives set for undertaking the work as well as in size of staff and their skills and abilities needed to do the work under the project. Thus, it affects the professional relationship of staff who are involved in the planning and executing the work undertaken by the institution. Similarly, these programmes based on the short and small scale as well long and large scale, those require different number of personnel and varied amount of funds. These are the adjustments required in the form of administrative organizational structure.

Principle of Investigation

Data of the related issues are required for planning in any organization. Therefore, an enquiry for collecting facts about the clientele, about the situation and related areas is essential. This necessarily becomes the sound platform for what has to be done. It is required to visualize the future plan of the activities of programme in the light of the facts collected though inquiry. Those facts will be so arranged in a manner that they make well profound articulated plan.

Principle of Planning

Organizations and institutions requires appropriate visualization i.e. appropriate forecasting which is the base of sound and perfect planning. Both the components, human as well as material should be properly organized so that they can be easily put into action. Thus, the process of planning also is of prime importance. Planning further ensures the human and material order which is easier to follow and which provides logic for the process and action. Command on the organization of human and material is possible and easier due to planning. This also assists in making and supplying materials and human source to various departments in time in order to make work effective and to pursue the goal of institution/organization.

Principle of Hierarchy

It is an arrangement or classification of things according to relative importance to each individual ranked. It is a system in which every individual is ranked one above the other according to the authority assigned to him or the status given to him in terms of responsibility. This helps in making individuals conscious and responsible about the duties and work assigned to them.

ACTIONS IN ADMINISTRATION

An Administration includes actions by the staff involved in the organizations to achieve goals framed by them.

Luther Gullick indicated the letters of the word POSDCORB functional elements included in administration.

The POSDCORB is consisted of the first letter of the following functions:

P –Stands for *Planning* i.e., working out in broad outlines, the things to be done and the methods to be adopted for accomplishing the purpose in hand.

O –Stands for *Organization,* i.e., building up the structure of authority through which the entire work to be done is arranged into well defined sub-division and coordination.

S –Stands for *Staffing*, i.e., appointing suitable persons to various posts under the organization and the whole of personnel management.

D –Stands for *Directing*, i.e., making decisions, issuing orders and instructions for the guidance of the staff.

CO–Stands for *Coordination*, i.e., interrelating various parts of the work and eliminating overlapping and conflict.

R –Stands for *Reporting*, i.e., keeping both the superiors and subordinates informed of what is going on, and arranging for the collection of such information through inspection, research and records.

B –Stands for *Budgeting*, which is more concerned with the financial affairs of the organization or formal administration.

These actions should be taken up by all the organizations working for human being as these are common to all fields of administration.

EFFECTIVE PROCESS OF ADMINISTRATION

Regular Issues of Memoranda By Main Administrators

This would help the administrative staff to get acquainted with the current theme and concern of the organization for development. This will help to progress more and more further. There are various means to communicate to others such as circular letters, notice boards or formal report. These help to keep people informed about policies, rules, programmes, events and all other activities planned in an organization. It is a better practice which makes every staff to follow instructions laid down for handling routine work regularly.

Continuously Receiving Support and Care From Long Established Relations and Members of Organizaions

Successful work towards achievement of objective will rely on the support and care from relation and members of organization who always stand in all situations for the fair, clean and perfect administration. It supports also in avoiding unbearable consequences which might cause due to revised strategy of the project or programme implemented by the organization.

Obtaining And Holding Internal Organisational Unity

Internal organizational unity is required for taking up fast decision and implementation of the actions by the administration. The decision may be in regard to the types and content of the programme activities, the methods of implementation and the expanding it for clientele. An administrative unity is required for adopting new techniques of administration rather than sticking to old traditions and past practices.

Quick Decision Making

Whenever the projects are planned by the organization the administrative technical sanctions are required. The same procedure should be made faster to take the decisions. Moreover, immediate decisions are required in critical conditions to control the situation. It is also necessary for smooth and easy routine administration of the project.

Rewards To Sincere Workers

Often human psychology affects the administration work culture. The creative, regular and efficient workers continue to work efficiently may be due to rewards they receive for their sincere work otherwise they work in inefficient and ineffective manner. Therefore, rewards should be given to sincere workers to encourage them to accomplish the objectives of the project and to bring fruitful results.

Effective Coordinators

Coordination is an important task of all the administrators. The present position set up of an organization is in position to extend the hands to other organizations as well as has the scope to utilize the services from the other organizations. This can be done only through proper coordination. For this purpose the administrator needs the information about programme content and programme objectives then he is able to distribute the share of each organiser in programme execution. Each share of the organiser in programme execution is communicated to them through orientation programme.

Efficiency in Work

Efficiency in administration proves fruitful as all types of services offered by the organizations are faster according to changing needs of clientele which help in continuity in programmes. It creates lasting effects in the clientele for their development. Efficiency of the organizations becomes essential among the staff for effective administration.

Maximum Utilization of Resources

It is important for every administrator to collect and create resources which have utility under the programme planned. Simultaneously, he also has to see that the resources collected or created have the proper and maximum utilization for effective programme implementation. Otherwise use of resources will lead to de–employment.

Profound Proficiency

An able officer will have profound proficiency in administration from all angles. The administrator is able to function successfully with deep proficiency he has in all functions. This rewards to the administrator with confidence and dialogue to capitalize on opportunity which leads to increase more proficiencies to meet the administration challenges. Thus, internal problem of the organization of pulling and handling of the person could be avoided in programme activities. Supervision and evaluation processes will be made clear through orientation to each administrator to have better coordination.

Utility of Feedback

For every successful administration "Feedback" is essential. Considerations of feedback helps in checking and improving the implementation which lead to attainment of objectives framed by organization. Dahama has also had indicated it by expressing that administrator who ignore or otherwise fail to attend to feedback can expect serious consequences. Failure to attend to Feedback leads to inefficient, ineffective and sloppy communication. This in turn, leads to loss of morale, lowered productivity and further degeneration of communication throughout the organization.

Accepting Challenges for Modern Society

It may be difficult stage to offer change in social practices initially but later on it proves for the betterment of the society. Therefore, taking up such challenges by the administrators in organization which may have opposition in the beginning but will have acceptance later on. The realization on the part of the society makes society accepted of the same. The unity and structure of administration help to accept these challenges. Thus, it will be stronger and solid and proves worthy of accomplishing objectives.

ADMINISTRATIVE MACHINERY

Planning In Organization

Planning will be the responsibility of all the members from top officials to down workers as well as with whom the programme is coordinated with other organization for the society. For this purpose the representative from the beneficiaries also will be involved along with the staff and administrator of the organization.

Members of Board of An Organization

Trustees from the board of private organization would be having responsibilities for planning and permitting implementation of the programme. Moreover, day to day financial and administrative power necessary for implementation of the progamme of action would be vested with them.

Supervisor

The supervisor may be selected from among the experienced and sincere staff members. The function of supervisor would include planning and organizing programmes for the beneficiaries. While supervising, a supervisor may check and guide the activity to help the beneficiaries.

The System of Programme Evaluation

It would ensure that all management personnel, organizers and supervisors jointly and concurrently review the progress of the programme. Experienced teachers from academic institutions as well as government officials such as District Development Officer, District Rural Development Agency personnel who are in collaboration would be associated for external evaluation.

Funding Agency

Usually the organization itself finances the programme, but they may collect donation at time for some specific development activities. The other voluntary agencies or government agencies in collaboration with the organization may provide fund for the activities or may provide supplies and materials required for the programme to the organization.

Management Information System

It would be instituted to ensure continuous flow of information required for improving management. Suitable measures need to be taken for careful analysis and interpretation of information data and feedback received from the beneficiaries as well as the field officers.

PROBLEMS IN ADMINISTRATION

Lack of Skills and Understanding of An Administrative Function

Whenever personnel function, they must be aware of the general administrative work culture. The basic administrative skills are required by every member of the staff personnel. First of all, every year the personnel should meet for sharing information about the need of a higher level of administration adequancy skills as well as understanding and performance of the administrative function. Well conceived information directs the organizational resources and programmes which help the personnel to administer smoothly.

Absence of Administrative Adequancy

Organization precedes the breaking up tasks into convenient unit and subunits and linking them again to secure team work. This raises the problem of the basis on which one should distribute the work and regroup it into convenient units. The work of each unit has to be characterized by some similarity which may relate to purpose, programme activities, methods, process and beneficiaries. These become the policies for adequancy of administration. An absence of adequacy of such policies leads to problems in administration.

Lack of Internal Organizational Resources

The services and resources under private voluntary organization are dealt with various age groups of the society with relation to different aspects of development. The organizations are formed on functional basis. There are major programmes which are made up of minor activities. Mid-Day-Meal programme is a major progamme which takes care of minor activities such as including nutritious meal for children, increasing regular attendance of children in the school, helping to develop their health status through meal progamme offered by school, etc. To organize such programme various internal resources are required to followup the work. These needs to be taken care by the administration.

Lack of Leadership among the Members of Administration

Administrators must balance the use of limited funds, internal organizational resources, skills and present and potential sources into programme. To take the decision about these matters, the administrators must use their reasoning power and take leadership to lead the administration successfully. Leadership helps to take up administrative challenges. Without leadership success of programme of the organization is not possible.

Inability to Make Intelligent and Timely Decisions

Should programme be one that will accommodate different groups of society? How to support the demands of the groups specially related to traditions or less pressed? These are certain questions raised in the administration. The personnel needs to have intelligence and ability in taking quick and correct decisions which serve the purpose of the matter for which the decision is taken.

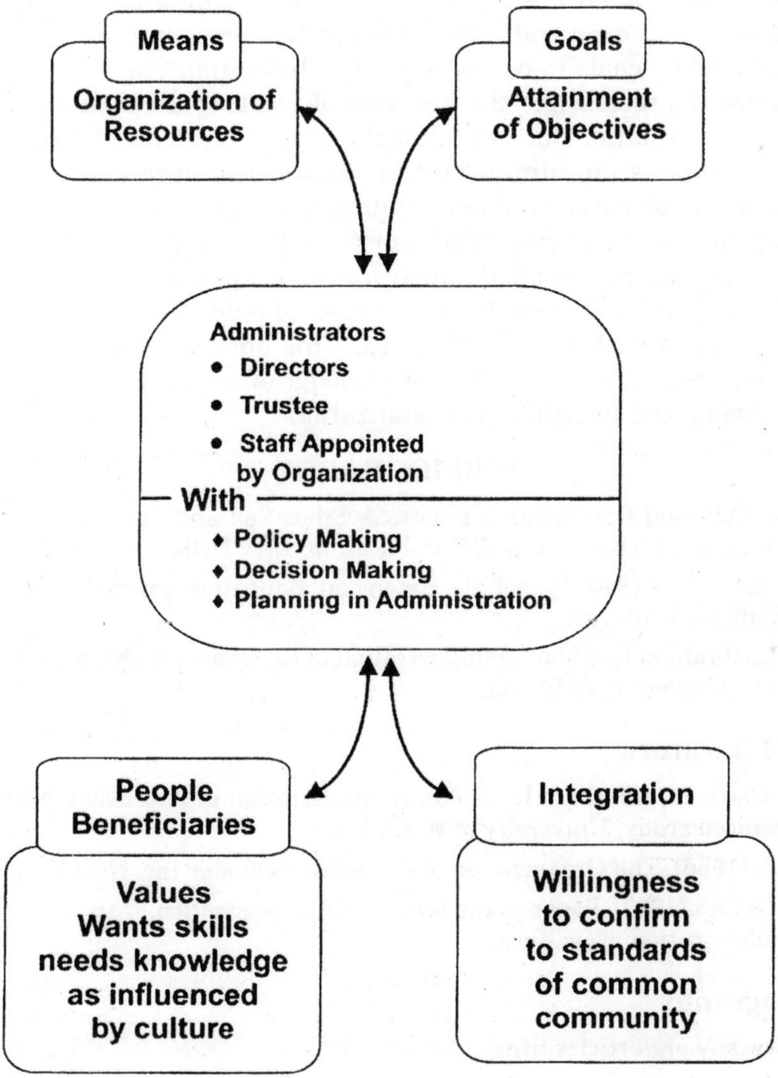

Sloppy Communication

Proper and correct communication is effective and accomplishes the work. Where in sloppy communication does not give clarity, create confusion in minds and lowers the production. These brings obstacles in the implementation of programme. The administrators therefore should use proper and effective communication.

ADMINISTRATION ROLE MODEL

The model presented here helps to explain the process of administration in private voluntary organization. It shows that major role of administration is to keep the means of attaining objectives in tune with dynamics of social change. In addition, the model shows the relationships should exist between the functions. Decision-making is influenced by the culture and the natural integrative function present in society. Action is influenced by goals to be attained and the adaptation of means. The management process has the key role of relating decision-making to action. These relationships exist for the organization and for clientele.

An emphasis on administration within the organization would necessarily involve a clear understanding of the nature of administration and particularly the process of administration. A management emphasis also implies that the role of administration to keep the means of attaining objectives in pace with the changing times, should effectively relate the administration with its beneficiaries. This administration emphasis would require that personnel have knowledge of human behaviour, social action theory and principles of organization.

BIBLIOGRAPHY

Dahama O.P. and Bhatnagar O.P. (1985), Education and Communication for Development, Oxford and IBH Publication, New Delhi.

Waghmare S.K. (1980), Teaching Extension Education Prashant publishes Vallabh Vidyanagar.

Clark R., Abraham R. (1960), Administration in Extension. NAEC for Advanced Study, University of Wisconsin.

Cited Literature

Getzel, Clark R., Abraham R. (1960), Administration in Extension. NAEC for Advanced study, University of Wisconsin.

Williams (1956), The Organization Man. Simon Schuster Inc. New York.

Luther Gullick (1997), Paper on the Science of Administration, Institute of Public Administration, New York.

Webliography

http/www.sify.org/articles.htm.

MEGHA SIDHPURA & ANURADHA MATHU

6 Role of NGO's in Women Empowerment

INTRODUCTION

"Voluntary Service of Others Demands The Best Which one is Capable of and Must Take Precedence Over Services to Self."

—Mahatma Gandhi

"Voluntary Action" is an instrument for not only satisfying the needs of the community and solving its difficulties but also participating in the affairs of the community whether it is social, economic or political and so on. The organization of people and its constructive actions take the shape of a voluntary organization. VOs have acquired wide acceptance internationally. But the concept of voluntary social services is very ancient. They have been engaged in the developmental work for many years and decades. As the governmental agencies have not been able to reach the people particularly women and other vulnerable groups with regard to social development, there is a desire now to handover the management of programmes of social services, especially where direct contact with people living marginally is involved, to voluntary organizations. In recent years, NGOs have increased in considerable numbers acquired greater importance and significance and put up many new experiments in social development and rural development.

The United Nations nomenclature of an NGO refers to any international organization not established by inter-governmental agreement including organizations, which accept members designated by Governmental authorities, provided that such membership does not interfere with the organizations free expression of views. NGOs are different from the market induced organizations and other organizations of the state. They are formalized organizations beyond the market and the state, receiving their resources partly from voluntary contributions of the society. The term NGO in India has been used to denote a wide spectrum of organizations which may be non-governmental, quasi or informal, non-profit or profit oriented bodies, with a legal status and registered under Special Acts (like Companies Act, Societies Registration Act, etc.) To be eligible for funding from various agencies, it should have legal status (i.e. legal personality).

In the Indian context Chowdhary (1971) defined a voluntary organization as an organization which, whether its workers are paid or unpaid, is initiated and governed by its own members without external control.

Smith and Freedman (1972) defined voluntary organization as "Structured, formally organized. Relatively permanent, secondary groupings as opposed to less structured, informal, ephemeral or primary groupings, identified by presence of offices filled through some established procedures; periodic, scheduled meetings; qualifying criteria for membership, and some formalized division and specialization of labor."

According to Sundaram (1986) a voluntary organization, properly speaking, is an organization which, whether its workers are paid or unpaid, is initiated and governed by its own members without external control.

David Sills (1987), a sociologist defined voluntary organization as "a group of persons organized on the basis of voluntary membership without state control, for the furtherance of some common interests of its members."

Michel Banton, an anthropologist, characterized it as a group organized for the pursuit of one interest or of several interests in common. Usually, it is contrasted with voluntary groups, castes, social classes and communities."

Prabhakaran (1992) defined a voluntary organization as an agency., organized or unorganized, structured or unstructured, which works for the welfare of a community in any given area of its own volition. It may be just an individual or a collection of individuals or it may have a more formal structure.

In the Handbook of NGOs, Nabhi (2003) defined Non Governmental Organisation, "NGOs include groups and institutions that are entirely or largely independent of government and that have primarily humanitarian or cooperatives rather than commercial objectives. They are private agencies in industrial countries that support international development; indigenous groups organized regionally or nationally; member groups in villages. NGO include charitable and religious associations that mobilize private funds for development, distribute food and family planning services and promote community organization. They also include independent cooperatives; community associations, water-user societies, women's groups associations."

The term Voluntary' means that people out of their own volition and their free will come together around a particular problem or community head, define its contours, find solutions or remedies, prepare plans, organize themselves, develop funds, monitor and evaluate the plans and programmes may be wholly internal or supplemented by outside agencies. The touchstone for such voluntary ventures is people's initiative without outside control but only assistance or guidance based on needs perceptions on terms and conditions and the procedures of grant giving, people's action or initiative may be promoted or weakened. (Choudhary, 2000).

Thus the concept of voluntarism may be termed as an informal creed or system with infrastructure, methods and procedures laid down by the people in an indigenous manner to tackle their problems. The initiative taken spontaneously by an informal gathering or a group may ultimately result in an organization called voluntary agency or in today's parlance-a Non governmental Organization. The spirit of voluntary initiative or action can be maintained as long as, the structure of an NGO is small, its chain of commands and communication are without outside dictates such as through the condition of grants. Public cooperation is somewhat broader terms, which become operational through an organized network of voluntary agencies and sometimes-local bodies like Panchayats (Choudhary, 2000).

HISTORY OF NGO's

The history of voluntary agencies as we know them dates back to the middle of the nineteenth century although traditional community supported local groups serving the needy has been a part of old Indian culture.

Before independence there were a few thousand social welfare agencies in the voluntary sector as registered societies and trusts looking after orphans, widows, the sick, the handicapped etc. based on concept of compassion and pity. The rich and influential citizens who funded these ventures were motivated by various considerations such as achieving salvation purposeful utilization of their wealth and perhaps getting social recognition.

Another stream or category of voluntary in India was those managed and funded by Christian missionaries who received state patronage with a desire and motivation of serving the poor and the downtrodden rejected by their families and communities.

After independence, the First Five-year Plan document recognized the role of private voluntary organizations in the fields of women welfare and social education. These organizations under the plan were expected to meet the herculean task of public cooperation, public opinion, democracy and planning. The following plan envisaged entrusting social welfare extension projects to VOs. The Third Plan again reiterated the role of VOs in community cooperation. The following two plan documents accentuated the VOs' vital role in rural development and social welfare, acting as publicity and propaganda media to remove poverty in rural areas. In the Sixth Five Year Plan, the government reposed faith in these organizations in the fields of child and health care, animal husbandry, social forestry, women and child development.

Unto Sixth Plan the Government, however, paid lackadaisical attention towards voluntarism, in the absence of parameters and yardsticks to legitimize the relevance of the VOs. Till then, it is opined that there might be a hiatus between planners and VO's practitioners. It was however, only the Seventh Plan, which showed the firm commitment of the Government to engage VOs in implementing antipoverty and minimum need programmes not only acting as alternative machinery to development bureaucracy but also as "eyes and ears" of the beneficiaries. In this plan certain preconditions were laid down for the VOs eligibilities. These include appropriate legal recognition, minimum experience of working, serving and economic needs of the community, professional competence, democratic outlook, of constitutional means, commitment to secular outlook and democratic modus operandi.

The next plan document emphasized the due role of VOs in developmental activities of education, fisheries and sericulture. The Ninth Five Year Plan admitted that Panchyati Raj Institutions, cooperative societies, Self-Help Groups and VOs could play a paramount role in decentralized democracy and participatory development. The Tenth Five Year Plan document reveals that VOs are expected to play different role models by executing planners' missions. These are: social mobilization, strengthening SHGs capacities, Imparting Training for Entrepreneurial Abilities, Sharing managerial experiences with development bureaucracy, ensuring people's active involvement in development efforts, independent monitoring and evaluation.

WOMEN

The human development paradigm, which puts people at the center of its concern, is now becoming a universally acknowledged strategy for the development of nation. The growing consensus among development thinkers is that people are-and should be-the starting point, the center and the goal of each development intervention (Cernea, 1985). The real wealth of a nation is its people, both men and women, and the purpose of development is to create an environment to enable them to enjoy long, healthy and creative lives. However, the harsh reality is that, "in no society do women enjoy the same opportunities as men" (Human Development Report, 1995:29).

In India, for centuries, Women have been pushed aside from the race of development in the name of customs, traditions and religion. As a result, they have been denied the opportunities for their social, economic and political development leading to a lower status in society. As women comprise nearly half of the total population of the country, this denial has contributed in no small measure to India's continuing underdevelopment, in terms of three main indicators of development, namely, life expectancy, educational attainment and income, India occupies a dismal ranking of 134th among 174 countries. (Ibid: 53).

In 20th century, the terms 'Women empowerment', 'women welfare'. 'Gender justice' have come in lime light in social, economic and political development analysis of both developed and developing nations. Traditionally women in almost every society have remained second grade citizen. Social network wants to keep women dependent on men in all spheres if life right from birth to her last rites. In actual terms women had become slaves of men, whose sole aim was to use them for bearing and rearing–up–children and fulfilling there sexual desires. Neither they were allowed to get themselves educated nor they were given legal rights in the property, government and in administration. Their freedom and status exploited by marying them in tender age and keeping them inside the house, exploiting their labor and dignity to maximum possible extent.

Empowerment means giving legal and moral power to an individual in all spheres of life-social, economic, political, psychological, religious and spiritual-which are essential for the survival and overall development of the mankind. Every society has known racism, sexism and authoritarianism. In broader terms empowerment is nothing but a religious, cultural and legal struggle against operation, injustice and discrimination. Empowerment express the bold idea that all people have claimed to social arrangements that protect them from the process of enhancing human capabilities to expand choices and opportunities so that each person can lead a life of respect and value. According to Kapoor (2002), "Women's empowerment could over resource material, human and intellectual like knowledge, information, ideas and financial resources like money and access to money and control over decision mankind in home, community, society and nation and to gain "power". Bliwala has rightly observed (2002)," The term women's empowerment has come to be associated with women's struggle for social justice and equality".

According to the country report of Government of India presented at Fourth World Conference on women at Beijing," Empowerment means working from a portion of enhanced powerless to one of power. It would promote women's inherent strength and positive self image."

Social movement of women's right propelled the 20th century progress towards equality regardless of gender, race, religion, ethnicity or age, with roots back over the centuries. The issue of empowerment of women becomes significant as women constitute half of the population and unfortunately they had been discriminated lot.

NGO's AND WOMEN EMPOWERMENT

Traditional welfare services covered the needs of widows , destitute and old women through homes, condensed courses, literacy classes, maternity and medical services for women in need. As a matter of fact this effort helped a limited number of women. In the seventies and eighties a movement led by women activists resulted in several legal, economic and organizational steps for women development. The concept of "women empowerment" is receiving due attention because women are discriminated against in many spheres. Experts felt that empowerment must be two-fold, it must be externally induced so that women can exercise a level of autonomy and there should be "self-empowerment" so that they can look at their own lives and see the ways in which their acceptance of the status quo has contributed to their disempowerment (Sundaram: 2000).

The concept of women empowerment took birth and shook the bureaucracy, political parties, legislature and judiciary. Thus women started with the result that women's issue and problems were debated at various forms of NGOs. This resulted into establishment of National and state commission for women:

1. A division of women's development the ministry of HRD.
2. A division for research and training in National Institute of Public Cooperation and Child Development.
3. Women's studies centers in universities aided by UGC.
4. Women cell as part of police infrastructure.
5. Women legal aid cells in district courts.

In addition to all India and local voluntary agencies a large number of Mahila Mandals promoted by the erstwhile Ministry of Community Development and Central Social Welfare Board, are working at the grass-root level. A large number of voluntary agencies have in the past worked in the field of women welfare. In fact this was the only input in women's welfare. These organizations have to be more aware of developmental needs and problems of women and their role in this voluntary effort, there is much desired so far as women's needs, problems, and aspirations are concerned.

NGO's & WOMEN EMPOWERMENT ROLE OF NGO's IN EMPOWERMENT OF WOMEN

Involvement of Women in Income Generating Activities

Women from urban and rural area should be given training for income generating activities like handicraft products, jute products, clay work, embroidery work, sewing, etc. This would lead them to earn some money and so they will be economically independent. This way also they can utilize their time effectively for some productive work.

Starting Women's Co-Operatives and Banks

Women should be organised and they should be motivated to save and invest their money. This way they can start self help groups (SHGs). Cooperatives, banks and small scale industries operated by women, will empower women and increase their economic status.

Sensitize Women for Leadership

NGOs should offer leadership training to the women. Women are always dependent on men for each and every social and economic matter. Now in todays world women should recognize their own abilities and skills. They should be equal participants in the decision making process both at home and outside the home.

Promote Health

Women have always been ignorant for their health. It is a main cause for their poor health status. Their poor economic conditions, improper dietary practices, problems related to reproductive process etc. are the issues which need to be taken care. Voluntary organizations can bring awareness regarding major health issues and also they should provide proper interventions to solve the problems.

Promote Child Care Agencies

Women use to leave their children at home when they go out for work/ labour. Proper child care agencies like crèches, day care centres etc. should run with the help of NGOs so that women do not have to worry for their children and on the other hand the other woman who runs crèches or day care centre will earn.

Providing Counselling Services

Today women are facing lot of problems in her marriage and family life, related to her reproductive health etc. She faces lots of violence by her family members–in laws, by colleagues at workplace, etc. So, NGO should provide legal and other counseling services to solve her problems.

Open Functional Literacy Classes

Literacy is the first step in the process of empowerment of women. Illiteracy is the bottleneck in the development of women. So, NGOs should open functional literacy classes which will provide literacy related to her work or occupation.

Demystification of Technology

Since the technological marginalization of female at work in endemic in both agricultural and non–agricultural informal sector, NGOs should be involved in over–coming gender differences in the application and generation of technology to reduce the drudgery of the poorest working women in back breaking tasks such as gathering of fuel, fodder and water.

STRENGTHS OF NGO'S

The NGOs have gained respectability among the respective governments as well as the donor agencies mainly due it their strengths. An account of such competencies can be listed as follows:

Grass Root Presence

The ability of NGOs to mobilize the popular participation is virtually due to their presence among the people. The field personnel who work with the people can gauge their requirements and are available to their needs. Thus, the beneficiaries have more faith on these workers rather than the civil servants who visit them occasionally.

Motivation

Individuals have founded NGOs with strong commitment to social service. The staff, though working for salaries, are not mainly driven by the pecuniary benefits, Such motivation can be hardly found with the government officials who are on a string of two or three year posting. Likewise the beneficiaries too, who lack business acumen, need constant pushing without which they can hardly surmount the hurdles posed by the support system. Even today, the performance of the paid staff is better than the civil servants.

Target Group Approach:

When benefits of developments failed to "trickle down' to the masses, these NGOs have entered into the fray to initiate "bottom up' development efforts. Enterprise development technique is one of such effort directed to economic upliftment of the target population. If open to every one in the community, there is danger of such benefits being taken only by the elite.

WEAKNESSES OF NGO's

Leadership and Succession

The founders of NGOs usually are of highly talented and motivated. However, their management style is not necessarily be democratic. They can serve the community better when they build broad-based rather than individualistic organizational structure.

Flexibility and Responsiveness

Freed from the bureaucratic hurdles, NGOs are usually adapted to informal system of governance.

Heterogeneity

Their operations are demand based rather than imposed from higher-ups, thus find enough leverage to introduce a variety of EDPs. Tailor-made training programmes for each target group have helped these NGOs to optimize their resources.

Dependence on Customer Satisfaction

The future enterprise development activities related to satisfied clientele. Surprisingly, the NGOs are more accounted for the result than their public sector counterparts, probably for their dependence on others for financial assistance.

Death of Programme Integration

Stimulation, support and sustenance activities of entrepreneurship development are highly interacting, supplementary and crucial to each other. Lack of enough knowledge on the part of NGPs may lead to the absence/negligence of the above activities.

Inadequate Training Opportunities

Entrepreneurship development requires highly talented and motivated staff. However, human resources recruitment and development is actually one of the neglected areas in many NGOs. This affects the whole range of activities connected to entrepreneurship development.

RECOMMENDATIONS

1. The increase in the number, expansion and diversification of activities of the voluntary agencies has not necessarily equalized the disparities between them. There are not only regional imbalances in the growth of the voluntarily sector but within a particulars state, the growth of this sector has not been even. It is also well known that a majority of voluntary agencies are urban based and that relatively few have taken up the issues of women. It is recommended that the focus of voluntary agencies move from urban to rural areas, as the situation of rural women warrant immediate support, There is also need for the Government to encourage voluntary action for development of women by provision of adequate financial and structural support.
2. There is an urgent need to improve the effectiveness of voluntary action. Improvement will have to be brought about both in the organizational structures as also in the quality of services offered.

Voluntary workers need to be professionals, equipped with appropriate skills for managing women's projects and sensitivity towards women's issues.

National and state level institutions and training organization should provide adequate facilities, research and training relating to women's issues. They should take up activities guided by the felt needs of women and those that can make a qualitative differences to women's lives, rather than be confined to traditional areas of support and action.

3. Voluntary action should be directed particular towards preventive rather than purely curative measures. Efforts of voluntary agencies should also be geared towards generating self-reliance rather than to create dependencies. To improve their capabilities in planning and implementation of programmes, voluntary agencies are in need of expertise and technical guidance as much as financial assistance.
4. The process of grant–seeking and receiving is considered by a number of voluntary agencies as a frustrating experience. There is an urgent need to review the working of the grants–in–aid system. Wherever needed, modifications should be introduced rules are simplified, grants released on time and the needs of a particular programme.
5. Voluntary agencies have tended to neglect the participative potential of women in the development process as well as concretizing women on their rights and roles. There is the need for such efforts that could increase the awareness of women and improve their participation as equal citizens in national development.
6. At present, there is no proper mechanism of coordination among different voluntary agencies. There is also the need for a continuous flow of information from government to voluntary agencies and vice–versa through such mechanisms as a clearing house for information.
7. A focal point is desirable in the rural areas to encourage women's voluntary activities. Mahila mandals and women's groups at the village or community level should be organized or revived and encouraged to register and function as women's institutions for undertaking socio–economic programme.

   Particular attention need to be given to the training of the mahila mandal functionaries and women's group organizers and provide them an orientation to development perspective rather than purely welfare approaches.
8. The CSWB which has been the coordinating agency for voluntary action for women and children, must respond to the new trust of Government policy meant for women and recast is its own programmes.

9. Greater coordination and cooperation among NGOs is called for to avoid duplication of services. This will ensure more efficient utilization of funds and greater coverage of programmes.
10. Voluntary agencies must be increasingly involved in the provision of employment and supportive services for women.
11. The National Literacy Mission must involve women's organizations in a big way.
12. The volunteers be involved to act as a catalyst/intermediary in organizing women for collective action.
13. There is need to document the success stories of major NGO's in India and learn from their success and failures. Further, it is necessary to analyse the cost benefit of NGO projects versus governmental projects.
14. In order to ensure that the security and integrity of the nation are preserved, there is a need to adopt suitable policies to ensure that voluntary agencies abide by the rules governing the receipt and utilization of foreign grants and submit audited accounts, returns and reports periodically.
15. In order to have sufficient infrastructure and facilities, there is need to mobilize more resources for voluntary agencies who are engaged in welfare and development of women.
16. There is a need to decenteralize the planning process to stimulate local people's participation in planning, implementation, monitoring and evaluation of development project. A suitable mechanism should be evolved to involve voluntary agencies and other people's institutions at various stages of developmental programmes / projects. Voluntary agencies should further ensure the participation of poor women in the development process.

ROLE OF HOME SCIENCE EXTENSION & COMMUNICATION IN THIS AREA

1. Home Scientists can work extensively with neighbourhood groups and can show persistence in influencing the decisions of relevant government agencies.
2. Home Scientists can work in the NGO and help people to identify their needs and problems.
3. As a programme planner and co–ordinator also she can work for the benefits of the people/beneficiaries.
4. She can act as a motivator and can motivate beneficiaries to adopt desired changes and practices for their own benefits and development and at the end development of nations.

5. Home Scientists can work as a counselor for legal or any other problems.
6. Home Scientists can organize training for the volunteers of NGOs working in the different areas.
7. She can design various developmental messages and multimedia strategies (packages) to reach to the target group.
8. She can do research in this area to find out problems in the existing/ present situation may be related to working of NGOs, their programmes, strategies methods, process, beneficiaries, etc. and can also suggest solutions/alternative for the same.
9. She can develop curriculum for the any of the subject area i.e. to health and nutrition, reproductive health, income generation activities, legal awareness, etc.
10. Home Scientists can identify active NGOs and their positive factors so that they can suggest other agency to adopt the same model or practices. They can also help in co–ordination of the agencies working in the same areas.
11. Home Scientists can open up their own NGO to serve the people.
12. Home Scientists can organize seminars, workshops on the topic related to the NGOs and their concern areas. In a way they can provide platform for the NGO people to discuss their issues and problems.

BIBLIOGRAPHY

Bhatia, Anju (2000), Women's Development and NGOs. Rawat Publications, Jaipur and New Delhi.

Chauhan, S. and Bansal, G. (2002), Various Dimensions of Women's Empowerment. Social Welfare, Vol. 49, No. 5, August, pp. 10–17.

Chowdhary, D. Paul (2000), Overview Voluntarism, Welfare and Development. Social Welfare Vol. 47, No. 11, February, pp. 3–10.

Kaul, A. Educational, Economic and Social Impact of Voluntary Training Agencies offering Income Generating Programmes on Low Socio Economic Status Women of Baroda City.

Krishnamurti, V. (1986), Voluntary Action in Rural Development: A Survey. Kurukshetra, Vol. XXXIV, No. 2–3, pp. 33–36.

Lawani D.T. (1999), NGOs in Development, Rawat Publication, Jaipur and New Delhi.

Markowitz (2001), USA. Finding the field: Notes on the Ethnography of NGOs, Human Organization, Journal of Society for applied Anthropology, Spring.

Muttalib, M.A. (1987), Voluntarism and Development. Theoretical Perspectives. The Indian Journal of Public Administration. Vol. XXXIII, 3, pp. 501–511.

Nabhi (2003), Handbook for NGOs, An Encyclopedia for Non–Government Organizations and Voluntary Agencies, A Nabhi Publication, New Delhi.

National Perspective Plan for Women (1988–2000) Report of the Core Group set up by the Department of Women and Child Development, Ministry of Human Resource Development, Government of India (1988).

Pandya, R.M. (1996), NGOs–Towards Self–Reliance. Social Welfare. Vol. 43, No. 5, August, 22–24.

Report: National Conference on Voluntarism and Social Development on 22–24 February 2000. Social Welfare, Vol. 47, no. 1, April 2000, pp. 19–22.

Roy, Sanjit (Bunker) (1987), Voluntary Agencies in Development–Their Role, Policy and Programmes. The Indian Journal of Public Administration, Vol. XXXIII, 3, pp. 454–464.

Sen, S. Voluntary (1994), Organisations and Women Development. Dissertation (MSW)..., M.S. University.

Singhal, C.S. (1998), Assam: Survey of NGO activities. Social Welfare, Vol. 45, No. 10, January, pp. 24–29.

Siwach, R.K. (2003), Prospective Role of VOs in Tenth Plan. Social Welfare, Vol. 50, No. 11, February, pp. 13–15.

Srivastava, R.C. (2000), NGOs: Securing People's Partnership for Progress. Social Welfare, Vol, 47, No. 11, February, pp. 15–18.

Srivastava, S.P. (1999), Nature of Voluntary Action in India Today: A Critique Social Action, Vol. 49, January–March.

Srivenkataramana, T. and Raj, N.N. (1997), NGOs are Vital to Social Development. Social Welfare, Vol. 44, No. 4, July, pp. 15–17.

Sundaram, I.S. (2000), Voluntarism in the new millennium. Social Welfare, Vol. 47, No. 11, February, pp. 11–14.

Suresh, K.A. (1990), Participation of beneficiaries in the Developmental Programmes of NGO in Kerala. Journal of Rural Development, Vol. 9, No. 5, September 1990, pp. 911–915.

SUJATA SRIVASTAVA

7 Universalisation of Elementary Education: Role of NGO's

Education and development are closely related. Education is a vital input in human resource development and is an essential component for our country's growth and prosperity. India requires economic, political and social stability for its development, where education plays an integral part.

Elementary or primary education plays a critical role by laying the foundation stone of education.

Article 45 of the constitution stipulates that the 'state shall endeavor to provide, within period of 10 years from the commencement of the constitution, for free and compulsory education for all children until they complete the age of 14 years.

MEANING AND CONCEPT OF UNIVERSALISATION OF ELEMENTARY EDUCATION

Let's try and understand the whole concept of universalisation of elementary education in greater detail.

In the Indian context UEE implies that all children in the age group of 6–14 years, irrespective of cast, creed colour, gender, socio-economic states or their rural-urban set-up be provided with elementary education.

Universalisation of elementary education focuses on free education. India being a developing country free education primarily connotes, no tuition fees. However in different states there may be welfares schemes in operation wherein books, stationary may be provide to all or the disadvantaged section. Many states today have the free mid-day meal in operation. Infact today twelve crore of India's children are being fed by the mid-day meal schemes.

Universalisation of elementary education involves the following three steps:

Universalistiaon of Provision: This indicates that all children in the age group of 6–14 years must have access to primary schools within a walking distance of one kilometer. There has been a rapid expansion of primary schools to cover the remotest corners of the country.

Universalisation of Enrolment: All children between the age group of 6–14 years must be enrolled and enjoy the benefits of primary education.

Universalisation of Retention: Universal access to primary schools and enrolment alone does not ensure the goals of primary education. Once children join primary school they must complete primary education. If the child leaves the primary school in between, the whole idea of universalisation is defeated.

WHAT POLICY DOCUMENTS SAY?

Since independence there have been number of policy recommendations to achieve universal elementary education. Education commission (1964-1966) stated that the 'state shall strive to provide free and compulsory education for all children upto the age of 14 years. It further states that each state, and even each district should prepare a perspective plan for the development of primary education taking into account the stage of development already reached and local conditions and problems.

The National Policy on Education (1968) maintained that strenuous efforts should be made for the early fulfillment of the directive principle under Article 45 of the constitution, seeking to provide free and compulsory education for all children up to the age of 14. Suitable programmes should be developed to reduce the prevailing wastage and stagnation in school and to ensure that every child who is enrolled in school successfully complete the prescribed course.

The National Policy on Education has laid great emphasis an universalisation of elementary education, assuming that the universal elementary education is achieved by 1990. It further emphasized that unless large-scale wastage is reduced to minimum and other objective conditions are fulfilled the target of universalisation of elementary educating will remain a pious will.

The National policy on Education (1992) again provided a comprehensive frame work for the development of education up to the end of the century and a plan of action assigning specific responsibilities for organizing, implementing and financing its proposals. It gives unqualified priority to primary education and adult literacy programmes.

National Curriculum Framework (2005) feels there is a deep disquiet about several aspect of our educational practices, like inflexibility of school, learning as an isolated activity, discouragement of creative thinking etc and states that the basic concern of education is to enable children to make sense of there life and develop their potential, to define and pursue a purpose and recognize the right of others to do the same–stand uncontested and valid even today.

UNIVERSALISATION OF ELEMENTARY EDUCATION: ITS VALUE

It had been universally accepted that the success of UEE is an important indicator of the social, economic, political and cultural development of any country. It is a well-known fact that primary education contributes to national development. The developed countries all over the world have realized the contribution of effective primary education in their rapid progress. For a developing country like India UEE has immense value. Elementary education is the basic foundation on which other levels of education will be constructed. The basic education offered has to be of superior quality if it has to lead to the growth of the individual and the nation as a whole. The quality of life of an individual depends on this. India is a democracy and constructive participation of individuals in the political arena is critical. Elementary education would ensure intelligent voting and the election of the right powers, putting the country in safe hands. Thus quality of followers and leaders should improve. Basic skills in individuals would be developed and enhanced leading to vocational efficiency. Scientific temper would be inculcated which would give direction to individuals at every step, eliminating darkness and ignorance. Elementary education inculcates different values in individuals, which is vital for their very existence in this universe.

UNIVERSALISATION OF ELEMENTARY EDUCATION: AN UNFULFILLED DREAM

The importance of basic education is embodied in the Article 45 of the constitution, which assures provision of free and compulsory education for all children till the age of 14. Since independence this has been one of the important goals of educational development in India. However this goal has remained elusive. This task should have been completed by 1960 but due to several problems it was mission incomplete. The target date was then revised to 1970, then to 1976, then to 1990. Later the National Policy on Education (1986) revised the date to 1995.

Alas! The goal of UEE have still not been met and Sarva Shiksha Abhyan was launched to achieve this goal and aims to provide elementary education to all children in the 6-14 age group by 2010.

According to the 2001 census while the all India Literacy rate is 65.38 per cent, it is considerable lower among certain categories SC/STs (52 per cent): Muslims (59 per cent): females (54 per cent) and rural areas (59 per cent) Innumerable factors have led to the non-achievement of the goals of UEE. Some of these important factors have been discussed below.

Wastage and Stagnation

It is not sufficient for children to just enroll in primary schools but successful completion of the primary classes is the aim to work for. According to the 2001 census the dropout rate of boys in classes I-IV was 39.71 per cent and 50.33 per cent in I-VIII classes. The dropout rate of girls was 41.90 per cent in classes I-V and 57.95 per cent in classes I-VIII.

Though the official policy forbids children to repeat the same class and are automatically promoted till class V, the repetition rates considerably higher after that. The high dropout and repetition rates lead to wastage and stagnation in primary education.

Girl Education

Enrolment of girls in primary schools has shown a sharp increase from 5.4 million (class I to V) in 1950-51 to 49.8 million in 2000-2001. Girl enrolment was 0.5 million (upper primary, class VII to VIII) in 1950-51 and 17.5 million in 2000-2001. However the female literacy rate in India is still 54.16 per cent (2000-2001). There are many reasons, which can be attributed for this state of low literacy. The socio-cultural milieu in our country has traditionally put a lot of taboos on girls and it still continues specially in the rural set-up.

School Infrastructure

There has been a great expansion of educational facilities since 1950-51. The number of primary schools were 2,10,000 in 1950-51 and increased to 6,38,738 in 2000-2001. The number of upper primary schools were 13,596 in 1950-51 and have increased to 2,06,269 in 2000-2001. In spite of this phenomenal expansion the quality of infrastructure qualities is sub-standard in many places.

Quality in Teaching–Learning Process

Research evidence in primary education revel that a lot of qualitative improvement is required in the teaching and learning, which goes on today. Statistics reveal a dismal trend. It is disheartening to note that 35% of India's rural children between ages 7 and 14 cannot read a simple paragraph, something which they should have learnt to do in first year of school. Another 52% cannot read a simple story, which they should have learnt by grade two, while 41% cannot either do two digit subtractions with borrowing or divide three digits by one digit. The overall rural India is behind by two to three years, which is deeply disappointing for a country aiming to achieve great heights. The classroom environment is unattractive and the transaction of the curriculum does not interest and challenge the mind of learner. The teaching methodologies do not foster creativity and critical thinking in the learners.

Problem of Teachers

It is paradoxical that a country where 40 million are unemployed still faces shortage of teachers in the rural areas. If teacher are on the rolls of the school often it is only for name-shake. Teacher absenteeism is rampant. This hampers the serious goals of primary education

Poverty

India is a developing country. Forty million of our 1.2 billion population is unemployed. India has one of the lowest per-capita-income in the world. Every extra pair of hands brings extra income to the family is a premise held by many parents. Therefore poverty affects the enrollment and retention of children in primary schools.

It has been increasingly felt that the government alone would not be able to shoulder the responsibility of meeting the goals of UEE. The last decade has seen the involvement of the Non Government Organizations like never before.

Role of Non–Government Organizations

One of the prominent features of the last decade has been the active involvement of the national and international NGOs in education. In fact the NGOs have slowly emerged as the new significant partners to the government body. Today they are an active force to be reckoned with. The NGOs have played a major role in bringing about qualitative improvements in different areas of primary education.

Development of Textbooks and Curricular Material

A lot of initiative has been taken to develop instructional material keeping in mind the interest of the learner. The focus has been to include different activities, which would stimulate the mind of the learner, arouse curiosity and spirit of enquiry. Due importance has been given to projects and assignment which would promote cooperative learning and self-learning. The curricular material includes illustrations and visuals with which the child can easily identify.

Community Mobilization and Advocacy

The NGOs have contributed immensely in making the masses aware of the importance of education. Different strategies like folk theatre, skits, and other literacy campaigns have been used. The community has not only been mobilized to a great extent but it has further led to community participation, furthering the cause of primary education.

Training of Teachers

Serious efforts are being made to give in-service training to the teachers to update their knowledge and skill. These quality initiatives leave a distinct mark, improving the teaching-learning process. Various workshops are organized focusing on content and pedagogy.

Promotion of Girl Education

There has been an increase in female literacy since independence and girl education has made headway. However a wide disparity between the education of boys and girls still remains. To bridge this gap and to put an end to the discrimination against the girl child is the goal of these voluntary agencies. Different interventions are being made and schemes are being implemented on a priority basis to reduce gender inequality.

Adult Literacy

Adult education programmes have been the center of attention for quite some time now. Even today thirty-five out of every hundred of the population is illiterate. These people are totally indifferent to education and do not realize its importance for their children and this is one of the factors which comes in the way of UEE. Massive programmes for removing adult illiteracy are being launched at regular intervals.

Strengthening Non–Formal Education

The scheme of non-formal education (NFE) was introduced in 1979-80 to those children in the age group of 6-14 years who had remained outside the formal system of schooling. The prime focus of the programme was the educationally backward states, urban slums, hilly, tribal and desert areas. The programme was not only implemented by the states/UT's but full support was given to the NGOs to run non-formal co-educational centers and girls' centres. Their sustained work in this area is laudable.

The Benefits and Limitations of Non–Government Organizations

Non-government organizations have total autonomy to function in ways they think best. There is no government control and intervention in their day to day concerns. There is no beaurocratic checks at each step thus enabling faster realization of goals. The lack of red-tapism ensures quick decision making and time-bound targets can be met.

At the same time we have to keep in mind that many NGOs today are functioning within boundaries and have their own limitations.

The sources of funding for their various developmental activities is a matter of grave concern for many small NGOs. They have to function within the limited parameters which could affect the quality of their work. Often it has been observed that these organizations are not able to attract quality human resources for the want of high salaries. This could adversely affect the entry of committed and dedicated workers into the system.

The government often looks at many of these organizations with suspicion. There have been innumerable incidents where unnecessary queries have been made by government agencies and work has been disrupted. These roadblocks frequently become a source of demotivation for people working passionately for a cause.

A few measures have been suggested to enhance the effectiveness of Non-Government Organizations in India.

ENHANCING EFFECTIVENESS OF NON-GOVERNMENT ORGANISAITONS IN INDIA: SOME MEASURES

One cannot refute the role, which NGOs have replayed in India in the field of elementary education. They do have certain advantages and at the same time have limitations too. Hence if suitable steps are taken by government to enhance their effectiveness, it would go a long way in helping us to achieve our long cherished dream of UEE.

Relaxing Bureaucratic Procedures

First of all, it is almost necessary on part of government to relax some bureaucratic norms and regulations in case of such organizations. The donations given to them are exempted from Income-Tax Act but still they have to pass through official channels with regard to different matters. Red tapism, cumbersome procedures, complexities of rules and sluggishness on the part of government administration leads to wastage of time, money and energy of human power. Many times it proves to be a barrier for the NGOs. Therefore government needs to take such steps, which would motivate them to work with higher efficiency, zeal, enthusiasm and productivity. This would be helpful not only to the existing organizations but further encourage new organizations to be active in this field.

Optimum Utilization of Mass Media

Further, government at central, state and at local self body level enjoy control over mass medias such as Radio, T.V., Printed literature (weekly & monthly bulletins) etc. They need to be utilized maximally to attract NGOs' to contribute in greater way to the goals of UEE such as enrollment, retention, quality education etc. The prime need of the hour is involvement of these organization in the area of providing quality education. Although, over years, the drive for 100% enrollment has been a success to a great extent in may states e.g. Gujarat but due to low quality of education and poor infrastructural facilities as well as inefficient utilization of resources, 100% retention still appears to be a distant dream. In this regard, NGOs can be motivated especially through mass media to contribute in an active way. The government should declare some awards/prizes to recognize their services as this proves to be a great motivational force. This should be declared at the institutional as well the individual level.

Developing Partnership

The most important strategy on the part of government should be to develop spirit of cohesion rather than conflict with these organizations. Active collaboration or partnership would enhance total productivity as it would help to nullify their own limitations to a great extent, if not totally. Government can develop a partnership venture with NGOs where have not only the financial but human resources on the part of government can be involved.

The government must have a long term and short-term action plan in consultation with NGO's where UEE would not be a responsibility of education department alone but also of Ministry of Health and Family Welfare, Social Welfare, Environment etc. This is precisely because education does not exist in isolation but is one of the social subsets and therefore integrated efforts would be of great help to all. Involvement of anganwadi workers, primary school teachers and employees of social welfare and environment with NGO's would go a long way in improving the quality of education and help to achieve the target of 100% retention.

The time has come to realize that the goals of universalisation of elementary education cannot be met without effective partnership of non-government organizations in India. Lets walk hand in hand to make this dream come true.

BIBLIOGRAPHY

Aggarwal, J.C. (2004), Modern Indian Education Delhi, Shipra Publication.

Aggarwal, J.C. (2004), Development of Education System in India. Delhi, Shipra Publications.

Joshi, M., Pradhan, N. (2000), et.al. Management of Primary Education: A Challenge, Vadodara, Good Companion.

Sharma, S. (2004), History of Education. New Delhi, Anmol Publications.

National Curriculum Framework (2005) New Delhi NCERT.

Ministry of Human Resource Development, National Policy on Education 1986. New Delhi, MHRD.

Ministry of Human Resource Development, National Policy on Education 1992. New Delhi. MHRD.

Ministry of Human Resource Development, Report of Education Commission. 1964-66. New Delhi, MHRD.

Ministry of Human Resource Development, National Policy an Education. 1968. New Delhi. MHRD.

SARJOO PATEL

8 NGO's: Development Instrument

"A small body of determined spirits, fired by unquenchable faith in their mission, can alter the course of history". These were words of Mahatma Gandhi for the committed Voluntary Organizations.

Arnold Toynbee, once commenting on the process of degeneration in our civilization, said that our civilization could be saved by means of proper guidance and commitment by the "creative minority" in which a "selective group" of leaders restrain themselves from corruptive influences, commune with God and return spiritually regenerated to inspire the masses. It is indeed these "Selective Group" of leaders from Voluntary Organizations, which have ever been making sterling contributions to bring about desired changes in society.

NGO's: A NEW HOPE

Non governmental organizations have become the new hope of development cooperation. NGO's are increasingly assuming tasks which earlier were the domain of government sectors. In the case of NGO's engaged in the development policy, it is not only their standing that has become greater, their number, budget and influence and their closeness to governments–have also gained in quantity and strength. NGO's are now 'in' with government cooperation agencies. NGOs are seen as the miracle weapon' in the battle against increasing poverty in large parts of the world. Whoever travels through developing countries today, sees at many cross roads signs that point in all directions to the locations of local NGO's. Not all NGO's are competent, not all are grassroots oriented, and not a few are simply labels for private business sector initiatives or the sinecures of representatives of the state elite. This does not mean that there should be no competition to find the best solution to a problem. On the contrary, specific process should be made transparent and discussed so that one can differentiate between reports of short lived success and approaches aligned on the long haul. Indeed, perhaps that would enable learning from others and lead to good ideas being taken up by several (Narasaiah, 2003).

NGO's: ADVANTAGES AND DISADVANTAGES (COUSINS, 1991)

Advantages

- They have the ability to experiment freely with innovative approaches and, if necessary, to take risks.
- They are flexible in adapting to local situations and responding to local needs and therefore able to develop integrated projects, as well as sectoral projects.
- They enjoy good rapport with people and can render micro-assistance to very poor people as they can identify those who are most in need and tailor assistance to their needs.
- They have the ability to communicate at all levels, from the neighborhood to the top levels of government.
- They are able to recruit both experts and highly motivated staff with fewer restrictions than the government.

Disadvantages

- Paternalistic attitudes restrict the degree of participation in programme/project design.
- Restricted/constrained ways of approach to a problem or area.
- Reduced replicability of an idea, due to non-representativeness of the project or selected area, relatively small project coverage, dependence on outside financial resources, etc.
- "Territorial possessiveness" of an area or project reduces cooperation between agencies, seen as threatening or competitive.

RISE AND ROLE OF NGO's IN SUSTAINABLE DEVELOPMENT

The Non-Government Organisations (NGOs) have taken deep roots in human civilization in supplementing and complimenting the work of Government agencies. Their contributions in micro-level development has been highly appreciated. Their role in times of calamities, especially the speed with which they provide quick relief to the suffering humanity has earned them a place of respect in the Society. All this is due to several advantages they have over Government agencies e.g. greater flexibility and freedom to adopt themselves to changing needs and ideas, greater human touch, close personal contact, better rapport with people, greater potential for mobilising community support etc. (Gugnani, 2000).

Added by advances in information and communications technology, NGOs have helped to focus attention on the social and environmental externalities of business activity. Multinational brands have been acutely susceptible to pressure from activities and from NGOs eager to challenge a Company's labour, environmental or human rights record. Even those business that do not specialize in highly visible branded goods are feeling the pressure, as campaigners develop techniques to target downstream customs and shareholders.

NGOs are those organizations which pursue some sort of public interest or public good, rather than individual or commercial interests. One characteristic these diverse organizations share is that their non-profit status means they are not hindered by short-term financial objectives. Accordingly, they are able to devote themselves to issues which occur across longer time horizons, such as climate change, malaria prevention or a global ban on landmines. Public surveys reveal that NGOs often enjoy a high degree of public trust, which can make them useful for the concerns of Society. The NGOs are now-a-days fulfilling a fundamental needs in a nations life by endeavoring, by supplementing and complimenting existing services, by being the instruments of change and by serving as catalyst for community action which ultimately is the best way of achieving progress in any Society.

Many NGOs are devoted to the cause of women welfare and make people innovative, participatory and try to make them independent. They also can help the Government in forming policies for women because of their intimate knowledge of the local situation. The NGOs have in particular played a significant role, both nationally and internationally in growing the feminist movement towards gender equality, which can only be achieved by making women economically independent, indirectly rising the economic status of the family. (Chandrasekhar, 1989) Thus the NGOs are chief means to attain goal of sustainable development alongwith organized and well executed governmental drives.

STRENGTHENING THE CAPACITY OF NGO'S

Non-governmental organizations (NGO's) have played a major role in pushing for sustainable development at the national as well as international level. There are few things the NGO should think for strengthening its capacity. First and foremost is the purpose or clear vision of what is to be done. Even if it begins with little more than an aim to help a certain group or community, an NGO's ability to muster commitment, resources and results depends largely on its defining what it wishes to accomplish, and for which beneficiaries. The organization's aims will undoubtedly evolve overtime, yet they must be tied directly to the priority needs held by the particular beneficiaries of that NGO. Secondly, the long-term efficacy of an NGO requires an effective management structure staffed with capable persons. The roles, responsibilities and relationship of all staff must be well articulated and understood for internal operations and interactions with beneficiary groups, officials, and other partners. Thirdly, an NGO's influence is measured by its achievements, requiring capacity in planning, implementation, and monitoring and evaluation, along with the resources to accomplish them. Finally an effective NGO is judged on the openness and reliability of its relations with strategic partners like Government, NGO's, and Private Sector as collaboration, advocates, or allies. Attention to these issues has traditionally focused on strengthening the internal structure and operations of target NGO's. Increasingly, the work of developing NGO's focus on ensuring that the policies, practices, and other structural features of the broader framework in which NGOs operate are conducive to effective NGO initiatives. This approach has resulted in modifications to other existing approaches.

Working towards the achievement of full participation of Civil Society ideally involves individuals and groups from many organizations, like NGO's and community–based organizations, the media, private associations, government, and others interested (Muskin, 2001).

ENHANCING NGO'S POLICY ADVOCACY SKILLS

William. A. Douglas and David Payton suggested some points for enhancing NGO's policy Advocacy skills. NGO's should keep a number of points in mind for both the initial planning and subsequent implementation phases of their projects. Some points are self-evident and serve as reminders; all should be considered within the cultural and political setting in which the project takes place. These points are as follows:

- Time and diplomacy are required to help NGOs advocating on similar issues to form coalition and combine their strength. Consider these factor when laying out the project's time-line.
- Advocacy-building efforts must take into account, and overcome, the legacy of fear in societies recently emerged from repressive rule. Engage in one-on-one discussions with local leaders to judge what they view as risky.
- An abundance of good materials are available for teaching advocacy skills. Use them, rather than waste time and money "reinventing the wheel."
- The trend of training, technical assistance, and grant support helps build NGO confidence, allowing its members to apply skills learned in their local institutional and socio-political context. Avoid over-reliance on a single approach.
- The effectiveness of training depends on the time and effort put into preparing NGOs before training. Plan and budget accordingly.

- Formal and informal channels through which advocacy takes place vary from culture to culture. (As the salesman says in the opening scene of Meredith Wilson's classic show The Music Man: "But a gotta know the territory"!). Become familiar with local realities.
- NGOs may initially attempt to achieve advocacy goals rather than what their limited resources will allow. Help NGOs to narrow the target.
- Emotion and reformist zeal must be tempered by tactical sagacity. Help NGOs make prudent decisions about the selection and sequence of tactics for use during advocacy campaigns.
- Follow-on assistance and short refresher training programs are as important as the training itself and just as costly and time-consuming. Budget to ensure adequate resources to reinforce the initial instructional phase.
- To ensure that participants retain what they learn in formal training sessions, minimize lectures and maximize participatory teaching techniques such as role plays, small group work, case studies, and practical activities such as writing a press release.
- Formal training sessions can also be used as advocacy platforms. Invite advocacy targets to be teachers or guests.
- Media coverage of advocacy campaigns need not be purchased. NGOs can learn how to show reporters that their work is newsworthy, and thus receive free coverage.
- Use prudence in judging which advocacy activities are suitable for support with foreign funds especially if they are foreign government funds. Consider how one might feel about foreigners funding a similar advocacy in one's own country.
- Foreign donors should not expect that raising local NGOs' advocacy skills will in and of itself change the prevailing basic power structure of the society" this results from revolution, not advocacy.
- A mix of local and external perspectives is productive. Foreign advocacy advisors can combat local fatalism by showing that significant change is possible even within existing power structures, and the experience of local NGO personnel can suggest how best to promote such change.

CONCLUSION

NGOs can be proud of their contribution to the consolidation of human rights in many Societies, and of their efforts for civil rights and for more efficient local organization with a greater capability to handle conflicts. NGOs also have won great credit by pointing out to government sector deficiencies and weak spots in developmental practice. Without the

NGO's pressure and that of their lobby, the cross–sectorial topics of the environment, women and poverty–which are now firmly fixed in development cooperation–would not have entered the international political debate so quickly not have been implemented in projects and programmes. NGOs should get together and define and agree on criteria for the quality of their work. It is also important to carry out evaluation programmes that would enable to describe clearly the impact of the efforts made by NGOs. NGOs were not born yesterday, but the rising number of conflicts that have reverberated in recent decades around a world globalised in the neo-liberal mould has led them to multiply and diversify into highly visible bodies. The role of NGOs should be to foster the emergence of a world wide civil Society, the first step towards making globalisation a more democractic affair (Narasaiah, 2003).

BIBLIOGRAPHY

Barbara, H. (1987), "Women in Development: Issues for Economic Sector Analysis".

Chandrasekhar, R. (1989), "A Book on Women's Resource and National Development".

Chaudhary, P.K. (1986), "Women Sweepers of Patna" Social Welfare, Volume 33, No. 2.

Cousins, W. (1991), "Non Governmental Initiatives" in ADB, The Urban Poor and Basic Infrastructure Services in Asia and the Pacific", Asian Development Bank, Manila.

Dayal, R. (1987), "Resource Book on Women's Development, Co-operation with Government Donors and Voluntary Organizations".

Dixon, R.B. (1980), "Assessing the Impact of Development Projects on Women" Agency for International Development, Washington.

Douglas, W.A. and Payton, D. (2001), "Enhancing NGO's Policy Advocacy Skills: Lessons Learned" cited in "NGO's in Development", SIT Occasional Papers Series ,Published by School for International Training, USA.

Gugnani, H.R. (2000), "Indian and International Non-Government Organization in the Social Sector", Educational Consultants Consortium, Delhi.

International Labour Office, "A Report of the Office Training and Women".

Khedgkar, V. (1987), "A study of Voluntary Organizations impact on Development of Womens" S.N.D.T., Mumbai cited in Shah, M. (1996)."A study of the improvement in economic status of families of women trained in income generating activities by the Voluntary Organizations", Unpublished Masters Thesis, Department of Home Management, Faculty of Home Science, The M.S. University of Baroda.

Muskin, J. (2001), "NGOs in Development: The case of World Learning", cited in "NGO's in Development", SIT Occasional papers Series, Published by School for International Training, USA.

Narasaiah, M.L. (2003), "The Role of Micro Credit and NGOs in Economic Development", Discovery Publishing House, New Delhi.

Shah, M. (1996), "A Study of the Improvement in Economic Status of Families of Women Trained in Income Generating Activities by the Voluntary Organizations" Unpublished Masters Thesis, Department of Home Management, Faculty of Home Science, The M.S. University of Baroda, Vadodara.

Website Browsed

www.google.com.
www.worldlearning.org.
www.sit.edu/publications

SIRIMAVO NAIR

9 Walking with Hand in Hand

World's major achievements have been great success always through participation and team efforts.

"If local people are involved, the community will really listen. Link volunteers speak community's own language. If the motivation comes from both sides, we can achieve our aims. They help in reassuring community members because they belong to the community."

—***Dr. V. Anantha Kumari***

Human nature calls for better livelihood all the time. The urge to live in better standards keeps flowing till the end of ones life. Major transition occurs in this phase. One tends to the thinking which brings "live & let live" policy. These thoughts usually are the outcomes of experience shared by self, by community and masses. When such number of bodies associates together the evolution of an NGO occurs. Nevertheless to say it takes time to settle 'niche' which it carves for itself. To find a place, to adjust to the needs, provide facilities and grow along generally the target goal of any such body, sustenance alone at time would be difficult here because the issues dealt by this unit would be sensitive, Hence it calls for 'Team efforts'.

Natural growth in population and their increased densities are resulting in unplanned development of big cities. Thousands of people migrate to the cities majorly due to poverty, bad living condition etc. A study published in India formal of community need by Siddharth reported that population in rural India grew by 18% whereas that of urban scenario was 31% in between 1991-2004.This clearly indicates urban growth is overtaking rural growth. This can happen in any country which is on its developing path.

The 9th five year plan of India had estimated that urban population will be 605-618 million during 2021-2025. In the past, poverty was assumed to be mainly rural phenomena, owing to its relatively greater

Figure 1: Percent Decadal Growth by Residence in India: 1901-2001

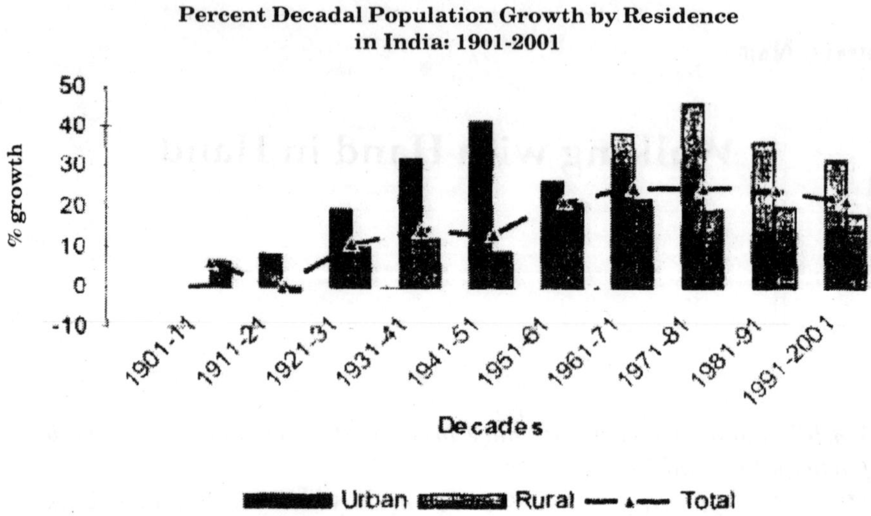

(*Source:* Siddharth Agarwal, 2004).

magnitude and visibility in comparison to the urban poverty which is largely camouflaged within its rich neighborhoods. Although the majority of people, in absolute numbers, still live in the rural areas, a large and rapidly growing segment of the population lives in cities. Many of these do so in conditions of extreme poverty, without access to adequate shelter, other basic services and health services.

According to census of India 2001, of the total population 32% dwells in UP, MP, Orissa, Bihar, Jharkand, Chattisgarh, Rajasthan, Uttranchal etc of this 43% of urban poor dwells in these states. This needs a lot of focus especially on the health impacts of this population.

Various learning experiences from major cities of India like

Figure 2: Urban Poverty in EAG States

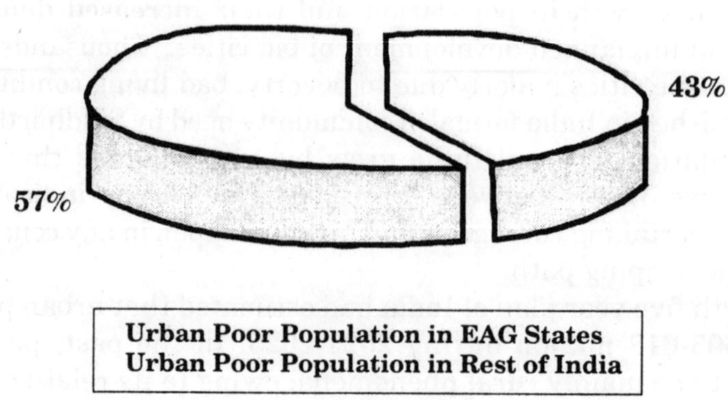

Bangalore, Delhi, AP, Indore etc has contributed to various population programs. Urban averages marks sharp disparities between the rich and poor in urban settings. By many health indicators, urban poor populations are comparable to nearby rural populations-or worse in many cases. There are multitude of healthcare service providers such as the Municipality, Ministry of Health, Private Sector, NGOs etc with ill defined roles and poor coordination. The range of health problems in urban areas demands integration of the poor as a priority into urban health planning and for RCH services.

The reach and effectiveness of immunization services in urban slums are strained by a number of challenges. Disease transmission can be interrupted with a lower immunization coverage rate in less densely populated areas, whereas the coverage rate needs to be much higher in urban areas to have the same effect, owing to higher population density and the consequent ease of disease transmission.

The example of health programs in Madhya Pradesh can be cited here. The vaccination of children against six serious preventable diseases (tuberculosis, diphtheria, pertussis, tetanus, polio and measles) has been a cornerstone of the child health care system in India. The reanalysis of NFHS 2 data, Madhya Pradesh reveals that only one-fifth of all children aged 12-23 months had received complete immunization. 43 percent of children from urban poor households had been vaccinated against measles by the age of 12 months as compared to the urban average coverage of 55 percent. Dropout and left out rates are far higher among urban poor households, in comparison to the urban average.

Public sector services for the urban poor in India, has suffered overtly. The centralized planning have been inflexible, lot of political interference, failure to integrate programs meant for family welfare and nutritional health services etc. The public sector share is hardly about 20%. The scheme on urban family welfares is functioning since 50s. Currently there are 1083 UFWCs (Urban Family Welfare Center). With the total urban population of 290 million, this works to one UFWC/HP (health post). Through Indian population project VIII which covered 7 million slum populations in 4 mega-cities and 94 small towns. It was seen that Bangalore had 55 health centers with the existing 37 and yet improving health services varied from place to place.

The reasons were:

- Inadequate physical and social access.
- Low demand for services among slum dwellers and weak community linkages.
- Poor quality (time, attitude, atmosphere)
- Insufficient reach to the underserved slums
- Weak monitoring and tracking of coverage

- Low focus on behavior change
- Little emphasis on sustainability
- NGOs active in small areas etc.

NGO Partnership in Health Programs

A lot of experiences and lessons are learned from partnership programs.

The following are the few examples from various parts of the country:

1. Bangalore-NGOs were involved in running UFWC under city cooperation with financial support from Govt. of India and Govt. of Karnataka.
2. In Andhra Pradesh, the volunteers and women's health group linked activities which were interrelated and promoted them through NGOs.
3. In Delhi, the NGOs like Mamta and Asha operated with partial support from govt. Thus enhancing partnership programs.
4. In Indore, the world coordination model involving improving immunization services were made functional. The NGOs coordinated with Municipal Corporation, health dept., ICDS, local traders and community based organizations.
5. In Gujarat, SEWA and SAATH focused on institutional capacities at slum level and created an effective build-up to manage all the development activities.

All these programs were successful. Some of them are still continuously running and has proved beneficial to the society.

The above mentioned situations proved the benefits of partnership programs of the NGOs with the govt. Further the NGOs contributed in the Reproductive and Child Health (RCH) programs by adapting the following steps:

(a) Identifying and mapping vulnerable slums.
(b) Improve sanitation and other basic amenities.
(c) Enhance demand and utilization of services in building capacities of the functionaries.
(d) Manage primary level programs independently.
(e) Building effective partnerships and convergence.
(f) New models for replication are to be developed.
(g) Capacity building, institutional strengthening and sustainability should be emphasized.
(h) Strengthening and developing urban Health Mission Improving Strategies.
(i) Develop the field for urban health programs.

The conclusions based on RCH programs were suggestive that the NGOs can play an important role in identifying the pockets on a priority basis; they can act as effective community mobilizers, can create awareness and demand for quality health services. Thus, the urban health programs can be strengthened.

Another study carried out in Hyderabad was also reviewed. Here the NGOs were engaged in community development, women's initiatives and health improvement. The IPP VIII project staffs were also actively involved into this program. Of the 662 slums, 22 NGOs managed and acted as intermediaries between health staff and community members. Each NGO took care of maternal and child health programs atleast in 20 slums. They motivated community women to form Women's Health Groups (WHG) known as 'Mahila Arogya Sangams'. They train community health volunteers and the link volunteers. Link volunteers serve as communicators of important messages and information related to health, family planning etc.

The Partners in IPP VIII - Hyderabad

IPP VIII government staff	Health staff	NGOs	Link Volunteers & women's health groups	Community members

Integral Involvement: The Multiple Roles of NGOs in Hyderabad

Unlike many development projects in which NGOs are engaged in isolated tasks, such as managing a health center or vocational training program, in IPP VIII Hyderabad, NGOs are involved in all community-based activities. Their responsibilities include the following:

- Oversee maternal and child health and family planning activities in 20 or more slum communities.
- Identify, train and manage Link Volunteers.
- Organize and manage women's health groups.
- maintain a regular dialogue with community members and health staff through:
  - monthly meetings at the Urban Health Post for NGOs, health staff, and IPP VII Women's Development Officers;
  - monthly WHG meetings in the slum for Link Volunteers, NGOs and women from the community;
  - monthly meetings in the IPP VIII project office for NGOs and project officials;
  - quarterly meetings in the IPP VII project office for NGOs and Medical Officers;

– annual meetings of all the Link Volunteers in the city

- Raise awareness of health and family planning issues by organizing:
  – health camps
  – competitions for Link Volunteers and adolescent girls in the slums
  – special programs, such as World Health Day and the Pulse Polio Campaign:
- Register vital events.
- Manage IPP VII community-based health and development activities such as:
  – revolving funds for WHGs
  – nursery schools
  – schools for former drop-outs
  – adolescent girls' workshops
  – first-time mother's workshops.
- Establish additional community development activities according to community needs, such as legal literacy programs and income generation schemes.

Source: Urban health resource center

Encouraging Participation: How Did it Happen in Hyderabad:

Getting NGOs and women from the slums involved in the project was not easy. Numerous steps were taken:

1. The administration of the project created a dedicated, all-female management structure for overseeing women's participation and community-based activities:
   - One program officer with management skills and experience working with government and NGOs and in the field.
   - Three assistant program officers for extensive field-based work.
2. Project staff developed procedures to promote NGO involvement:
   - A request to the state government to issue an order outlining government-NGO collaboration, thus providing the legal framework for approving NGO activities in a government project.
   - Guidelines and selection criteria for NGO participation.
   - A standard contract for NGOs, specifying terms and conditions of collaboration, including the administrative, technical, and financial responsibilities of the NGOs.
   - Reporting requirements and a standard monthly reporting form for NGOs.
   - An annual action plan for all community-based and NGO activities.

3. Project staff selected and prepared NGOs for collaboration with the project by:
   - Developing a comprehensive profile of NGOs in Hyderabad, with help from other government departments and development agencies.
   - Organizing a two-day workshop for NGOs to introduce IPP VIII and discuss possibilities for collaboration.
   - Providing a 10-day training program to prepare the selected NGOs for project work.
4. NGOs established networks of community health volunteers and women's groups in the slums by:
   - Holding IPP VII orientation meetings in each slum.
   - Holding additional meetings in slums to measure sustained interest of Link Volunteer candidates.
   - Working with community members to select one Link Volunteer for every 20 families.
   - Training Link Volunteers for four days.
   - Initiating WHGs in each slum.
5. NGOs established other IPP VII innovative schemes in slums, such as adolescent girls workshops, first-time mother's workshops, and nursery schools.
6. Project staff expanded collaboration with other groups by:
   - Holding orientation meetings for other influential groups in the communities, such as local private medical practitioners, women entrepreneurs, and female community leaders.
   - Collaborating with other government departments and private groups to bring other community development activities to the slums, such as the HUDA Urban Forestry Nursery Scheme.
7. NGOs and community members were given the flexibility to plan and establish community activities:
   - NGOs identified and began additional development schemes needed by the slum communities.
   - WHGs planned and funded community schemes using revolving funds.

Source: Urban health resource center.

The NGOs and link volunteers hold 2 meetings every month for 2 hours, to ensure regular communication between all the groups and also to address their related issues. One meeting is held in the slum so as to facilitate attendance of the women groups in respective communities. Urban health positions bring the link volunteers and NGOs together. They also provide with a platform to women to discuss their other community concerns. Link volunteers and NGOs along with Women development officers and health facilitators work out appropriate solutions and actions for any major issues.

It was interesting to note that these partnership programmes brought in a lot of benefits to many communities without any additional duties. The project also threw some light on the following benefits-NGOs are able to effectively manage community based network of health volunteers, women groups because of the understanding of the cultural contexts, community mobilization, promotion of local participation etc. They further manage to fill the gaps like addressing controversial topics, issues of poorest populations etc.

The involvement of partnership programmes in the IPP VIII, in Hyderabad proved highly beneficial. Resources, financial and moral support was gained. Successful schemes were expanded to larger populations. The level of awareness went up tremendously. Few responsibilities in the project like identifying, managing project activities, functioning as intermediaries, managing all the networks, conducting baseline surveys, etc has helped the project to go on a long way. This calls for attention to the government functionaries and authorities to draw more plans in similar lines and implement them at a state wise level.

In Gujarat, various NGOs are working towards benefits for children at different levels. In Vadodara, Shishu Milap is one such organization which is aiming such a big progress. Various activities are conducted by this organization to update and move the children towards attaining minimum education and basic amenities. Disha, is another organization which takes care of under-privileged children. For children between ages 3-6, are enrolled in an organization known as Vatsalya. All these organizations contribute to upliftment of children in various sectors.

Various international organizations are also known to take care of under-privileged children on a partnership basis as well as independently. In India, we have partnership programs for improving health status with UNICEF, micronutrient initiative (MI), WHO, ICMR, etc. Worldwide supporters and sponsorers are involved in projects maintained by the above mentioned bodies. For e.g. MI works with specific achievements like:

- Virtual elimination of Iodine deficiency disorders.
- Virtual elimination of Vit. A deficiency and its consequences.
- Reduce Iron deficiency Anemia in women by one-third of the reported levels in 1990.

The progress through partnerships are aimed with the following tips in mind:

- Commitment, capabilities and programs to control micronutrient deficiencies where none previously existed.
- Successful promotion staple food fortification with cost effective interventions.
- Strengthen national programs in Asia, Africa and Middle East.
- Technical assistance to various countries etc. are a few to list.

Some of the activities of the NGOs focus on broader development concerns such as education and women empowerment, while others focus on reproductive and child health concerns. They were further able to respond to developmental needs of the slum communities which differed from one area to the other. Interdepartmental help and support was seeked and delivered from these collaborative approaches. The strengthening of community net work, developemental activities etc has helped in betterment of community. This has increased the credibility and effectiveness of community programmes.The women who have worked gained recognition and importance in these fields. This has boosted their work culture and morale.

The following steps are to be born in mind while involving an NGO-They should be able to develop a standard contract. Specifications regarding administrative, technical and financial responsibilities should be defined. The outlines laid should be flexible and feasible. It should be tailor made as to particular requirements of the communities. Reporting should be systematic and accessible. If these guidelines are followed smooth functioning of partnerships between NGOs and government functionaries can be achieved.

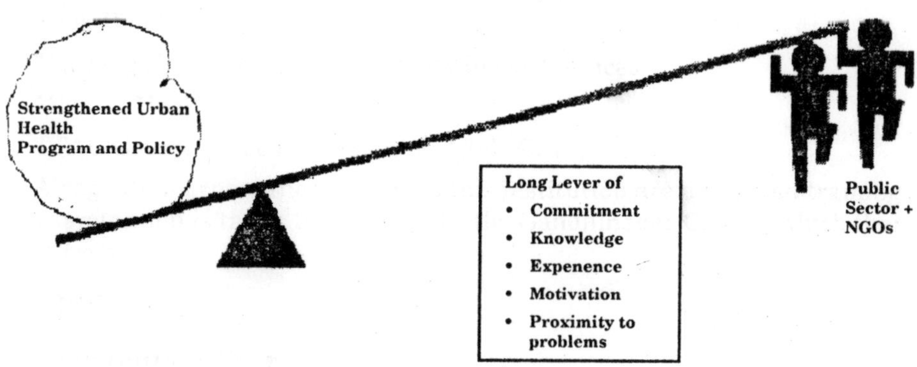

BIBLIOGRAPHY

Kirrin Gill. If we walk together: Communities NGOs and Government in partnership for health.

Kirrin Gill. The IPP VII Hyderabad experience.

Siddarth Agarwal. Building public sector NGO partnership for urban RCH services.

Siddharth Agarwal and Kirti Sangar. Need for dedicated focus on urban health with national rural health mission.

Urban Health Resource Centre. Selected literatures on health of Urban Poor.

Part – II
Empirical Studies

RAMESHWARI PANDYA

10 NGOs - Towards Self Reliance

INTRODUCTION

Beginning in 1958 with Delhi Pilot Project financed by Ford Foundation, there has been a series of Urban Community Development Project in India. Community Development in India could be seen as an effort to mobilize *manpower and participation of village or city people for economic, political and social reconstruction activities. The ultimate of these programmes is composite national development leading to an overall process of modernization. These are the projects of local significance initiated and carried out by local people. Development is achieved by moving in stages towards modernization through mobilizing sizeable people's participation and their efforts towards improving conditions for community integration and self–direction.

Voluntary associations and community councils are structured groups in which numerous individuals work towards some common objectives. What do people actually do in their non–working hours? Dr. Saxton Graham has made such a study in Butler Country and in his findings more leisured persons are found in the upper than lower classes, but only 25% of Buttlers population belongs to one or more organization. Most persons are "bench sitters" spending a large portion of their leisure time watching video, television and motion picture which are passive, non–creative and non–commercially organized activities. More urban than rural folk engage in recreational and religious activities, which are most likely to produce warm and personal relationships and enriching experiences.

The literature suggests that the rapid growth of urban areas in developing nations is accomplished by social disorganization and that individuals living in these urban centers experience great stress as a result of their being caught between two worlds–the modern and the traditional. Inhabitants of urban centers may leave traditional patterns and learn to adopt new patterns. There are certain organizations which have developed in urban areas. They take the form of voluntary association which are either rooted in traditional patterns or which are Western in form they are said to provide meaningful substitutes of traditional identities and patterns of living and to act as socializing agents for the adoption of new roles mere in harmony with the urban environment and a modern society. Voluntary organizations play an important role in the lives of modern men living and working in an urban environment. In the industrialized cities these associations have flourished without precedents. One of the outstanding characteristics of urban living is said to be the great number of variety of clubs, organization, societies, leagues and similar associations into which people group themselves and through which they pursue their interests.

PHILOSOPHY OF THESE PROJECTS

Self help has been the philosophy of these projects since the beginning. The projects proceed with the assumption that any neighbourhood, no matter how poor, can do something to improve itself by its own efforts and that any approach for outside help should be resorted to only after it has exhausted its own resources fully. This is not always an easy message to get across to poor people who sometimes felt that the government should freely meet their needs because they are poor. The success of the projects depends almost entirely upon the work of each individual community organizer who had to stimulate guide and sustain the whole process by working with individuals and groups and bring in outside help when needed. The task requires a great deal of patience, sensitivity and commitment to the aims of the projects.

HOW VOLUNTARY ASSOCIATION ARISE ?

Urban groups and associations arise and exist to help the urban people to adjust to their social and cultural environment. The rise of special interests are fewer in rural areas, a small number of such interest groups are found there, people who are socially and culturally conscious tend to form into groupings of their own kind, cities foster many such special interest groups. City life and conditions also give rise to many welfare associations. It has been theorized that voluntary organizations flourish in a social setting in which the community loses its cohesive and organized character and ceases to function as an all inclusive social group. The growth of big urban centres have created the conditions fertile for the extensive development of associations.

Social differentiations, heterogeneity and large urban aggregates are some of the major factors responsible for this development. The loss of economic, educational, protective and recreational functions of family, neighbourhood community largely contribute to the growth of voluntary associations. Consequently, voluntary associations have been increasingly relied upon to make up for these losses. These voluntary associations are also considered to be individual as well as providing a direct way for the individual.

VOLUNTARY ORGANIZATIONS AND SEGMENTATION

One chief reason for segmentation of the social world of many urbanites lies in the number and importance of the voluntary association in which they participate. Many men with similar interests want to associate with others of like interests and of the same economic class–lawyers with lawyers, executives with executives, regardless of local area of residence. City life proves to be a particularly fertile breeding place for voluntary associations not only because of similarity of specialized interests and problems as the part of many person but because most of these people do not normally come to know one another personally through family or neighbourhood.

Thus, a whole series of association parallels the various branches and activities of government and extends into many areas where government is relatively inactive. The people involved often meet face to face but do not have such intimate contacts. They see each other as persons in certain categories.

FUNCTIONS OF VOLUNTARY ASSOCIATIONS

It is difficult to categorize the associations and their functions as such because they tend to overlap each other. However, one can always identify the main functions from the subsidiary ones which can help in placing them in almost exclusive categories for analysis purpose.

N.K. Bose in his social survey of Calcutta sponsored by the Anthropological Society of India, points out a similar preponderance of voluntary organizations. Members of different linguistic groups have built up, in course of time, a little less than two thousand voluntary institutions to cater to residents, educational, recreational, welfare, religious and cultural needs.

It is always found that professional, recreational and welfare organization have the largest membership. Studies reveals that formal organizational membership with other variables, suggest that this significantly associated with respondents urban exposure and experiences, socio–economic status and education.

An obvious explanation of this correlation pattern can be the fact that people with good education, high income and status occupation usually have an easy access to voluntary organizations especially those organization which function on a relatively more secular and specialized interest–based pattern. These organizations such as Rotary and the Lions have a restricted and selective membership based on the factors discussed above. Although NGOs are plentiful, they do not reach all elements of the population equally. It is generally the people in the higher income brackets, the better educated those having high SES and greater urban exposure and experience that are more active in formal organizations.

Voluntary agencies in India have evolved as a result of a historical process that has brought them to their present shape and the role in the nation's development. If we look at the journey of development we find that in early 50s many of the voluntary organizations were engaged in relief work like drought or flood or were engaged in welfare activities like running Educational Institute or orphanage, destitute homes etc. However after a decade the focus of objective was changed they realized the importance of self reliant citizens. This was important that people should be able to procure the benefits of institutional welfare. Even after emphasizing the need of economic self reliance it was very strongly felt that until unless social structure of the country changes. India cannot follow the path of development.

Because of this realization during 1970s many voluntary organizations began to gear themselves towards a new type of education of making people aware and conscious of disparity in society. How the weaker section are deprived of their rights and until and unless they are also given their due place in the society the development and change in the society is not possible. This was the main cause that several activist groups built around these considerations, subsequently came into existence in the voluntary sector.

From the mid 1970's onwards there was an new trend which emerged gradually it was group of activists. Majority of them were around women and combating atrocities. These voluntary agencies were able to mobilize women. The activist groups have successfully from state and judiciary. The increasing interest of the government in promoting the role of voluntary organization and development of women is very clear. Government has strongly felt that it cannot assume the entire responsibility of service provision. As a result a meaningful partnership with the voluntary sector is essential goal.

Voluntary organizations are structures in which numerous individuals work towards some common objectives. Voluntary organizations play an important role in the lives of modern women living and working in an urban environment. A study was conducted in Baroda city.

OBJECTIVE

The objective of the study was to analyse the performance of women's voluntary organizations in terms of structure, functions and overall activities.

METHODOLOGY

A questionnaire was made and 18 voluntary organizations of Baroda city which were working exclusively for women were studied.

RESULTS AND DISCUSSION

A range of human care services is being provided in the fields of education, health, economic and women's upliftment, etc. It is difficult to categories the associations and their functions as such because they tend to overlap each other. However, one can always identify the main functions from subsidiary ones which can help placing them in almost exclusive categories for analysis purpose. The various voluntary organizations have undertaken several programmes to attain their objectives. They may be divided into these categories.

1. Cultural and Religious Programmes
2. Economic Programmes
3. Welfare and Relief Programmes

These categories are not manually exclusive. The investigators have differentiated them for the purpose of convenience.

Table 1
Percentage Distribution of Voluntary Organizations According to the Type of Activity Undertaken

N = 18

Type of Activity	*N*	*%*
Economic Activities	15	83.5
Social Activities	14	77.9
Religious Activities	13	72.3
Cultural Activities	12	66.7
Health and Nutrition Education	10	55.6
Counselling Services	6	33.3

As indicated in Table 1, more than 80 per cent of the agencies are involved in economic activities. These include assistance in the form of providing raw materials for preparing masalas, snacks, uniform, providing equipments like sewing machine, typewriter, etc. activities related to health and nutrition education are undertaken by little more than 50 per cent. The health education is imparted through meetings and discussions. Nearly one third of the various agencies have provision of counseling services for family, social and marital problems.

Different organizations have schemes of self supporting economic activities. Sewing classes seem to be most widely offered course. Embroidery classes are held in about more in 70 per cent voluntary organizations. This is followed by course is of Aya training as seen in Table 2 only 17 per cent organizations were offering this course.

Table 2
Percentage Distribution of the Voluntary Organizations According to the Courses Offered by Them

N = 18

Course Offered	*N*	%
Sewing	15	83.5
Embroidery	13	72.3
Knitting	10	55.6
Typing	10	55.6
Book Binding	10	55.6
Adult Education	10	55.6
S.C. Tuition	05	27.7
Hand Painting	05	27.7
Aaya Training Centre	03	16.8

Table 3
Percentage Distribution According to the Extent of Service Provided by the Various Voluntary Organizations

N = 18

Content of Service	N	%
Provide Training only	18	83.33
Placement after Training	03	16.66
Training and Refresher Course	00	00.00

The most striking finding of Table 3 is none of the agencies have facilities of retraining for refresher course for the women. More than 80 per cent of the agencies have facilities for training of the individual.

Table 4
Percentage Distribution of the Beneficiaries According to Their Characteristics

N = 18

	Characteristics	*N*	%
Age	Below 20 years	03	16.8
	21 – 30 years	05	27.7
	31 – 40 years	06	33.3
	41 and above		
	Age is no bar	16	66.7
SES	Belong to LIG	17	94.4
	Belong to MIG	17	94.4
	Belong to HIG	04	22.4
Education	Illiterate	17	94.4
	Primary	15	85.5
	High School	13	72.3
	College	03	16.8
Caste	Brahmin	03	16.8
	Baniya	06	33.3
	Patel	07	38.9
	SC/ST	03	16.8
	Cast no barrier	11	61.11

As far as the age of a woman is considered to become a member of organization, it is no bar in more than 66 per cent organizations. So women from all age groups are present. Maximum of women who came to take advantage of the different organization are either illiterate or educated till primary level and from lower or middle income groups. The women from Patel and Baniya caste are in majority and they also dominate various shehers of public life of Baroda.

Table 5
Distribution of the Type of Course and Time for the Course in the Various Voluntary Organisations

N = 18

Nature		*N*	*%*
Type of Course	Only Theory is Taught	00	–
	Only Practicals are Done	11	61.2
	Both (Theory & Practicals)	07	38.9
Time of Course	Fix Timing	14	77.9
	Learner chooses time according to convenience	17	94.4

Sixty per cent of the agencies offered only practical courses. This holds true as all the agencies are undertaking some or the other skill developing and practical oriented courses. Majority of the agencies (94%) reported that the learner chooses time according to their convenience. The women beneficiaries after finishing the household chores as and when they find free time they come to take part in the activity.

Table 6
Distribution of Beneficiaries According to the Number and Purpose of Attending Activities

N = 18

	Characteristics	*N*	*%*
Average Number of Beneficiaries			
	Less than 20	03	–
	21 – 40	02	11.2
	41 – 60	06	33.3
	More than 60	07	38.9
Purpose of Attending			
	Income Generation	16	88.8
	Recreational / Cultural	06	33.3
	Legal help	04	22.4

When average number of beneficiaries are analysed it is found that majority of the organisations have more than 60 women on an average.

Income generating is the main objective for which the women come to the organisation. The chance of getting extra income by working in leisure time have attracted many women to these voluntary organisations.

Besides income generation, women come to take part in recreational, cultural and socialization in their leisure time. These women enroll themselves so that these centres could provide them entertainment by offering cultural programmes. Competitions are held, with a view to encourage members to take up various activities. Various organisations organize dance, music, drama, and Garba competition, reciting of Geeta, Bhajanas. Besides these celebrations, the voluntary organisations have programmes like baby–show, fun fair, cooking contests and beauty classes, etc. All these activities give them chance to take part and show their talents. Also, it gives them a feeling of satisfaction.

Counselling centre provides just and viable counselling to the distressed women. Out of eighteen women voluntary organisations contacted by the investigator, four of these organisations reported that women come to these agencies for getting legal help also.

There are other than the routine activities not so commonly found in all the voluntary organisations in Baroda city as listed below:

- Giving Hall on rent for marriage
- Running Working women hostel
- Running own show rooms to sell their goods
- Organising Street plays, Dharana, Gherao.
- Running Balwadis.

ROLE OF HOME SCIENTISTS IN THESE ORGANIZATIONS

The significance of voluntary organizations in the life of modern women is seen. The changing kinds of participation of women in education and social activities can be seen from the post–independence club activities. At the turn of the century women's clubs were limited to cultural and educational opportunities of upper class women.

Today the great variety of women's organizations reflect the greater range and differentiations of women's activities, interests and services in our society. Because they wanted to change to work with others, they wanted to develop latest talents in art, hobbies and organizational planning and the pride in being part of a special group.

Home Scientists can work extensively with neighbourhood groups and can show persistence in influencing the decisions of relevant government agencies. Home Scientists can help in some project areas where the problems may be of Juvenile delinquency or atrocities on women and while outside agencies may deal with such cases, much can be done by the local community itself. A citizen juvenile delinquency committee can be formed to discuss the problems with the young people and the families involved. Home Scientist (who will be having knowledge of child development and psychology) can help to discover conditions in the family and community that may have given rise to delinquency.

Home Scientists can work in the different voluntary organizations and help people. For example, the income generating activities like tie–dye, different type of printing and making of handicraft and decorative articles.

In Baroda one of the oldest agency "Lalita Devi Society" is doing very good work in the field of recreation, education and income generation. Home Scientists can help other agencies to establish rapport with such agency and learn its positive points, so that they can also run as efficiently.

In Baroda district, the social welfare authorities have the established "Mahila Mandals" where women sing songs and Bhajans during meetings. This is because they are not trained. Seminar and workshops can be conducted to teach them different activities which could be performed by these women. Home Scientists can give them training to perform their functions properly. The Balwadi workers can be taught about soft toys, wall hanging, soap making, pot holders and magazine holders, use of embroidery. They can be given education about child care and health and nutrition education and many such important topics.

Although public authorities have chalked out a number of programmes for the welfare of women and they have been implemented also. These ladies can be suggested new topics like file making and making of bakery items. Alongwith this they can be given information about various places where they could go and get more orders for sale.

The Balwadi workers can be taught about clay moulding, and soft toys. Education about child care and health and nutrition education can be given to them so that they can perform their work more effectively.

In Baroda district, Social Welfare organisations run several Mahila Mandals. In these Mahila Mandal's women only sing songs, Bhajans and Kirtans during meetings. This could be because of lack of training. Seminars and workshops can be conducted by Home Scientists to tell them about different productive activities which could be performed by these women.

SUMMARY AND CONCLUSION

A detailed analysis of activities, services and projects of the voluntary organisations reveal striking similarities which indicate that they share a common cultural pattern. These similarities appear in recreational interests, income generating activities, religious, educational and social patterns of Baroda.

The voluntary organisations are one of the basic community structures found in modern urban society. A voluntary agency is a non–political, non–commercial and non–government organization engaged in various human care services to the people. These are the projects of local significance initiated and carried out by local people.

The objective of this study is to analyse the performance of the women's organizations in terms of their structure, functions and overall activities.

More than 80 per cent of the agencies are involved in economic activities. These include assistance in the form of providing raw materials for preparing masala, snacks, uniform, providing equipment like sewing machine, typewriter, etc.

Majority of the agencies reported that the learner chooses time according to their convenience.

Majority of the voluntary organizations have more than sixty women on an average. Age and caste are no barrier for the women to take part in the activities. Maximum of women who came to take advantage of the different associations are either illiterate or educated till primary level and from lower or middle income group.

None of the agencies has facility of retraining or for refresher courses for the women. Not very commonly found activities are giving Halls on rent for marriage and other functions, working women hostel, balwadi, health centre for women and children.

A detailed analysis of activities, services and projects of the voluntary organizations reveal striking similarities which indicates that they share a common cultural pattern. These similarities appear in recreational interest, income generating activities, religious, educational and social pattern of Baroda.

BIBLIOGRAPHY

Alfred Desouza (1978), The Indian City Poverty, Manhar Publications, New Delhi.

Almelu, S. (1987), Vocational Training for Women Placement within easy Reach. Social Welfare, Vol. XXXIV, No. 8, Nov., pp. 34–35.

Chandra S. (1977), Social Participation in Urban Neighbourhood. National Publishing House, New Delhi.

Gupta et al. (1987), Role of Women in Economic Development. Yojana Vol. 31, No. 18, Oct. 1–15, pp. 28–32.

J.K. Friend, J.M. Power (1982), Public Planning Dimension. Tavistock Publications, London.

Marvin B. Sussman, Thomas Y. (1989), Community Structure and Analysis. Thomas Y. Cromel Company. New York.

Paul M. and E.H. Mizruchi (1980), Urbanism, Urbanization and Change – Comparative Perspectives. Addison Weslly Publishing Company, New York.

Tiagi, S.R. (1988), Stree Seva Mandir. Social Welfare. Vol. XXXV, No. 9, Dec., pp. 20–22.

William E. Cole (1980), Urban Society. The Riverside Press. Cambridge. Massachusetts.

MEGHA SIDHPURA & RAMESHWARI PANDYA

11 Development Role Played by NGOs in Baroda–A Study

INTRODUCTION

Voluntary action in India has been an inbuilt culture of Indian life and tradition. We all know that even prior to independence Voluntary Agencies were providing social services. During that period their main focus was on social reforms like spreading awareness against child marriages, sati pratha, etc. However after independence there were policies and commitment which strengthened and supported the voluntary agencies and their movement. The voluntary agencies have played very important role in the national development because of their direct rapport with the people. The voluntary organizations have an extra advantage as they can plan and execute their programme according to the local needs and resources and do not have to waste time in rigid bureaucratic red tapism. This is the reason people work with great motivation and commitment and spirit. Much of importance is given to the NGOs and much written and discussed about their efforts; therefore it was necessary to uncover the facts and real picture of the NGOs.

The Department of Home Science Extension and Communication works in collaboration with the NGOs in various ways. Students of the department are also placed during their study and are also recruited by the different NGOs. We all know that administrators are the pillars and beneficiaries are the hearts of the NGOs, as they are the most appropriate people who can throw light on the following unanswered questions such as:

- What is the status of NGOs and their problems?
- Who are the beneficiaries of the NGOs?
- What is the opinion of the beneficiaries regarding programmes, staff members and timings of the NGOs?

- How much beneficiaries have improved and what problems do they face in the different NGOs?

Hence, it is in this direction study was undertaken regarding the beneficiaries of the three selected NGOs working for welfare of women in Baroda. An attempt is made to study the different aspects of the NGOs and their problems. This study throws light on the most crucial aspects of the NGOs namely their functioning and beneficiaries. Hence, the findings of the present study will add to the knowledge about the NGOs and their role which they play for the welfare of women *leading to sustainable development.*

Beneficiaries are the crux of the NGOs. They are raison d'etre of any organization. So, their opinion about the selected aspects of the organization, improvement found in them, the problems faced related to the organization and their valuable feedback for the organization will help for further improvement in planning and implementation of future programmes and services. The information related to all the above aspects will provide strategic guideline to the administrators of organizations and government policy planners.

OBJECTIVES OF THE STUDY

1. To study the *profile of the beneficiaries* of the selected NGOs working for the welfare of women in Baroda.
2. To study the *overall opinions* of the beneficiaries regarding the selected aspects of the NGOs:
   - Programmes
   - Staff members
   - Timings
3. To study the *overall differences* in the opinions of the beneficiaries regarding selected aspects of the NGOs with respect to the selected variables:
   - Age
   - Marital status
   - Educational qualification
   - Family Size
   - Monthly family income
   - Personality dimension
4. To study the *opinions* of the beneficiaries regarding the selected aspects of the NGOs with respect to the following variables:
5. To study the *improvement* found by the beneficiaries in them after joining the NGOs.

6. To study the *differences in the improvement* found by the beneficiaries in them after joining the NGOs with respect to the selected variables.
7. To study *problems* of the beneficiaries related to the NGOs.
8. To study the *differences in the problems* of the beneficiaries related to NGOs with respect to the selected variables.
9. To seek the *suggestions* from the beneficiaries for the improvement of the NGOs.
10. To collect the *profile* of the selected NGOs working for the welfare of women.
11. To study the problems of the selected NGOs related to the selected aspects.
    - Finance
    - Staff Members
    - Miscellaneous

DATA COLLECTION

Data was personally collected by interviewing the respondents. Thus extensive field work was done during December 2004 and January 2005. The total time taken to interview a beneficiary was 30–40 mins. To collect information related to the NGOs, 2–3 meetings were arranged with the administrators, almost 40–45 mins were taken for an interview.

SELECTION OF THE SAMPLE

The sample for the present study comprised of 100 beneficiaries of the three selected Non-Government Organizations working for the welfare of women in Baroda.

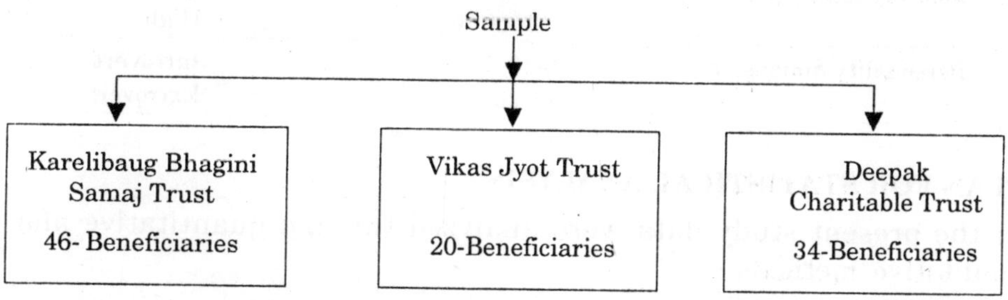

CONSTRUCTION OF THE TOOLS

For the quantitative data related to the beneficiaries, an interview schedule consisting of five sections was prepared. To collect the profile checklist and open-ended response system was used. For the personality dimension two point scale, prepared by V. S. Sahntamani and A. Hafeez (1978) was used. Further three-point scale was prepared, to study opinions related to the selected aspects like programmes, staff members and timings, improvement found after joining the NGOs and problems faced related to the NGOs. To collect the suggestions checklist and open-ended response system was used.

To collect the qualitative data regarding the selected NGOs, interview schedule was prepared; where in set of open-ended questions related to their profile, programmes, methods and problems were included. Problems were studied in detail under three selected aspects, viz. finance, staff members and miscellaneous.

SCORING PLAN AND CATEGORIZATION

Table 1
Categorization of the variables under study

Sr. No	*Variables*	*Basis*	*Category*
1.	Age	≤ 20 years	Young
		21-30 years	Middle
		31-40 years	Upper middle
		≥ 41 years	Old
2.	Marital status	—	Unmarried
		—	Married
		Divorcee Widow	Others
3.	Educational qualification	≤ 10th standard	Low
		≥ 10th standard	High
4.	Family Size	2-3 members	Small
		4-5 memberse	Medium
		≥ 6 members	Large
5.	Monthly family income	≤ 1500 Rs.	Low
		≥ 1500 Rs.	High
6.	Personality dimension	0-10	Introvert
		11-20	Extrovert

PLAN FOR STATISTICAL ANALYSIS

In the present study data were analyzed through quantitative and qualitative methods.

FINDINGS OF THE STUDY

The discussion has been divided into two parts:

1. Beneficiaries
2. NGOs

PROFILE OF THE BENEFICIARIES

Findings revealed that nearly one third of the beneficiaries belonged to young and upper middle age group whereas little above than one fourth were from middle age, that means beneficiaries approaching the NGOs hold from different age groups. The probable reason would be that the NGOs could cater to the needs of the beneficiaries of all age group.

It was also found that majority of the women were married. It is a known fact that married women have to shoulder greater household responsibilities than unmarried girls do, yet more married women are found to be coming to the NGOs to attend programmes. However, among them widows and divorcees were considerably less in number. The reason could be their widowhood or divorcee status that inflicted on them a lot of restrictions restrain their movement outside. Hence, problems related to single parenthood would cause further impediments preventing them to attend the programmes. Likewise, many parents did not prefer sending young unmarried girls to NGOs. They felt insecured while sending them alone to NGOs for participation in public activities.

Of the beneficiaries almost half of them belonged to families of medium size with 4 to 5 members in a family. To add to it majority of the families reportedly earned more than 1500 rupees per month. So, it is understood that per capita income in these families was too inadequate to survive particularly when the inflation rate is very high.

It was also reported that more than half of the beneficiaries were employed to support their families. It was because their family income was too low that women had to help their spouses to raise enough for their economic needs. These women are employed as anganwadi workers health workers, maid servants, farm–labourers or workers in catering businesses, etc.

Kaul (1990) and Bhatia's (2000) study too reveals similar findings about the beneficiaries with respect to their age, educational qualification and income level.

The findings reveal significant fact that a good majority of women possessed extrovert personality. The women could become open, free, practical and confident with readiness to work in groups. This made them more extrovert energetic and active participant to contribute significantly to the social cause.

Looking at religions composition among the beneficiaries it was found that a high majority of them were Hindu and very few of them followed the Islam faith. Compared to Hindu women, fewer of Muslim women approached NGOs and participated to earn benefits. The reason is that Muslim families are more conservative than Hindu families. Secondly, following the riots in Gujarat in 2002, the communal harmony was much disrupted and damaged heavily. As a result if NGOs were located preferably in Hindu dominated areas. In this light, Muslim families might not feel safe to send their daughters, wives or daughters–in–law to NGOs although it might earn them a number of benefits.

There are number of objectives that motivated the beneficiaries to join the NGOs one is that they felt a need of various kinds like training, legal advice, counselling, health related services etc. Secondly, some beneficiaries joined the NGOs for satisfying their own interests, which otherwise would not have due realization. Some of them were interested in mahendi artwork, embroidery work, etc. So they joined the classes run by the NGOs.

Desire for self development was yet another reason that the beneficiaries' responses revealed. They joined personality development classes, Spoken English classes and mahila sangathan activities that the NGOs conducted.

It was revealed through the present study that the NGO's run various welfare programmes and provides need–based services to women. The findings of the study reflect that women participated in different programme according to their needs and expectations. They also availed benefits in view of their different problems and purposes from the services rendered by the NGOs. It is indicated that one third of the beneficiaries participated in awareness generation programmes which were mostly for HIV/AIDS awareness. The NGOs therefore seek to outreach workers to approach these women and make them aware of HIV/AIDS. It might be possible that some of these women have only heard the term HIV/AIDS but they do not have its knowledge. Hence, in order to know about HIV/AIDS they might have joined the programmes conducted by the NGO.

It was found that beneficiaries were more interested in vocational training programmes run by the NGOs. More than one fourth of the beneficiaries joined sewing classes thinking that they will be able to raise adequate livelihood with tailoring and stitching. Some of the beneficiaries attended embroidery classes and beauty parlour classes. While some other beneficiaries received training for anganwadi worker, some of them are working as anganwadi workers.

Banking is another area of public need that needs to be explored in remote rural areas. The NGOs initiated it by setting up Self Help Group called "Bachat Mandal". One fourth of the beneficiaries became members of Self Help Group (Bachat Mandal) that the NGO's constituted. While women joined saving banks they thought if they saved and deposited money in the saving bank they could at least secure some amount of money which could be useful as and when needed. It can provide for a secured future.

Women faced many problems related to their reproductive health. NGOs organized health camps. They also sent their health workers to visit door to door. The beneficiaries felt more comfortable talking to the health workers on their visits. Some of them even discussed freely their health related problems and got solution in terms of counselling and treatment. This contributed significantly to public education and awareness as regards health and hygiene of life and environment.

Some women approached the NGO's to get assistance for legal advocacy. Legal advocacy or counselling is yet another crucial area for the illiterate in remote rural areas particularly in problem areas like property ownership, divorce, mental and physical harassment, etc. Most women are not aware of their rights. On the other hand for their poor economic conditions they could not afford to hire a lawyer. Thus, they were unable to stand for their own rights. In this light legal assistance extended by the NGOs proved most precious to them.

Methods are the most important aspects of any welfare or developmental programmes. Beneficiaries were approached through various methods, such as home visits, discussions, demonstration, field tour, video shows, group level methods and mass level methods. More than half of the beneficiaries were approached through home visits. For programmes like HIV/AIDS awareness, literacy, saving banks, health services, etc. beneficiaries were contacted at their homes. They were also collected in a nearby place or a faliya or a lane for public meeting at which discussions were held. Discussion was the most frequently used method for the various programme. It proved very effective allowing participation of the beneficiaries in need and giving voice to their concerns and confusions. Beneficiaries also attended the demonstrations held for tailoring and embroidery, recipe of food items and even usage of condom. All these methods yielded good results in terms of good response of the beneficiaries in need.

Anganwadi workers, members of saving banks, members of mahila sangthans, etc. were taken to the field tours in order to have better insight into the respective fields. The NGO's also organized video shows that almost one third of the beneficiaries watched. It became a popular method and the most effective means to impart to people instruction with delight.

About one third of the beneficiaries also reported that during implementation of programmes different mass level methods were also employed. Mass level methods are helpful to cover large population. At the same time, they are helpful in creating awareness among people, specifically women, on their specific issues and concerns such as girls education, importance of balanced diet, care to be taken during pregnancy, prevention of AIDS, legal rights of women etc. They can be explained and understood with the help of posters, exhibitions, booklets, campaigns, etc.

Administrators at the NGOs, however, report that they do involve beneficiaries in different stages of the programme. At the planning stage beneficiaries may help NGOs to identify need based programmes that would suit their expectations. During the implementation they can be helpful in reaching them out to the other women. They also help NGOs to build rapport with women. In the last stage of evaluation opinions and response regarding the effectiveness and benefits of the programmes may be shared among members of the NGOs and the women participant in order to have clear vision and insight into the goal to be achieved.

Suresh (1990) however reports in his study that the rate of participation was very low in selected organisations in Kerala. In these programmes, beneficiaries were hardly taken into confidence for monitoring, supervision, evaluation and follow–up.

OPINIONS OF THE BENEFICIARIES

Over a long association with the NGOs the beneficiaries form definite opinion about the NGOs. It would be interesting and also helpful to have a look at the opinions that the beneficiaries formed. They focus on three selected aspects, viz. programmes, staff members and timings. The beneficiaries' opinions may be held important when they throw light on the above stated aspects of the NGO. It would be encouraging to know that more than half of the beneficiaries, that is about 65 per cent of them hold favourable opinions regarding these selected aspects of the NGOs.

They expressed high opinions regarding each aspect. This shows that they might be highly satisfied with the programmes, the staff members involved in them and the timings of the NGO. However, there remained significant difference in the overall opinions of the beneficiaries with respect to a monthly income of their families.

Income of the beneficiaries' families may affect their priorities and needs significantly. It is the priorities and needs that motivate them to participate in different programmes. This allows them different experiences leading to different perceptions and insight into the selected aspects of the NGO. This further leads them to forming different opinions.

The findings also revealed that no significant difference was noticed in the overall opinions of the beneficiaries regarding the selected aspects of the NGOs with respect to their age, marital status, educational qualification, family size and personality dimension. Irrespective of difference in these aspects of the beneficiaries they found the NGOs equally useful to them. The beneficiaries might have received equal treatment from the NGOs. This might have encouraged similar and equally favourable opinions about the programmes, staff members and timings of the NGOs.

The studies presented by Sen's (1994), Bhatia's (2000), Kaul (1990), Brahmbhatt (1996), Mehta and Das (2003), Siwach (2004) reported almost similar findings that beneficiaries expressed favourable opinions about the NGOs. Thus, there seems to prevail unanimous opinion among women beneficiaries that the NGOs exert positive impact on their minds through various programmes and through motivated efforts to help them improve their life.

Opinions Regarding "Programmes"

The NGOs conducted various programmes as detailed above for the benefit of women. The objective was to improve their lots, raise their confidence level and make them economically independent. Such welfare programmes received hearty response from the women beneficiaries. In order to check their opinions, responses were collected from them, the findings reveal that high majority of the beneficiaries held more favourable opinion about "Programmes" of the NGO.

The responses collected from the beneficiaries reflect that the NGOs offered various programmes including educational, vocational and the welfare kind to reach out to the maximum number of women. The responses meaning that programmes were need based and interesting were reported with very high intensity indices. The reason may be that the variety of programmes that the NGOs conducted might have addressed the demands and needs of the beneficiaries. It might have made them more focused and concentrated in spirit. This implies that NGOs modify programmes with the time and see to incorporate the changes that occur in the society. They also seek to focus on the needs of the people in view of the specific government policies and programmes announced from time to time.

The findings further report that programmes were well planned, organized, implemented and evaluated. It may be because the NGOs obtained collaboration of international and national level programmes and schemes that added high standard and qualify management to their programme with planning, implementation and evaluation patterns. There was more a touch of professionalism and bias–free approach reflected from among the organizers and workers involved.

Opinions Regarding "Staff Members"

"Staff members" form another crucial point in the triangular work area in which the NGOs have to work. They form a crucial link between planners of the programme and their beneficiaries. Thus they play a very important role to carry out any programme or services. They are the channels through which information is passed on to the beneficiaries. Hence, opinion about them again counts as significant aspect of the present study.

The responses collected from the beneficiaries reveal that a majority of the beneficiaries expressed more favourable opinions regarding "staff members" of the NGOs. Very high intensity indices have been reported for them stating that they were efficient enough to plan appropriate methods to suit the objectives of the programmes and needs of the beneficiaries. The more encouraging fact was that they were friendly considerate to deprived women of rural society who were very needy. This could be because NGOs hire qualified staff keeping in mind the jobs to be performed. Secondly, they provide regular training to their staff members. A good training enables a worker to plan appropriate methods to meet a particular objective with due efficiency and results. The findings reveal that at different stages of programmes, the staff at the NGOs employed different methods.

Further, the staff was working very well with their intrinsic motivation to help and serve people. This raised considerably among them a sense of involvement and commitment. The beneficiaries report that they established a very healthy relationship with the staff members and volunteers of the NGOs. They could approach them and talk to them freely. It allowed increased interaction between them. They could develop a personal rapport with the staff. They could share their concerns, problems and issues as well with due frankness.

Opinions Regarding "Timings" of the NGOs

"Timing" at which the NGOs would hold programmes required serious consideration because women who attend the programmes of the NGOs hail from rural and slums setups. As it has been discussed earlier a majority of them have to play a dual role as a care taker of a family and as a working woman. When they are employed anywhere it becomes clear that they have to manage their timings of households duties as well as work place. A good majority of the beneficiaries expressed a favourable opinion about timings at which the NGOs held various programmes.

The timings were suitable to the beneficiaries. The reason might be that the NGOs plans its activities and programmes keeping in mind the leisures or free hours that women enjoyed during a day in a village or in urban slums.

The intensity indices that reflect on the time that the beneficiaries utilized for the programmes was the highest. The programmes were organized regularly and timely. Today in fact NGOs have grown more punctual and regular in conducting programme because majority of the programmes are grant–in–aid and NGOs are accountable to the funding agencies in terms of timings and timely outcome of the programmes that they finance.

IMPROVEMENT FOUND AS REPORTED BY BENEFICIARIES

Any project or welfare programme has to be result–oriented. The result is visible through improvements affected in a target group of people. Further, its success can be measured through the feedback that can be obtained through responses or opinions of the beneficiaries. In order to obtain realistic picture of the success of the programmes the responses were collected from the beneficiaries and formulated in terms of the findings of the study through scrutiny and analysis.

The findings of the study reveal that after joining the NGOs a majority of the beneficiaries noticed more improvement in their conditions. The first change they noticed in them was that earlier they were not able to come out of their homes as there were many restrictions laid on them. It was because of the good efforts put in by the NGOs that women started coming out of their homes slowly and steadily to attend programmes. It increased their general awareness and also developed in them self confidence. This was reported by them in their responses with very high intensity indices. The women could overcome from their seclusive nature and break their isolation. As a result they could develop communication skills with which they can now share their thoughts, concerns and issues of common interests with their friends, relatives and family members besides the staff members of the NGOs.

Further they gained information, knowledge and also developed some skills because of different programmes and services. Through active participation they could enhance their educational level and also become more independent with awareness for their own rights. For instance, women initially joined the Self Help Group scheme launched by the NGOs, they did not know any thing about the banking procedures. They did not have confidence to carry out transaction. But in the course of time they learnt about the formalities and the system and now they can go to bank and do all works independently. This finding can be supported by what Joshi (2004) observes in "The capacity building support and involvement in economic activity have helped the women to gain respect and self–confidence. They can now go to bank for deposit or withdrawals for loan." On the other hand women who attended adult education classes learnt basics like alphabets, numbers, etc. to enable them to spell their names, or do simple calculations.

By attending programmes women became aware of their own legal rights. It was widely reflected by the beneficiaries that they would not tolerate any injustice or misbehaviour inflected on them. On the other hand, they also started involving themselves in decision-making process in their families as well as in a society or a community. They invited members of their community to form a community based women's activist group called Mahila Sangathan through which other beneficiaries are playing a significant role in the development of their own area and people.

Kaul (1990), Sen (1994), and Bhatia (2000) reported that the beneficiaries found improvement in them after attending programmes or receiving services offered by the NGO. Wadiwale (2004), Mehta and Das (1997) too observe similar trends. They report that beneficiaries could develop good ability to socialize with people, could make use of time more fruitfully by working and earning. They became more knowledgeable, confident, decision makers, planners, problem solvers and better organizers. Many personal attributes were gained by them.

The findings related to improvements experienced by the beneficiaries are also supported by Gaonkar (2003). She found that Self Help Groups (SHGs) have made lasting impact on the lives of the women particularly in the rural areas of Goa.

While reviewing the experiences of watershed project in Uttaranchal, Joshi (2004) finds social, economic, political and administrative empowerment and leadership that developed in women who joined Self Help Groups (SHGs).

PROBLEMS FACED

Problems that arise in the course of imparting programmes and services by the NGOs and also that of receiving benefits and services by women form an inevitable factor that hardly can be ignored. However, the lesser the problems arise the higher stays the index of success. The present study reveals encouraging fact that majority of the beneficiaries faced fewer problems in relation to the NGOs.

Also for all the items low intensity indices were found. The highest intensity indices reported was for the items stated as "transportation is not provided to the beneficiaries." The reason may be that beneficiaries came from far away places to attend the programmes. So, it might be difficult for some of the beneficiaries to spend money on transportation. Another reason could be that if the transportation was provided to the beneficiaries then their family members would not feel tensed and concerned for them. And if no transport was made available to the beneficiaries they would walk down to the NGO, which is time consuming and tiring. A few beneficiaries faced another problem that was of delay in receiving services. The reason might be that most of the programmes or services of the NGOs are grant in–aid. The NGOs were also facing a problem of delay in receiving funds from government or funding agencies. As a result sometimes the beneficiaries faced difficulties.

Curiously enough, it was reported by some of the beneficiaries that fees charged to participate in the programmes were very high. The findings however reveal that the NGOs did not charge any fees for a majority of the programmes, however for programmes like sewing class, beauty parlour and computer literacy class etc. they charge very nominal fees. The beneficiaries coming from a poor section of the society might find it difficult to pay the fees for the course. On the other hand, those young beneficiaries who were not working had to be dependent on their father's or husband's salaries. It might cause problem for them as to how to manage the fees for a programme of her interest.

Difference in the Problems

It was further found that age and marital status of the beneficiaries marked significant differences in the problems faced by them in relation to the NGOs. Differences with respect to age may be for the reasons that needs and demands of an individual vary with her age. Medical science has demonstrated that the older can make new connections, absorb new truths, and acquire new skills. They are also ready for innovations. On the other hand, the younger mostly live in a fantasy world. They always expect something fantastic from life and every surrounding thing. The reason is that they hold less experienced, realistic and mature attitude than the older do. So, Hence beneficiaries too reported differences in the problems according to their age wise characteristics. Here, it was found that young people reported more problems than others.

Further, the findings also reveal that married women reported fewer problems than the unmarried ones and others. According to their marital status women confront different living conditions which may cause to them problems of varied dimensions and proportions. An unmarried woman may desire for self–development, while married woman may have educational or vocational interest in mind. A widow may have approached an NGOs looking for some kind of income generation activity. They might have preferred to participate in vocational courses or preferred to receive counselling from Women Guidance centre (Mahila Margadarshan Kendra). The NGOs have also helped widows to register under widow pension scheme. So, in all these programme or services, widows might have faced some other kind of problems. Thus, differences were noticed in the problems faced by women with respect to their marital status.

SUGGESTIONS

A few suggestions may be worked out in view of change in women's aspirations and expectations in life with the changing time. If suggestions are accepted and incorporated with due sincerity, they may present any kind of stagnancy in the improvement affected and keep the efforts fresh and vital enough to render expected results. Beneficiaries suggested that new innovative programmes and services like personality development classes, spoken English; computer literacy classes etc. may be started. The beneficiaries may expect above programmes for the welfare of women keeping in mind today's demand. It indicates that women living in rural and urban centers are becoming alert and more aware and more concerned about overall development of their personality. The Director of Deepak Charitable Trust reported that now women living in rural areas are now involved in dairy project, where they have to keep daily account on computers and hence, they want to learn computer operation. It was further suggested that NGOs should create awareness regarding its activities among the people and It should encourage more and more number of women to take benefits of the different services. It implies that some of the beneficiaries still found women who avoided coming to the NGOs, reason might be that either they were not aware of it or they were not free to move out of homes.

Further, majority of the beneficiaries suggested that innovative communication strategies should be devised and employed in the programmes and services. It shows that the methods used by the NGOs attracted beneficiaries and they found them interesting and meaningful. They may strongly feel that if new communication strategies will be used then programmes will be more successful. It indicates that the beneficiaries too felt the importance of communication strategies in welfare and development programmes.

Kapoor (2004) reports almost similar findings as Adult learners suggested that computer education should be provided; more opportunities to express opinions, child care center facility, adequate transport facilities, etc. should be provided to adult learners who come for adult education classes.

NON GOVERNMENT ORGANIZATIONS

Profile of the NGOs

The three selected NGOs under study namely Karelibaugh Bahgini Samaj Trust, Vikas Jyot Trust, Deepak Charitable Trust based in Baroda were established during 1971–1982. In the Post independence time, the NGOs were flourishing in the country and their growth was tremendous. Under the socialistic democratic pattern of the state-nation, India was declared a welfare state and under it a number of schemes and policies announced for the growth and support of NGOs in the country. Lawani (1999) notes the reasons that the increase in the education level of public, proper canvassing of the provisions and schemes available, special enlargement by the concerned departments to take up the projects, encouragement for the grassroot level organizations like mahila mandals, youth clubs, etc. are the various reasons for the fast growth and development of voluntary organizations during the post–independent India.

Regarding growth and existence of NGOs, Gomes (1989), Narayana (1990), Maithani (1995) and Bhatia (2000) present similar observations in their studies.Their findings reveal that the NGOs under the study are operating at local level. These NGOs' area of work is limited either to a particular village /villages or an urban community. It may be for the limitation of funds available and the staff employed. It may not be possible to work for larger population.

It was further found that all the three selected NGOs work with the similar objectives of women welfare. Here, it should be noted that the objectives are formulated keeping in mind historical, socio–economic and cultural factors that is prevailing at a time. Ideologies and personalities of founder members too play vital role to influence the objectives.

It is encouraging to state that the NGOs in question are working hard to meet all the objectives as stated in their constitution. Reasons can be many; one of the probable reasons can be availability of finance. In the present study it becomes evident that majority of the programme of the NGOs are funded by Government or other funding agencies. They also receive donations from foreign and local persons. Another reason can be infrastructure facilities. The NGOs under study are found to be possessing good infrastructure.

Further the findings reveal that the NGOs have a well defined powerstructure. With a well-defined administrative hierarchy the responsibilities are divided, delegated and shared by the staff members down the line. This leaves hardly any chance for chaos or confusion. Lalitha and Kohli (1982) and Singhal (1998) present similar observation in their studies. They state that well defined formal organizational structure attribute a good shape to the NGOs and their programmes and services. These factors helped them to plan and run their programmes smoothly and efficiently.

The findings also indicate that the NGOs are well equipped and have good infrastructure facilities to carry out their programmes effectively and efficiently. It is obvious that NGOs needs minimum infrastructure and facilities are to enable it to deliver welfare services to beneficiaries. And in this respect, the NGOs under study do not face any problems. Further, their location in an urban centre like Baroda is an added advantage to them.

In a political and economic exploitation developing country like India women are among the people who are the most vulnerable groups. Therefore, NGOs are expected to provide interventions to empower women. It is evident from the present study that the NGOs under study encompass all the important thrust areas through their programmes and services. They organize various programmes and extend services to improve overall status of women, whether educational, vocational, health, legal awareness and assistance etc. Therefore, it can be concluded that the objectives of the NGOs do not just remain on the paper. They all are converted into well planned programmes and services though collective will and efforts in order to benefit deprived women in the society.

It is further observed in the present study that the NGOs employ different methods like home visits, discussions, circular letters, campaigning etc. to inform the target group of women about the programmes and to attract them to come and attend the programmes. Even in the implementation of the programmes the NGOs employed various methods and materials to make them focused and effective.

It may be noted here that the NGOs do not use popular methods like folk drama and puppet show so frequently. The reason may be a lack of professionally trained staff members who would use them efficiently. The administrators reported that they would like to provide training for the above mentioned methods so that more and more women can be attracted towards the NGOs and their activities to get the maximum benefits and improve their lots.

The present study throws light on the fact that the NGOs revise their programmes regularly. The project team prepares written reports which focus on negative and positive aspects that may further be taken up for discussion at the meetings with the director or the manager. Based on it the evaluation is carried out by the organization. Then the progress reports are prepared and submitted to the respective government departments or funding agencies. The reason is the NGOs stay accountable to those funding agencies that finance their projects and the funding agencies are much concerned about the proper utilization of funds as well as overall benefits rendered to the beneficiaries.

It is observed that the beneficiaries are hardly involved in the evaluation stage. This implies that beneficiaries are not granted opportunities to express their opinions or problems as regards the NGO's programmes and the other aspects. Lalitha and Kohli (1982) reported that periodic evaluation of programmes is essential to tone up the performance of these organizations with a view to incorporate suitable changes and modification therein.

The findings further reveal that in view of the selected NGOs no similar pattern of participation was noticed. It shows that the NGOs adopt different philosophies in different stages of programmes related to participation of beneficiaries. The reasons may vary, sometimes the NGOs may provide opportunities but because the beneficiaries on their part may not be so willing and interested in the participation.

The vis–a–vis situation may also be found. However social reformists and social–workers attach prime importance to the situation that the beneficiaries are allowed participation in the decision making process.

PROBLEMS

The findings of the present study further reflect on what the NGOs are lacking in some areas and what kind of problems they face related to those particular aspects. They have reported on their weaknesses and problems related to different areas like finance, personnel and others to include co–ordination, identification and implementation of the programme. It was found that the NGOs are not facing similar problems and the extent of their problems too differ. Hence the problems may be discussed in the sections titled as finance, staff members and miscellaneous.

Finance

Regarding the finance aspect the administrators of the NGOs complain about delay in receiving funds. It is a major problem that the two NGOs except Deepak Charitable Trust confront severely. Because of delay in funds the NGOs face difficulties in starting and completing the programme in time and running it smoothly. The administrator of the Karelibaug Bhagini Samaj further expressed that they have to pass through lengthy and tedious procedure to get funds and even after the utilization of funds unnecessary formalities have to be carried out. It is understood that as a part of their accountability the NGOs need to report back to funding agencies or the Government Departments that finance their projects and inform them about specific programmes. They also have to report on every single expenditure that they incur however small it may be.

The Deepak Charitable Trust, on the other hand, reported only one problem related to the finance. It is a different matter that the trust has its own funds which may be available to them as and when needed. Therefore they may not face many problems related to the finance. They in fact enjoy relative freedom. However, the administrator reported that they sometimes find difficulty in producing the utilization certificate because the appointed Chartered Accountants are not aware of the procedures and formalities as related to the NGOs.

Thus, from the findings it can be inferred that except one problem of delay in receiving finance the NGOs are not facing any other problems. It shows that the NGOs under study enjoy a good financial status. They get enough finance for their programmes through grants, funds or donations. Or it may be said that NGOs undertake only those programmes for which grants are available. Thus they do not have to worry about arranging funds for the proposed programme.

Staff Members

Since personnel form backbone of any organization their value cannot be undermined for its success. Qualities in personnel are a valuable asset to the organization. They give a touch of quality and efficiency to the working of an organization. Therefore, they count much for the success and fame that an organization achieves. The qualities of personnel working in NGOs include a sense of dedication and commitment and interest in the social services. In earlier times personnel were expected to have spirit of service and they did not require any special education or training. But now much importance is attached to professionally trained workers. Here, it should be noted that professionally trained workers expect high salaries, status and also opportunities for their own growth and development in their career. They would never want to confine their future in a service motivated organization operating in less challenging environment. They would rather dream for advancement and success that would give them a feel of accomplishment.

The NGOs under the study reported that they face problems to some extent in getting full time staff members, who are suitably trained and sincere and committed to work. For instance, the Bhagini Samaj faces a problem of stability of staff members to greater extent, as they keep on changing jobs.

Similar findings are reported by Chaudhary (1972), that voluntary agencies are under staffed and are inefficient. Because of lack of qualified staff the voluntary agencies are unable to maintain minimum quality standards of work.

CONCLUSION

The findings of the present study clearly depicts that the NGOs hold their definite objectives related to the welfare of women. They conduct many programmes and offer services through various methods in order to achieve their set objectives. But a review of available literature reveal that majority of the NGOs rely on government grants and funds from funding agencies for their programmes and services. They lack in independent source of funds. Thus they are heavily dependent on funds and support of the government as well as other funding agencies. When you receive financial support you fall to the obligation of the funding partners. Under obligation, you have to accept their policies and conditions. Rather they are imposed or dictated on you. In addition, you also owe accountability of what you do. This eventually restricts their innovativeness and freedom of planning and implementation.

The opinions of the beneficiaries regarding selected aspects such as programmes, staff members and timings and problem faced by them reflect that they are satisfied with the functioning of the NGOs. They report improvement in different aspects of their life. Here, it is worth to mention that the efforts of the NGOs towards welfare of women are greatly successful despite the fact that they face problems like delaying funds and unavailability of fulltime trained staff. Thus the efforts of the NGOs should be recognized and appreciated duly. The media are expected to carry out responsibility of motivating public opinion in the favour of selfless service that the NGOs render to the society.

The findings of the present study are directly applicable to the thrust area of the Department of Home Science Extension and Communication, as department is associated with number of NGOs in and around Baroda. Further, the findings might be helpful in fieldwork programmes and their planning, implementation and evaluation as undergraduate and postgraduate students of the department are doing fieldwork in collaboration with a number of NGOs.

To conclude it can be said that NGOs have undertaken many programmes and services through different approaches for the welfare of women. Considering the findings reported by the administrators of the NGOs as well as beneficiaries it can be concluded that NGOs just do not have plans on papers only but in reality they want to improve the status of women. Opinions and improvement found by the beneficiaries suggested that they are very satisfied with the programme and services offered by the NGOs. Therefore, present study implies that NGOs' efforts towards welfare of women are of great success and should be appreciated.

BIBLIOGRAPHY

Bhatia A. (2000), Women's Development and NGOs. Rawat Publications, Jaipur and New Delhi.

Brahmbhatt, U. (1996), Study of marriage counseling service provided by Karelibaug Bhagini Samaj Trust, Dissertation (M.S.W.).... M.S. University, Baroda.

Chaudhary, D. Paul (1971), Voluntary Social Welfare in India, Sterling Publication (P) Ltd. New Delhi.

Dhama, O.P. (1985), Education and Communication for Development, Oxford Publication; New Delhi.

Gaonkar, R. (2004), Role of SHGs in Empowerment of Women, Zuarinagar, Goa. Mimeographed paper read as ISTR Sixth International Conference, Contesting Citizenship and Civil Society in a divided world, Toronto. Canada, 11–14 July. (www.jhu.edu/nistr/conferences/toronto/abstracts/gaonkar.pdf).

Gomes, Lawrence (1989), Role of Voluntary and Other Organisations in Development. Yojana, Vol. 33, No. 23, pp. 28–31.

India, Department of Women and Child Development. Ministry of Human Resource Development. National Perspective plan for Women 1988–2000 A.D. Government of India, 1988.

Joshi, M. (2004), Women's Empowerment: Experience from Watershed Project. Social Welfare Vol. 51, No. 4. July, pp. 32–37.

Kaul, A. (1990), Educational, Economic and Social Impact of Voluntary Training Agencies offering Income Generating Programmes on Low Socio Economic Status Women of Baroda City. Ph.D. (Thesis)....., M.S. University.

Lawani B.T. (1999), NGOs in Development, Rawat Publication, Jaipur and New Delhi.

Maithani, B.P. (1995), Voluntary Organisations as Partners in Promoting Participatory Development, Kurukshetra, Vol. XLIII, No. 5, pp. 3–5.

Mehta and Das (2003), NGOs and Women Empowerment in Pandya R.M., and Mathu, A.A. (Eds.), Imbibing Value Education–various Perspectives, Kalpaz Publications, Gyan Book House, pp. 163–167.

Narayana, E.A. (1990), Voluntary Organisation and Rural Development in India. Uppal Publishing House, New Delhi.

Pandya, R.M. (1996), NGOs–Towards Self–Reliance. Social Welfare. Vol. 43, No. 5, August, pp. 22–24.

Rana, K. (2001), People's Participation and Voluntary Action. Dimension, Roles and Strategies. Kanishka Published, Distributed, New Delhi.

Robson, Lacke and Dawson (1997), User Involvement in the control of Voluntary Organizations (www.irf.org.uk).

Sen, S. (1994), Voluntary Organisations and Women Development. Dissertation (MSW)..., M. S. University.

Singhal, C.S. (1998), Assam: Survey of NGO activities. Social Welfare, Vol. 45, No. 10, January, pp. 24–29.

Siwach, R.K. (2003), Perspective Role of VOs in Tenth Plan. Social Welfare, Vol. 50, No. 11, February, pp. 13–15.

Suresh, K.A. (1990), Participation of Beneficiaries in the Developmental Programmes of NGO in Kerala. Journal of Rural Development, Vol. 9, No. 5, September, pp. 911–915.

Wadiwale (2004), Role of SHGs in empowerment of women, Social Welfare, April, Vol. 54, No. 11, pp. 20–25.

SANTOSH TIKOO

12 Utilization of Bank Credit by Women

Economic development requires the utilization of a wide range of resources that include the four factors of production-land, labour, capital and technology. Many development economists add that resources must be reallocated among richer and poorer regions, all available resources need to be used in entrepreneurial ways but one prime resource i.e. human capital is frequently underutilized.

Making fuller use of human resources especially of women has been singled out as a goal by many leaders in developing world. The challenge before us today is to make the activities performed by women more productive. Indian women are involved in all economically productive and social activities. In fact without their involvement, economic development of the country can never be achieved.

Improving productivity of women's work requires more capital inputs and introduction of improved technology. Availability of finance is an important and limiting factor. Assisting women for their economic upliftment continued to be one of the major concerns of banks. The bank emphasizes on providing credit facilities for greater economic self reliance of women, especially those belonging to weaker sections. Financial assistance is made available to women entrepreneurs for setting up traditional ventures such as manufacturing of hosiery goods, handloom goods, etc.

Being an unexplored field especially in urban areas, there is need to probe the credit practices of women to provide information to the banks, in the interest of customers. Studies conducted in the past (Grewal, 1986; Haq, 1984) have been very much limited in scope. Moreover, few studies have been taken up so far in this area by an impartial body. The present study was undertaken to determine the demographic and socio-economic characteristics of the respondents, to find out the reasons for availing and not availing the credit facility and to find out the problems faced by the beneficiaries in obtaining the credit.

The hypotheses formulated were: (1) Borrower and non borrower would account for significant variation in their mean monthly income, (2) There would be association between credit utilization and (i) education level and (ii) employment status of the homemaker.

METHODOLOGY

A combination of descriptive cum-evaluatory type of research design was used. Structured interview schedule was used for collecting the data. It was divided into 2 parts. First part contained questions regarding background information, second part consisted of reasons for taking and not taking the credit and problems faced by the borrowers. The total sample size was 50 women (25 borrowers and 25 non-borrowers). The study was conducted in Panipat. Frequencies, percentages, means, standard deviations were calculated and chi square test was applied to test the hypotheses.

RESULTS AND DISCUSSION

Demographic and Socio-economic Characteristics

Table-1 indicates that majority of the families of both the groups were of nuclear type. Though the present trend is towards nuclear families, yet we find that joint family system has not totally disappeared as 28 per cent of the borrower and 24 per cent of the non-borrower families were of joint type families. The mean size of families of borrowers was 5-6 whereas in case of non-borrower it was 6-24. Average age of borrower

Table 1
Percentage Distribution of Households of Borrowers and Non-borrowers According to the Demographic and Socio-economic Characteristics

Characteristics	*Borrowers (N = 25) Percentage*	*Non-borrowers (N = 25) Percentage*	*Total (N = 50) Percentage*
Types of Family			
Nuclear	72	76	74
Joint	28	24	26
Size of Family			
3-5 members	36	28	32
5-7 members	48	32	40
6-9 members	16	40	28
Mean:	5.6	6.34	5.92
SD	1.38	1.63	2.18
Age Structure			
25-35 years	40	44	42
35-45 years	30	36	36
45-55 years	24	20	22
Mean	36.0	37.6	40.0
SD	12.6	12.6	12.6

Characteristics	*Borrowers (N = 25) Percentage*	*Non-borrowers (N = 25) Percentage*	*Total (N = 50) Percentage*
Education Level			
Illiterate	24	44	34
Primary	28	44	36
Middle	12	8	10
High School	32	4	18
B.A.	4	–	–
Occupation			
Business	100	–	50
Domestic Servants	–	28	14
Stitching & Embroidery	–	72	36
Income Group			
0-500	–	100	50
500-1000	32	–	16
1000-1500	44	–	22
1500-2000	24	–	12
2000-2500	–	–	–
2500-3000	–	–	–
Mean	1210	250	
SD	374.16		

homemaker was 36 years and that of non-borrower was 37.6 years. The educational level of women has both social and physical significance. Twenty four per cent of borrower homemakers and 44 per cent of the non-borrower homemakers were totally illiterate. Thirty two per cent of borrower homemakers and 4 per cent of non-borrower homemakers studied upto high-school level. Data showed that education level of borrower homemakers was better than that of non-borrower females.

All the borrower homemakers were engaged in independent business i.e. handloom work, woolen and hosiery work, beauty parlour, electric shop and Karyana shop. Eighteen per cent of non-borrower homemakers were engaged in stitching and embroidery and 28 per cent of them were domestic servants. No one from the non borrower group was engaged in independent business. The mean income of the homemakers who had taken credit was Rs. 1210/- per month whereas it was Rs. 250/- per month in case of non-borrowers. This shows that majority of the beneficiaries were benefited by the loan scheme.

Reasons for Obtaining the Credit

It is evident from the table 2 that the major reason expressed for borrowing the credit by majority of the families (52%) was to purchase raw materials. The next second important reason given by 28 per cent was to make improvement in the work and rest of them borrowed to purchase machinery and tools. The major reason for borrowing credit from the bank only was less rate of interest, next important reason given by 72 per cent of respondents was that required amount was obtained followed by the reason that security was not bar. Fifty six per cent of borrowers were of the view that proper guidance was available in bank credit and 52 per cent of the respondents were of the view that bank credit was easily approachable. This data show that borrowers were satisfied with their source of credit.

Table 2
Distribution of Respondents According to Reasons for Obtaining the Loan, Opinions about Bank Credit and Amount of Credit Taken

Characteristics	*Borrowers (N-25) Percentage*
Reasons	
To purchase machinery and tools	20
To purchase raw materials	52
For further improvement of work	28
Opinions about bank credit	
Required amount is obtained	72
Easily approachable	52
Less rate of interest	76
Security is not bar	64
Proper guidance is available	56
Amount of Credit taken	
5000-10000	72
10000-15000	16
15000-20000	4
20000-25000	8

Above table also reveals that credit amount for 72 per cent of borrowers ranged between Rs. 5000-10000, 16 per cent of borrowers fell in the credit category of Rs. 1000-15000, 4 per cent in Rs. 15000-20000 and 8 per cent of borrowers took credit in between Rs. 20000-25000. So it is clear that maximum number of borrowers took credit in between Rs. 5000-10000. Credit amount was more for handloom, hosiery and woolen work but it was less for pottery work, and knitting machine. All the sample women had taken credit under women entrepreneur loan scheme. Almost all the borrowers were aware of the amount of credit, rate of interest, repayment period, subsidy and security pledged. They were aware of the fact until they would make complete repayment, they would not become the owner of the assets, they have purchased with credit.

Reasons for not Availing the Bank Credit

Data shows (Table 3) that 48 per cent of the families did not take credit because of the fear of complications associated with the credit. Twenty-eight per cent of the respondents were psychologically averted to taking credit and rest of them did not take credit due to high rate of interest. Non-borrowers showed inclination when they were asked whether they would like to learn the rules, regulations and other procedures for getting the loan. This calls for improving women's access to credit.

Table 3
Percentage Distribution of the Sample According to Reasons for not Availing the Credit

Characteristics	*Borrowers (N-25) Percentage*
(i) Sufficient income of the family	–
(ii) High rate of interest	12
(iii) Saving of purchase of different domestic and production items are sufficient	–
(iv) Fear of complications associated with taking of credit	48
(v) Lack of credit Facilities	12
(vi) Psychological aversion to taking credit	28

Table 4
Percentage Distribution of Borrower According to Problems Faced by them Getting Loan

Problems Faced	*Borrowers (N-25) Percentage*
(i) Too long time for whole procedure	92
(ii) Repayment regulations are inappropriate In frequency and duration	8
(iii) Workers do not give information and guidance	28
(iv) Rude behavior of the worker	8

Problems Faced by Borrowers while Obtaining Credit

One of the important concern of the present investigation was to check the problems confronted by the respondents in obtaining the credit.

It is clear from the table 4 that majority of the respondents (92%) felt that the whole procedure of getting loan was too long involving many formalities, 28 per cent felt that workers did not give the information about credit procedure, 8 per cent felt that repayment regulations were inadequate. It is not only the borrowers who had problems but bank personnel too had problems. Bank authorities replied that due to delay in repayment of loans, banks had to face great difficulty in the form of financial losses.

> *"In many cases, where the loan amount was less, the bank had written off the loan due to inability of borrower to repay the loan. Moreover in case of uneducated borrowers, the bank personnel had to fill up application forms and complete other formalities which meant lot of extra labour for them."*

It was also found (Table 5) that borrower homemakers had higher income than non-borrower homemakers (Chi-square = 55.4, significant at 0.01 level).

Table 5
Distribution of Respondents According to their Difference in Income

Credit holder	*Income Group*			*Total*	*Chi-square value*
	High	*Middle*	*Low*		
Borrowers	6	19	–	25	55.4*
Non-borrowers	–	–	25	25	
Total	6	19	25	50	

• Significant at 0.01 level, df2.

Table 6
Distribution According to their Educational Level and Credit Utilization

Credit holder	*Educational Level*			*Total*	*Chi-square value*
	Illiterate	*Less Educated*	*Highly Educated*		
Borrowers	6	10	9	25	8.59*
Non-borrowers	11	13	1	25	

• Significant at 0.01 level, df2.

Table 7
Distribution of Respondents According to their Employment Status and Credit Utilization

Employment Status	*Credit Holder*		*Total*	*Chi-square value*
	Borrowers	*Non-borrowers*		
Independent	25	–	25	50*
Not-indenpendent business	–	25	25	
Total	25	25	50	

• Significant at 0.01 level, df2.

Credit utilization was significantly affected by the educational level of the borrower (Chi-square = 8.59, significant at 0.05 level). The reason for this is that if the borrower is educated, she can easily fulfill the bank formalities. Those respondents who had their independent business, make more use of credit facilities than those who did not have such type of business (Chi-square = 50, significant at 0.01 level, Table 7). In the present study all the borrower respondents had some sort of independent business i.e. poultry business, handloom and woollen work, Kiryana shops, ready-made garments and cloth shops, book shops, electric shops and beauty parlours etc. Such was not the case in non-borrowers. They were engaged in stitching work, embroidery work and knitting work. For this work, they were able to get only meagre income.

SUGGESTIONS

The study has shown that better publicity about bank credit facilities for women is needed as many of the women are not aware of these banking facilities. Orientation and training of bank personnel is also needed to enable them to respond positively to women's needs and also of beneficiaries to familiarize them with banking procedures. The study has pointed out that along with credit, training skills should be provided to women to ensure maximum utilization of credit facilities. Group processing of loans using women's voluntary organisations as intermediates between beneficiaries and bank is also needed. With this not only large number of poor women will be benefitted but bank have benefits too through lower processing costs and smaller operations.

Role of NGO's

There are many NGO's working in Panipat and adjoining area e.g. Mahila Kalyan Samiti, Mata Sita Rani Seva Sanstha, Women institute of technology and social awareness (WITSA). These NGO's are working at a very small level. They provide training relating to sewing and computer and also solve the personal and family problems of women. They are also creating awareness regarding female foeticide and female infanticide. There is one another NGO called Empowerment and Sustainable Development Initiative (ESDI). This NGO is operating in Nilokheri near Karnal and it is helping the women in forming the self-help groups and helping them in income generating activities.

Of course the NGO's are there but their functioning is not very effective and efficient due to lack of funds. Government support for providing funds to these NGO's is needed so that they can achieve the target of making the poor and deprived women economically empowered.

BIBLIOGRAPHY

Batra, V.P. (1982), '*Women and Employment*'. Yojna 6 (1) p. 36.

Grewal, Q.S. (1986), '*Impact of Rural Development Programmes on Rural Women in Bhiwani District*'. Indian Journal of Agricultural Economics, 40 (3) p. 254-262.

Gupta, S.C. (1987), *Development Banking for Rural Development*. Deep Publications, New Delhi.

Haq, F.M. (1982), '*Rural Credit Ullahpura Bangladesh*'. Rural Development Abstract, 4 (3).

G. BARADHA

13 NGO and Senior Citizen

"Older people, who are healthy, are a precious resource. Healthy ageing is a central component of the Development Agenda"

Ageing is a natural process, in the words of Seneca 'old age is an incurable disease' but more recently Ross commented 'You do not heal old age, you protect it, you promote it, you extend it'. It is not a fact that growing old should be a time of dismay and withdrawal from everything around. Infact, for most people, growing old is a time to be enjoyed and savoured.

Ageing population has serious implications both at the macro and the household level, especially as the transition has been accompanied by changes in society and economy. The proportion of elderly persons in the country has risen from 5.6% in 1961 to 7.1% in 2001. In absolute terms, the year 1991 saw 55 million elderly persons in the country and touched 76 million in 2001 and expected to be 177 million by 2025. Fourty per cent of elderly live below the poverty line, 90% of them are from the unorganized sector, with no benefits at 60.55% of all women over 60 are widows, many without any support, 80% of them are from rural areas and 73% of them are illiterates and have to depend on labours.

As advances in medical technology have lengthened lifespans and cracks have developed in traditional support systems like the joint family and the village community, problems of the uncared aged have been impinging on the welfare agenda of the state. Life expectancy in India today is 62 years, but there are great variations between states. These variations not withstanding, the 60 years plus population in this country has been increasing at a faster rate (38 per cent) than the rest of the population (19 per cent). Population surveys indicate that 10–15 per cent of the elderly either are childless or do not have children living with them for various reasons.

PROBLEMS

Elderly persons, due to retirement from job and due to reduction in income have a feeling of loneliness, rejection and insecurity. This creates various problems in the elderly such as:

- Ageing
- Chronic diseases
- Psycho–social problems
- Feelings of tiredness and tension
- Feelings of worthlessness
- Loss of appetite
- Trouble in sleeping
- Dependency
- Increased expenditure
- Problems in concentration
- Headaches and vague aches and pains all over the body.

There is no doubt of the government's intention to meet the challenges of an ageing population head on. India is committed to the basic principles of the International Plan of Action on Ageing: financial security, health care, shelter and protection against abuse and exploitation.

The contribution that older people, by their experience, can make to the process of making our society and culture more human. Researches show that the aged are no different than the adults and their worries are the same as could be expected in a normal adult. It would thus be wrong to say that the old lines in the past and present does not affect them. they also need right to live with dignity.

RIGHTS OF THE AGED

- Be treated as a person
- Be treated as an adult
- Enjoy fair chances on own merits
- Right to a future
- Have fun and companionship
- Right to be romantic
- Right to be interested
- Right to professional help if necessary.

Therefore with changing demographic scenario that is likely in many states in first half of the 21st century or even before, it is clear that for a developing country like India with so much heterogeneity and diversity across and within the states, it could be a real challenge to meet the needs of senior citizens in terms of social support services including housing, healthcare, education and employment opportunities vis a vis psychological, biological, economic, cultural environmental and political requirements.

The government is taking steps to accord special facilities to old people such as concessionary railway and airfares, priority in telephone connections, hospital appointments and earlier court hearings. Media is also trying to present care and respect for older persons. Voluntary agencies have a important role to play. However fostering independence for older persons is important as the traditional family structure is eroding. It is important for senior citizens to follow the following steps for happier and healthier life.

ESSENTIAL FOR GOOD ADJUSTMENT

- Living within physical limitations
- Adjusting to a lower income level
- Achieving security in medical care without sacrificing economic security
- Expressing one's self creativity
- Extending family love to the brotherhood of man
- Retaining personal dignity in society
- Maintaining self interests
- Passing on torch to next generation

Although family support and care of elderly are unlikely to disappear in the near future family care of the elderly seems likely to decrease. The changing social structure, preponderance of individualistic, materialistic and negative values of the younger generation towards the elderly and compulsory retirement of the elderly contribute a great deal to the emergence of old age as a social problem in the country.

For a developing country like India, the rapid growth of older population's present issues must be attended to if social and economic development is to proceed effectively. Therefore Government and Non Governmental organizations have to play valuable role.

Under these circumstances, in order to establish an affluent and vital society with a pervasive spirit of solidarity in which every citizen can feel happy and proud to have lived a long life, it is necessary to ensure sound development of the economy and society and stable improvement of people's living conditions. Measures are to be implemented to constantly revise the socio–economic system to ensure it's suitability for the coming aged society, support individual independence and familial roles and sustain a secure lifestyle through an appropriate combination of self, mutual and public support.

To achieve this The National Policy of Older Persons was formulated in 1999, declared as the International Year of Older Persons by the Government of India. The policy drafted intervention in the following areas:

The National Policy on Older Persons is a comprehensive document with far reaching possibilities. The National Policy recognizes the NGO sector as an important institutional mechanism that can provide user friendly affordable services to complement the endeavour of the state.

NATIONAL COUNCIL FOR OLDER PERSONS (NCOP)

NCOP has been constituted by the Ministry of Social Justice and Empowerment to operationalise the National Policy for Older Persons.

Though the national co-ordinating bodies are doing social services, NGOs are doing laudable services, caring for the old.

ROLE OF NGO FOR EMPOWERMENT OF AGED

Individual Development (within the people)	*Area Development (in relation to the living environment)*
• Building hopes	• Creation of infrastructural facilities
• Skill development	• Betterment of facilities
• Entrepreneurial development	• Creation of job opportunities
• Attitudinal change	• Help in self employment
• Behavioural change	• Ensuring equitable distribution and utilization of facilities
• Intra–group development and harmony	
• Inter–group development and harmony	• Sustainability in the use of facilities created
• Capacity building	
• Confidence building	• Awareness of welfare measures
• Gender disparity	• Full utilization of welfare measures
	• Arrange short trips
	• Organize recreational activities
	• Conduct talent search competition

Multi services by NGOs for senior citizens has following strategies:

- Net working
- Research
- Direct services to senior citizens
- Training

DIRECT SERVICES

- Mobile health services
- Health camps
- Recreational services
- Awareness campaigns.
- Celebration of important days–world Elders' Day.

- Counselling.
- Effort to remove elder abuse, neglect, family relations, stress, health.
- Therapeutic services–e.g. Yoga, Physiotherapy.
- Hobby, talent search.
- Outreach services–Old age pension, facilities for the elderly, home based care.
- Day care centre for the elderly.
- Income generating programme.
- Family related activities: Intergeneration activities.
- Raise funds.
- Legal aid.
- Mobile resources.
- Integrated aged welfare and development on the pattern of Integrated child development services to be organized.
- Provide consultancy and training to voluntary agencies.

RESEARCH

NGOs can collaborate with educational institutions and conduct research on:

- Psycho social needs of the aged.
- Field practice to develop self help groups of senior citizens.
- Frequent demographic surveys to be done within the community.
- Networking of organizations working for the care of the elderly.
- National Seminar to develop Gerontological social work in India.
- Networking between NGOs, families and geriatric committees for upgrading the services of the elderly.

TRAINING

- Training for para professionals to work with older persons.
- Training for professionals to work for the situations of elder persons.
- Training of volunteers to work in the field of geriatric social work.

RECOMMENDATIONS

- The NGOs and para professionals may have to be increasingly involved in health efforts of older persons.
- Training and research programmes on community based health care for the elderly.
- Professional and scientific social work intervention has to be promoted in the prevention, treatment and rehabilitation of physical, mental and social health.

- Geriatric health awareness programmes have to be made an inevitable part of social work literacy.
- Geriatric experts may be made available at all levels of service.
- Interpersonal communication, spouse communication, inter-generational communication should be strengthened so as to promote highest sustainable standards of geriatric health.
- The family and the community have to take the responsibility for the care of the elderly as a challenge and more growth opportunities may be made available for improving the quality of their life.
- The care programme, should include family social work, family therapy, counseling etc. to prevent family disintegration and to uphold human resources development.
- Journalist and the mass media should care programmes of the older persons in it's totality.
- Physical beautification, environmental sanitation, personal hygiene, horticultural therapy, music therapy and occupational therapy have to be promoted and strengthened.
- Psycho–social and economic betterment and empowerment of women and families are essential to cater to the care of the older persons.

CONCLUSION

A multidisciplinary team approach consisting of the geriatrician, the demographer, the gerontologists, the professional social worker, the clinical psychologist, the social work journalist, geriatric nurse in well organized geriatric centres and their community outreach through people's participation is a good position for the future.

BIBLIOGRAPHY

Bhardwaj, T. (2005), 'National Policy on Older Persons–A Critical Review', in Social Welfare, Vol. 52, No. 7, pp. 3–6.

Bhose, J.S.G.R. (2003), NGOs and Rural Development–Theory and Practice. Concept Publishing Company, New Delhi, pp. 169.

Durairaj, N., Rengasamy, K.R. (1999), 'The Aged: Need love and Protection', in Social Welfare, October, pp. 6–7.

General Principles Concerning Measures for the Aged (2002), 'The Second World Assembly on Ageing 2002'.

Joshi, U. (1999), 'Creating Social Sensibilities for the Aged', in Social Welfare. October, pp. 3–5.

Modi, I. (2001), Ageing and Human Development–Global perspectives, Rawat Publications, Jaipur, pp. 276, 278, 285.

Webliography

http://socialjustice.nic.in/social/sdcop/benefits.htm

SARJOO PATEL & MANEESHA SHUKUL

14 Role of NGO's in Waste Management

INTRODUCTION

There is an environmental crisis on a global scale as recognised by the world about 25 years back (Khoshoo, 1986; Peng, 1992; Mohd Idris, 1992; National Report to UNCED, 1992). It still persists. Such a deterioration of environment is the result of the human beings own action. Its present deterioration has come about mainly due to industrialisation coupled with unrestrained growth of human population and the resultant degradation and mismanagement of the world environment. These have created several environmental problems. One such problem is solid waste disposal. The solid waste disposal has posed a ecological problem. It is a major and burning problem of today not only for a single country but for the entire world. But of various problems related to refuse in the Indian cities its collection and disposal are dominating. Saxena (1990) has rightly said that a waste is essentially a resource, although out of place. Being not available at its right place, such a resource, would give rise to ecological problems. Much of the solid waste end up in open dumps. Implications for public health and other problems have been linked to mis-management of solid wastes. The relationship between public health and improper disposal of solid wastes has long been recognized. Rats, flies and other disease vectors breed in open dumps and in residential areas or other places where food and harborage are available (Rao,1980). An extensive search of the medical literature has indicated an association between solid wastes and 22 human diseases (Encyclopedia of Environmental Science 1974) Nearly half of all open dumps contribute to water pollution and three fourth to local air pollution (Environmental Protection Agency, 1978). Open burning of solid waste frequently results in gross air pollution created by foul odour and fire either spontaneous or man made. Many residues resulting from mis–management of solid wastes are not readily eliminated or degraded. Some are hazardous to human health, others adversely affect desirable plants and animals. The ever growing thousands of open dump scar the landscape. There is litter along road side, sidewalks and beaches. Besides its ugliness and its threat to health, much of resources that may soon be in short supply are present in disposed solid waste. Apart from these great expenditure is involved in collecting transporting and disposing of waste.

QUANTITY OF SOLID WASTE

As noted by South Wick in 1976 in the United States 55 billion metal and plastic bottles and 7 billion automobile are thrown away every year indestructible. They threw 16 billion disposable diapers, 106 billion pens, 2 billion razors and blades, and 220 billion tyres (Karpagam, 1991). In the U. S. A. alone urban areas produced about 640 million kg of solid waste each day as noted by Schneider in 1970. This amount is sufficient to cover more than 1.6 square kilometers every day to a depth of 3 meters. According to Encyclopedia of Environmental Science (1974) American discard over 27.2 x 106 metric tons paper 3.6 x106 metric tons of plastics, 48 x 109 cans and 26 x 109 bottles. Waste generated per capita per day in U.S. is 2 kg, 1kg. in U.K., 700 gms in Australia and .50 kg in India (Kut and Hare, 1981; Southwick, 1976; Bhide,1975) The discarded aluminum from U.S. commercial airline fleet every three months. On an average an Indian generates 0.5 to 0.7 kilograms of waste (khoshoo, 1980). Simmons and Widmas (1989) estimate that a typical American generates 25 pounds of solid waste each week, 570 disposable diapers and throw away each second, family of five uses 1000 glass bottles and jars each year along with 2000 metal cans. Only 10% of the solid waste is recycled. Majority of the waste is generated in the industrial countries (Dela Court, 1990). Per capita consumption of plastic in India is about 12kg whereas in the west it is 16kg (Nidamboor, 1995) Tons of solid waste is disposed every day in the world today. If we look at the change in the scenario of solid waste it is found/observed that in 1990 the domestic waste disposed was 5,460 tons per day. Gradually it increased to 6000 tons per day in 1993, 6210 tons per day in 1995 and 7,430 tons per day in 1999 which reveals the increase in the solid waste. (www.google.com).

Nature has demonstrated its capacity to dispose, degrade, absorb or otherwise dispose of unwanted residues in the natural sink of the atmosphere, inland, water ways, oceans, and the soil. (Encyclopedia of Environmental Science, 1974) But the volume of waste generated by today's population is beyond the earth's natural capacity. As the Municipal authorities alone cannot tackle the problem of waste collection and disposal by themselves, the NGO's have come forward to help in waste management.

NON GOVERNMENT ORGANIZATIONS: IT'S ROLE

A non-government organization is an organization that is not part of a government. NGO's are therefore typically independent of governments. NGO's are usually non-profit organizations that gain at least a portion of their funding from private sources. Because the label "NGO" is considered too broad by some, as it might cover anything that is non-governmental, many NGOs now prefer the term private voluntary organization. Globalization during the 20th century gave rise to the importance of NGOs. Many problems could not be solved alone by the government. In an attempt to counterbalance this trend, NGOs have developed to emphasize humanitarian issues, developmental aid and sustainable development. Three stages or generations of NGO evolution have been identified by Korten's (1990) Three Generations of Voluntary Development Action. First, the typical development NGO focuses on relief and welfare, and delivers relief services directly to beneficiaries. Examples are the distribution of food, shelter or health services. The NGO notices immediate needs and responds to them. NGOs in the second generation are oriented towards small-scale, self-reliant local development. At this evolutionary stage, NGOs build the capacities of local communities to meet their needs through 'self-reliant local action'. Korten calls the third generation 'sustainable systems development'. At this stage, NGOs try to advance changes in policies and institutions at a local, national and international level; they move away from their operational service providing role towards a catalytic role. The NGO is starting to develop from a relief NGO to a development NGO. NGOs exist for a variety of purposes, usually to further the political or social goals of their members. Examples include improving the state of the natural environment, encouraging the observance of human rights, improving the welfare of the disadvantaged, or representing a corporate agenda. However, there are a huge number of such organizations and their goals cover a broad range of political and philosophical positions. This can also easily be applied to private schools and athletic organizations.

METHODOLOGY

Considering the NGO's recent development the present investigation was designed to study the solid waste disposal practices followed by the homemakers and their opinion regarding waste disposal facilities of the housing societies in which they live. Descriptive research design was used for the study. There are two NGO's in Baroda City who provide solid waste collection and cleaning facilities in some colonies. They are *Baroda Citizens Council* and *Beautiful Baroda Council*. In Baroda most of the colonies appoint their own sweeper for solid waste cleaning. So three colonies were selected purposively, namely Shreenagar Society where Baroda Citizens Council was providing services, Adhyapak Kutir where Beautiful Baroda Council was providing such services and Harkashi Society where the sweeper was appointed by the colony itself. The Sample of the study consisted of 120 homemakers 40 each from 3 housing society of Baroda City. From the list of total households in each colony the sample was selected through systematic random sampling method. Interview schedule was used as an instrument for gathering data. The schedule consisted of three sections. Section I contained questions regarding background information of the respondents, section II contained summated rating scale having statements showing practices followed by the homemakers regarding household solid waste disposal. Practice scale contained three categories of response namely Always, Sometimes, Never. The scores of I through 3 were ascribed to the statement which were negative and 3 through I were ascribed to positive statements. The possible range of some was divided into three categories having almost equal interval of number as below.

Practice	Range of Scores
Poor	Between 68 and 113
Fair	Between 114 and 158
Good	Between 159 and 204

If the score is high that means they followed good practice and low score means the homemakers followed poor solid waste disposal practice. Section III contained the summated rating scale regarding the opinion of the home makers about the solid waste disposal facilities of selected housing societies. The responses on opinion scale namely Agree, Undecided and Disagree were ascribed scores of 3 through 1 respectively.

The possible range of score was divided into three categories having almost equal interval of numbers as below.

Scores	Opinion	Range of Scores
1. Low	Unfavorable	12 to 20
2. Moderate	Neutral	21 to 28
3. High	Favorable	29 to 36

The content validity and reliability of both the scales (r=0.65) was established by split half technique.

MAJOR FINDINGS OF THE STUDY/RESULTS

Major findings of the study are presented below:

Background Information

The mean age of the total sample was 36.1 years, whereas the mean age of respondents from Shreenagar society was 36.6 and that from Adhyapak Kutir was 35.1 and Harkashi society was 36.6 years.

Nearly 43% of the homemakers were graduates and 35% of the homemakers had education above graduation. Probing further it was found that majority of the homemakers from Adhyapak Kutir had education above graduation whereas in Shreenagar and Harkashi Society majority were graduates. Nearly 60% of the homemakers were not employed. Majority of the homemakers from Shreenagar and Harkashi Society were not employed whereas majority from Adhyapak Kutir were employed. The mean monthly income of total sample was Rs. 10,428, whereas the mean income of Shreenagar and Adhyapak Kutir homemakers was almost similar but that of Harkashi society was comparatively much lesser. More than half of the respondents 'sometimes' read about waste problems in magazines and majority of them 'sometimes' read about such problems in Newspapers. Majority of the homemakers 'never' saw about these problems in movies, nor did they hear about these in radio. Nearly 40% of the homemakers always discussed about solid waste problems. Majority of the homemakers had low extent of exposure to the sources of information about the problems of solid waste.

Practices Regarding Household Solid Waste Disposal

Practices regarding cleanliness of dustbin and place of garbage disposal

Almost all the homemakers (99.2%) threw the solid waste in the dustbin and majority (72%) kept their dustbin clean and washed regularly. Majority of the homemakers followed fair practices regarding cleanliness of dustbin and place of garbage disposal.

Practices Regarding Disposal of Large and/or Intact Waste Items

Majority of the homemakers never gave the newspapers to the servant but a wide majority (97.5%) sold out the newspapers. Majority of the homemakers (91.7%) always sold off the emptied tins and 89.2% of them sold the polythene milk bags.

A little less than half of the respondents followed good practices regarding disposal of intact waste items but one tenth of them followed poor practices.

Practices Regarding Disposal of Paper

Majority of the homemakers (91.7%) always threw the food packages in the dustbin, and 83.3% never threw the paper food packages on the road. More than two third of the homemakers followed good practices related to disposal of paper-None of the homemakers followed poor practices regarding disposal of paper.

Practices Regarding Disposal of Waste Food Item

Majority of the homemakers (80.8%) always threw the peels of fruits and vegetables in the dustbin, and never threw them in front of the house. Majority of them also never threw leftover food and stale food on the road or neighbouring areas. A little less than half of them 'sometimes' washed and flown the food left in the thali in gutter and majority of the homemakers never threw it out of the compound. More than half of the homemakers 'sometimes' fed leftover food and fruit and vegetable peel to the animals. Majority of the homemakers followed good practices related to disposal of waste food item.

Practices Regarding Disposal of Waste Glass Article

A little more than half of the homemakers always sold small glass bottles of medicines. A wide majority (80%) never threw empty small glass bottles in the dustbin, majority never threw broken pieces of glass just out of the house and a little more than half of them (60%) always reused empty small bottles of glass in best possible manner. Two third of all the homemakers followed good practices regarding disposal of waste glass articles.

Practices Regarding Disposal of Miscellaneous Item

One third of the homemakers always threw dust collected after sweeping on the road or street. Majority of them always threw ashes, egg shells and hair after combing in the dustbin. Majority of the homemakers never separated bits of paper, cloth, rubber, plastic, glass, hair etc. either for selling or discarding. Majority of the homemakers stored empty shopping bags for other purposes. A wide majority of the homemakers never disposed off the sanitary waste anywhere. Two third of the homemakers followed good practices regarding disposal of miscellaneous waste item.

While looking at the Entire Practice Scale, it was found that two third of the Total Sample followed Good Practices regarding Disposal of Solid Waste and a little more than one third of them followed Fair Practices

The mean score on the total practice scale of the total sample was found to be 158.5. The mean score of Shreenagar and Adhyapak Kutir was similar whereas the mean score of Harkashi Society was much lower compared to the other two societies. It can be concluded that the homemakers from the colonies where solid waste collection facilities are provided by outside agencies had good practices regarding disposal of solid waste as compared with the society which had its own solid waste collection facilities.

Opinion of the Homemakers Regarding Solid Waste Disposal Facilities of Selected Housing Societies

1. The mean score on opinion scale of the total sample was found to be 26.6 which could be considered as neutral.
2. A little more than one third of the respondents had unfavourable opinion about the facilities provided in their housing colonies whereas nearly sixty per cent had favourable opinion.
3. The overall group opinion for Shreenagar society, where solid waste disposal facilities were provided by Baroda Citizens Council, was favourable. The opinion of respondents from Adhyapak Kutir colony was found to be favourable. In this colony the solid waste disposal services were provided by Beautiful Baroda Council. The opinion of homemakers from Harkashi society was found to be unfavourable for the solid waste disposal facilities provided by their colony where the colony itself had appointed a sweeper for solid waste collection and cleanliness.

   A comparison of mean of each item among the respondents of each colony revealed that the homemakers from Shreenagar and Adhyapak Kutir had favourable opinion for all the items. But the homemakers from Harkashi society had unfavourable opinion for most of the items.

Testing of Hypotheses

1. The solid waste disposal practices of the homemakers varied with their education, family income, housing society, and employment status but age and extent of exposure to the sources of information did not cause any variation in their practices as revealed through the ANOVA and t-tests.
2. The opinion of the homemakers varied with the housing colonies in which they resided as the F- ratio was found to be highly significant at 0.01 level.
3. Coefficient of correlation computed revealed a very high correlation ($r = 0.92$) between solid waste disposal practices of homemakers and their opinion regarding such facilities provided by Baroda Citizens Council, Beautiful Baroda Council and their own society. So it could be concluded that the practices and opinion of homemakers were positively correlated with each other.

CONCLUSION

The Non-government organizations should be encouraged to provide such services wherever the colony sweeper poses problems like irregularity as it was revealed that the homemakers from the colonies where solid waste collection and cleaning facilities were provided by outside agencies had good practices and opinion regarding disposal of solid waste as compared with the society which had its own solid waste collection facilities . The colonies where there are no sweeper should be encouraged to approach such agencies which can provide waste collection facilities which is a major problem nowadays.

IMPLICATIONS OF THE STUDY

For the Government

The Government should encourage and help the voluntary organizations such as Baroda Citizen's Council and Beautiful Baroda Council which extend their services for cleaning and collection of solid waste from housing colonies because the present study had revealed that those who were utilising the services of the aforesaid organizations held favourable opinion for them.

For the Non-Voluntary Organizations Providing Solid Waste Collection and Cleaning Services

As revealed through the findings of present study the residents of the housing colonies where these organizations provided the services had favourable opinion towards them, these organizations get a positive feedback for their services. Such an information can be utilised by them to propogate and support their program.

For the Municipal Corporation

Though the municipal authorities have provided containers in every area for dumping solid waste, a shortage is experienced. Generally people do not throw the garbage in these containers. The present study also revealed that more than one third of the homemakers did not throw the plastic food packages, disposable cups and plates etc. in the Municipal Corporation garbage collection bin. Hence the corporation can take help of the voluntary organizations to help it in the mega work of solid waste collection from Baroda city. It can also approach the educational institutions such as that of Home Management to make people aware to throw the household waste at proper place.

For the Housing Societies

Many of the housing societies of Baroda city face the problem of solid waste collection from every house, disposing it at a proper place, and cleanliness of the entire society. The present study revealed that the housing society which had appointed its own sweeper had unfavourable opinion towards it but the societies in which solid waste collection and cleaning services were provided by the non-government organizations viz. Baroda Citizens Council and Beautiful Baroda Council had favourable opinion for the services provided by these agencies. Hence those housing societies which face a problem in this regard can approach the aforesaid agencies to solve their problems regarding solid waste collection and cleanliness of their societies.

For the Field of Home Management

As the study revealed that education of the homemaker had an influence on the solid waste disposal practices, there is a need to educate the present and future homemakers which the field of Home Management can do in an effective way through formal and non-formal education. The Home Management department of Faculty of Home Science as one of the applied sciences can help to bring about the desirable change in the knowledge and practices of women. Through the non formal education programmes the present homemakers can be made concious of the problem of solid waste and the effect of filthy environment on their health.

For the Individuals

There are many things the public could do to reduce the quantity of waste generated on an individual basis. Each household can use the kitchen and garden waste to make compost, which in turn can be used as fetilizer. The present study revealed that majority of the homemakers always threw the peels of fruits and vegetables in the dustbin and many of them threw the leftover food in the dishes in the dustbin or threw it into the gutter. Such a waste could be very well utilised for making compost or even a vermiculture project. The present study revealed that nearly one third of the homemakers never sold small glass bottles of medicines and approximately one tenth of homemakers threw the broken pieces of glass any where out of the house. It is essential to make them aware to dispose the waste glass, metal and paper in such a way that it becomes easy to collect and then to recycle such a material. Recycling is economical and essential to meet the energy crisis. The present and the future homemakers should be made aware to change their life styles from "throw away" to "reuse". Also they must "want less" and "waste less". People must be made aware that "todays waste" can become "tomorrow's resources".

BIBLIOGRAPHY

Bhide A.D. et al (1975), "Studies on Refuse in Indian Cities part–11: Variation in Quantity and Quality "Indian Journal of Environment and Health, Vol.17, No. 3.

Dela Court (1990), Beyond Brundtland, New Horizon Press, Newyork, p. 50.

Encyclopedia of Environmental Science (1974), Mr. Graw Hill Book Co., New York.

Karpagam M. (1991), "Environmental Economic "Sterling Publishers Pvt. Ltd., New Delhi.

Khoshoo T.N. (1986), "Environmental Priorities in India and Sustainable Development "Indian Science Congress Association, New Delhi.

Korten D. (1990), Getting to the 21st Century: Voluntary Action and the Global Agenda, West Hartford, CT: Kumarian Press, p. 118.

Mohd Idris E.S.M. (1992), Living in the Environment 2nd ed., Wardsworth Publication Company, California.

National Report to UNCED (1992), Traditions, Concerns and Efforts in India, Ministry of Environment and Forests, Government of India, New Delhi.

News and Views (1993), "WEDO-Women Lobby Environment and Development, Policy Makers at UN."

Nidamboor R. (1995), "Coming Around Again", The Times of India, March 25.

Non–governmental Organization–Wikipedia, the free Encyclopedia Cited at www.google.com.

Paolucci B. and Hall (1977), Family Decision Making–An Eco-system Approach, John Wiley and Sons, New York.

Peng K.K. (1992), "The Third World Environment Crisis: Third world Perspective" as cited in Environment Crisis and Sustainable Development, Natraj Publishers, New Delhi.

Schneider H. (1970), Environmental Pollution as cited in Simonds J. (1978), Earth Space–A Manual of Environment Planning, Mr. Graw Hill Book Co. New York.

South Wick C.H. (1976), "Ecology and the Quantity of one Environment", D. Van Nostrand Company, New York.

Web Site Browsed

www.googlc.com

NIDHI GUPTA & RACHEL GEORGE

15 Voluntary Consumer Organisations: A Weapon to Fight Against Consumer Exploitation

The best way consumers can protect themselves is not relying on even the best intentioned government agency but by learning about the products they buy and using them wisely and by insisting on being heard.

—Thomas Larkin

INTRODUCTION

Ordinarily every person is a consumer because he uses or consumes economic goods and services. A person is not only a consumer when he buys and uses groceries or automobiles or clothes but he is also a consumer when he makes use of educational opportunities offered in a school or obtain legal advice from a lawyer, medical services from a physician. The retail merchant himself is a consumer when he buys food, recreation and other things for himself and his family. Therefore, a consumer is any person who engages in the process of spending money and using economic goods and services. The word 'Consumer' more elaborately may be defined as a person or group of persons who taxes, succeeds, buys, hires, for him or for his family's final use. Thus the term 'Consumer' is used to the person for whose cause marketing is constituted. Consumer is the focal point of all the activities, but they are unorganised. Therefore the protection of their interest and rights is vital to the general welfare of the people, which is the major goal of modern welfare state.

Consumerism is a social and legal force which aims at protecting the general interest of the consumers. Self policing and collective action are the most important components of consumerism. Despite development of consumerism, the common consumers fall prey to the exploitation at the hand of services/goods providers'. Thus the exploitation of the consumer has led to the formation and establishment of voluntary organizations.

Consumer Exploitation Galore

Consumer exploitation is not a new phenomenon in the global market. It has always been there in our country date back to the Indian civilisation. With the advancement of technology, production has become more sophisticated and innumerable types of goods are flooded to the market. Often the consumers are at great confusion to choose the right product since too many goods with different brand names and disguises are entering the market. In addition, the marketers are using highly sophisticated techniques, such as pressure salesmanship which is refined to such an extent that in the end, the customer invariably takes what is thrust on him.

Indian consumers are the worst victims of blatant exploitation adopted by the ruthless businessmen through unfair means. Some of the ways of exploitation are mentioned below:

Adulteration

Adulteration is the outcome of the shortage economy. Various types of additives are generally used for preservative purposes and for flavouring the products, but most of these additives are found to be carcinogenic and affect the various parts of the body.

Warranties and Guarantees

Warranties and guarantees are present in bold print but taken away in fine print. Letters of complaint are often skilfully ignored. Even in case of consumer durables, warranties are either inadequate or defective. More often than not, manufacturers fail to honour warrantees and guarantees.

Hazardous or unsafe Products

Many consumers sustain injuries or die due to electric shock, fire and other accidents either while using defective appliances or due to absence of adequate information for safe handling. The range of such products varies from toys, cycles, cooking range, ovens, and television etc.

Underweight

Underweight is resorted to in many ways including soaking of vegetables & sugar, using heavy containers and manipulation of seals. Even in the packed articles weights are not correct.

Duplicate Products

These products are sold in the rural areas by the businessmen in the lust of heavy profit. But it creates numerous problems to the consumers.

Bogus and Misleading Advertisements

Information available to the consumer through advertisement is usually inaccurate, unreliable, incomplete and unfair.

Sales Promotional Tactics

Offering discount, gifts, reduction sales, economy size, coupons or competitions based on draw etc., mislead than lead the consumer.

Service

Service quality is more difficult to evaluate then quality of goods. In contrast to commodities services are abstract. They can not be easily identified as good or bad. Its quality changes from customer to customer.

Consumerism

Consumerism has been defined as the social movement, which seeks to safeguard, and strengthens the rights of consumers in relation to the producer or the supplier of goods and services. The obligation rests on all consumers to take all possible steps to protect them before they buy rather than regret when it is too late. Consumerism enables the consumers to buy right products resulting in more goods of less expenditure. Consumerism will reduce the number of unsafe or unhealthy products. The need of the hour is to strengthen and promote consumerism. The wide spread exploitation of the consumer has led to the formation and establishment of voluntary consumer organizations (VCO). The main objectives of establishing the VCO is to protect the interest of the consumers.

Protection of Consumer

To protect the interest of the consumers Government has brought about number of legislations and has established the VCOs. This means that the consumers can be protected by:

Legislative Action of the Government

Government has passed a plethora of laws and regulations to protect the interest of the consumers but the existing laws are ineffective due to laxities of administration and attitude of agencies which are subject to enactment and coupled with this is the widely prevailing corruptions among the agencies administrating the law. The regulatory measures have created more scope for harassment and corruption without providing much relief to the consumers.

In order to overcome various limitations in the legislation and implementation machinery, a comprehensive act was passed by the Government of India in 1986.

Consumer Protection Act (COPRA) 1986

Consumer Protection Act, 1986 is an important piece of legislation in safeguarding the interest of consumers. The main significant features of this act are:

(i) The act is applicable to enterprises falling in the categories of public sector, financial institutions and cooperative societies.

(ii) The provisions are in addition to and not in derogation of provisions of other laws.

(iii) The Act is a comprehensive legislation with its main thrust on giving speedy redressal and compensation to the consumers.

Benefits of COPRA

The main benefits of this act are:

(i) Now it is not necessary to consult a pleader or legal expert.

(ii) Speedy and cheap relief is being provided by the authorities.

(iii) Forums/Commissions have to follow the fundamental Principle of Natural Justice.

(iv) It avoids procedural delays.

(v) It extends adequate compensation to the aggrieved party.

Machinery Constituted

Under this certain authorities have been established to provide safeguard to consumer interest. They are:

1. ***Consumer Protection Councils:*** The governments have constituted Consumer Protection Councils in order to promote and protect the rights of consumers such as right to safety, information, choice, to be heard, seek redressal and consumer education.

2. ***Consumer Disputes Redressal Agencies:*** Under the Act following agencies were established for the purpose of consumer protection. They are:

   (i) District Consumer Forum: District Consumer Forum will be established by the State government. The District forum will have jurisdiction to entertain complaints where value of goods or services and compensation claims, if any, is less than Rs. 5 lakh.

   (ii) State Commission: It will have jurisdiction to entertain complaint where value of goods and services and compensation, if any, exceed Rs. 5 lakh, but does not exceed to Rs. 20 lakh and to entertain appeals against the orders of any District forum within the state.

(iii) *National Commission:* The National Commission shall have jurisdiction to entertain complaint where value of goods or services and compensation, if any, exceed Rs. 20 lakh and appeal against the orders of any state commission.

Voluntary Consumer Organization

With the arrival of multi-national companies into the country and with the liberalisation of the Indian economy, consumerism has assumed more significance. This has resulted in the mushroom growth of voluntary consumer organizations (VCO). Corollary to the frustrations crept in the mind of consumers; various consumer organisations have emerged to shield the interest of the consumers. Herman Levin defines Voluntary Organization as the one which embodies the interest of the people through a group effort to organize services.

A consumer organisation is an ideal set-up of consumers to come together to offer collective resistance against all kinds of exploitation. The role of these consumer organizations is not only to educate and guide the consumers with respect to redressal of complaints, but also to make the consumer movement a reality, through co-ordinated efforts from all angle. The success of consumer movement depends solely on its ability to build a strong and collective resistance against all kinds of exploitation.

Generally, a consumer organisation has the following objectives:

(i) To promote co-operation and collaboration of all activities related to consumers' protection and interests.

(ii) To provide consumer education.

(iii) To share and exchange consumer related information.

(iv) To conduct research and product testing.

(v) To ensure the rights of every consumer to basic needs such as food, housing, health care and clean environment.

(vi) To develop spirit and confidence among the consumers to represent their case to Government, among the public, and against the private companies that exploit them.

(vii) To educate consumers to think critically to make their own decisions and to have the strength to resist hazardous trends and practices like smoking, drinking, gambling etc. that make their lives more deprived.

There are a good number of organizations that may be included either full-time or part-time, in the modern social movement of consumerism. The brief description of Consumer Association is given below:

Table 1
Types of Consumer Organizations and Principal Activities

Sr. No.	*Types*	*Activities*
1.	National	State legislation, consumer education, law enforcement.
2.	Local and cooperatives	Local legislation and law enforcement, consumer education, complaint handling, information and buying services.
3.	Corporate	Complaint handling, consumer education, company protection from consumer criticism.
4.	Laissez·· faire group	Deregulation, promotion of growth and investment.
5.	Social and political Groups	Worker-citizen control, comprehensive planning, limited output and technological growth, international-impact recognition.

Hence, an attempt has been made to evaluate the activities of consumer organization in view of the response of the consumers towards their various activities.

NEED OF STUDY

Most of the literature on consumer protection reveals that researches have been carried mostly on the general themes of consumerism. There is no evidence of any comprehensive research on the study of the opinion of the consumers about the activities of consumer organisations. This field remains largely unexplored. The need for this study is also felt in view of the following facts.

(i) Consumption function has increased

(ii) Rise in consumer exploitation.

(iii) Increased number of Voluntary Consumer Organisations.

(iv) Significant developments in consumer protection legislation such as enactment of COPRA, amendments in MRTP Act, Essential Commodities Act and PFA Act etc.

(v) Lack of reliable research in the field of Consumer Protection.

(vi) Momentum in consumerism in international scenario.

OBJECTIVES OF STUDY

The present effort aims at studying the opinion of the consumers about the voluntary consumer organisations. The main objectives of present study are:

(i) To study the emergence of consumer movement in India.

(ii) To analyse the opinion of consumers towards consumer organisations for protecting their interest.

(iii) To advance suggestions for improving the functioning of Consumer Organizations.

(iv) To identify the areas for future research.

METHODOLOGY

In order to achieve the objectives, both primary and secondary data have been utilized. Secondary data have been collected from various sources like publications of various consumer organisations, reports published by Consumer Organizations and government, books, journals and newspapers etc to study the emergence of consumer movement in India.

To analyse the opinion of consumer towards various activities of consumer organisations for protecting their interest, Likert's method of Summated Rating was used to develop the attitude scale. The carefully edited items were submitted to a panel of ten judges who were experts in their fields. A descriptive research design with survey method was adopted. The data have been collected from four organizations selected in the first stage through purposive sampling method. From the list of employee's the sample of 220 consumers was selected. A pre-coded questionnaire formed the tool for data collection.

The correlation coefficients of VCO opinion scale was 0.84 and reliability coefficients 0.91. Item selection was done on the basis of computed critical t-ratio. The final VCO opinion scale consisted of seventeen items. The data were then processed, tabulated and analysed using SPSS and FoxPro software. Frequencies, percentages and means were computed in relation to base line data, viz., age, education level, occupation, and personal income.

On the basis of the emergence of consumer movement in India and opinion of the consumers about VCO, suggestions for improving the functioning of Consumer Organizations and scope for the future research are given.

EMERGENCE OF CONSUMER MOVEMENT

Consumer movement is conceived as social movement which seeks to enhance well being and bargaining power of consumers. The word consumer movement has a history of over a century, but it gained momentum only about three decade ago. Sporadic efforts where made by various governments in consumer protection in their countries. The establishment of International organization for Consumer Union (IOCU) was the first step in the field of consumer movement, which helped in spreading the movement in different countries. It acted as a catalyst where from affiliated country could avail the services of this organization on various issues. On march 14th, 1962 President J.A. Kennedey equated the rights of the ordinary American consumers, later on IOCU expanded the list to eight rights which included (i) Safety,

(ii) Information, (iii) Choice, (iv) Representation, (v) Redress, (vi) Education, (vii) Environment, and (viii) Basic needs.

In our country the consumer organizations and the government are in the firm determination to protect the following consumer right which are of prime importance.

The Right to Safety

This right enunciates that the consumer is to be protected against the marketing of goods which are hazardous to health and property.

The Right to Be Informed

As per this right the consumer is to be protected against fraudulent, deceitful or grossly misleading information, advertising, labelling or other practices and to be given the facts he needs to make an informed choice.

The Right to Choose

The consumer is to be given access to a variety of products and services at competitive price. In those industries in which competition is not workable, Government regulation is substituted to provide satisfactory quality of goods and services at fair price.

The Right to Be Heard

According to this right consumer interest will receive full and sympathetic consideration in the formulation of government policy and fair and expeditious treatment in its administrative "Tribunals".

The Right to Seek Redressal

This right seeks redressal against unfair trade practices or unscrupulous exploitation of consumers. It also includes right to fair settlement of the genuine grievances of the consumer.

The Right to Consumer Education

This right seeks to acquire knowledge to be an informed consumer throughout his life.

The Right to a Healthy Environment

This right permits a life of dignity and well-being and basic needs and services. It guarantees an adequate food, clothing, shelter, healthcare, education and sanitation as demanded to remove the pollution from the world and to make it more beautiful.

CONSUMER MOVEMENT IN INDIA

The merciless exploitation of the consumers and the consequent discontent led to sprout of consumer movement.

The history of consumer movement in India goes to ancient times In Kautilya's times necessary regulations were in force for protection of consumer interest. Inspired by the Consumer Rights Bill passed on 15th March, 1962 by the American President Sri John F. Kennedy and impressed by the Consumer problems some enlightened house wives formed the consumer Guidance Society of India in 1966. Similarly, under the able leadership of late Sri J.R.D. Tata and Late Sri Rama Krishna Bajaj some progressive manufacturers and traders came together and formed the Fair Trade practices Association in Bombay in March 1966. These two very important events started the modern consumer Movement in India.

Mahila Upbhokta Sangathan, was the first consumer organisation established in Lucknow. The major consumer organisations which made impact on Indian consumer movement were Madras Provincial Consumer Organisation (1949), Consumer Guidance Society of India (1966), Consumer Unity and Trust Society (1984), VOICE (1983), Common Cause (1981), and ABGP (1975). From the middle of seventies voluntary organisations in the field of consumer protection have gradually but steadily been emerging in all parts of the country. At present there are over eight hundred such organisations which render assistance to the consumer. Consumer Education & Research Centre (CERC) set up in 1978; the centre is a public trust under the Bombay Public Trusts Act, 1950. The complaints cell attends to almost 500 complaints in a month. In appropriate cases the society files petitions, writes and complaints in the Supreme Court the High Court, the Monopolies and Restrictive Trade Practices Commission and the Consumer Dispute Redressal Agencies.

The Consumers Association of India

It was established in 1959. It has yet not done any work of quality testing and also the job of consumers' education. This Consumers Association should have been reorganised to counter act the aggressive efforts of traders and manufacturers.

The Consumer Guidance Society of India (CGSI)

The society was established in 1966 by a few enlightened ladies. The purposes of CGSI are to protect and promote the rights and interests of consumers, provide them with information, counsel and take-up their complaints with the offending party and/or the authorities and help them select goods and services which are fair return for the money they spend. The CGSI is a non-profit organisation and derives its income from membership subscriptions, sales of its publications, grants and donations.

Of all such organisations, the CGSI is the best organised union of consumers in the country. It is represented on the central committee for food standards, ISI certification makers' advisory committee, two ISI oil burning appliance committees, the ISI drugs and cosmetics committee and several state advisory committees.

But the progress of consumer movement in India has been rather very slow as compared with that of Western European countries and USA. In the West, consumer interests are given statutory recognition in the form of protective laws and supervisory and regulatory institutions. The consumers there are fully protected through quality control, a definite price policy, and well regulated channels of distribution linked with informative labelling, certification marks, and guarantees. Though these are there in India also, they are hardly effective. In the less developing country like India, the consumer movements are weak and poorly organized for various reasons. Naturally businessmen and traders start exploiting the consumers in more than one way. Slow growth of consumer movement may be attributed to the prevailing vicious circles of following reasons:

(i) Lack of general awareness in consumers.
(ii) Persistence of poverty.
(iii) Illiteracy.
(iv) Cumbersome legal procedure.
(v) Lack of consumer interest groups.
(vi) Lack of proper education and guidance.
(vii) Limited Government involvement.

In India there is a great need for the consumer movement to grow further. Even though there are many VCO all over the country, there are still many areas where consumers have not come together. Absence of consumer organisations has led the sellers and manufacturers to practise all kinds of malpractices and exploit the consumer in all possible ways. It is, therefore, necessary that consumer organisations are set-up in every nook and corner of the country to reverse this situation. The consumer movement at its highest level is only possible through the permanent consumer associations and organizations with adequate resources and support from the Government.

OPINION OF CONSUMERS ABOUT THE ACTIVITIES OF CONSUMER ORGANIZATION

According to Webster's dictionary, 'opinion' applies to a conclusion or judgment, while it remains open to dispute, seems true or probable to one's own mind. In the present study, 'opinion' refers to the conclusion or judgment reached by an individual about Voluntary Consumer Organizations (VCO).

The mean age of the respondents was estimated to be 37.6 years. A considerable percentage of respondents, i.e., one-third of them were Post-graduates. The ratio of male to female consumers of IR worked out to be 3:1. It was found that a major part of the respondents, i.e., 40 per cent belonged to middle order vocation while only 9.5 per cent were found to be semi-skilled workers The results revealed that while one-fifth of the respondents earned between Rs. 6001 and Rs. 8500 per month, 12 per cent of the respondents earned between Rs. 1000 and Rs. 3500 per month.

Out of the total 45 per cent respondents did not have any knowledge about consumer organization at national level while 65 per cent respondents knew about the local consumer organizations.

The opinion scales was measured on a five point continuum, i.e., 'strongly agree', 'agree', 'uncertain', 'disagree' and 'strongly disagree'. Scores 1 through to 5 were assigned to strongly agree through to strongly disagree respectively, if it measured a negative opinion and scoring pattern was reversed in the case of items that reflected a positive opinion. The scores were interpreted such that the higher the score, the more favourable the mental disposition of the respondents towards the construct in question. The possible range of scores on VCO scale was zero to 17. All those who earned a score of X-s or less were grouped under 'low' category while all those who earned a score of X + s or more were grouped under 'high' category. Those who earned scores in between these two ranges were grouped under the 'medium' scorer category.

The mean opinion score of the respondents was 58.39 with an S.D. of 4.63. A close look into the data revealed that a little more than three-fourth of the respondents were medium scorers while approximately one-tenth of them were either low or high scorers when classified using mean and standard deviation values. However, the distribution of the respondents when analysed by their observed score on the opinion scale classified as per the response categories revealed that none of them exhibited negative opinion about VCO. The opinion of the consumers about VCO was found to correlate positively with age (r = 0.1553*) and education(r = 0.1371*).

The respondents who held low opinion about VCO probably might not be well informed about VCOs and because of that their opinion tended to be biased. It could also be that their past experience with the procedure to seek redress through VCO might have been cumbersome or that they might not have been active members of VCO due to time constraints that they might have failed to seek redress to their grievances through VCO or third party assistance. Further, it also could be that they might have remained tradition bound in their complaining behaviour acts that expressed dissatisfaction without expectation of any reward rather than resort to third party complaining wherein a reward by way of compensation results in successful cases of complaints.

Table 2
Distribution of Respondents by their Opinion about VCO

Scores	*N = 220*	*%*
Low	24	10.9
Medium	172	78.2
High	24	10.9
Mean	58.39	
SD	4.63	
Range	45-72	
OAMIS*	3.244	

* OAMIS denotes the overall aggregate mean item score.

The respondents with relatively higher opinion about VCO might probably view them as one of the effective alternatives for third party option of complaining, for they might have witnessed its active involvement in solving consumer complaints. Thus, those with higher opinion about VCO tended to seek redress through third party to a greater extent. The opinion of the consumers about VCO was found to correlate positively with age and education. Their higher level of experience (age) and education might play a prominent role in their access to authority and third party options for complaining.

SUGGESTIONS FOR IMPROVING THE FUNCTIONING OF CONSUMER ORGANIZATIONS

Four pronged strategies should be adopted to ensure better consumer protection.

(i) **Self-help on the Part of Consumers:** What is essential for the success of consumerism is the awareness of consumers. Every consumer must habituate himself to check properly and if he finds any malpractices, he must immediately report to the authorities concerned. Then only the consumer movement will be successful. The consumers should be highly conscious of their rights and asserts them in case of any cheating or exploitation by traders.

(ii) **Effective Working of Consumer Organizations as Watch Dogs of Consumer Interest:** More and more consumer organizations must be formed at taluka, district, state and national levels and they should be run more effectively. The Indian Consumer Movement lacked a carefully planned programme of action. Hence, there is an urgent need for a proper co-ordination between all consumer organizations. This will, no doubt, facilitate an organized and united action by all organizations simultaneously to help to achieve to the objectives faster.

(iii) **Self-discipline on the Part of the Businessmen, Resort to Fair Trade Practices:** Consumer service/guidance centres should be set up by all the business and Government departments to maintain a close liaison with consumers with a view to create in them an organizational image and to win their confidence.

(iv) **The Government Intervention to take Legislative and Administrative Measures more Effectively:** Government should enact the laws in such a way that it is understandable to common man. It is the duty of government to reduce the gap between intent of the law and its implementation and improve the co-ordination between different government departments dealing with consumer protection matters.

FUTURE RESEARCH

In the present study certain aspects could not be dealt in detail in view of the study objectives and time and money constraints. These findings provide certain clues on the basis of which research can be carried out in the following areas in future:

(i) Case study of different consumer organizations.

(ii) In-depth study of effectiveness of each activity may be undertaken viz. consumer awareness and education, product appraisal, complaints settlement and consumer research.

(iii) Comparative study of rural and urban consumer organization.

(iv) Comparative study about working of major consumer organization.

(v) Appraisal of consumer protection measures adopted in different states.

(vi) Problems in the management of various consumer organizations.

(vii) A critical analysis of the strategies followed by different consumer organizations in protecting the consumer causes.

(viii) Cross cultural study on consumerism.

(ix) The impact of pressure groups on the functioning of consumer organizations.

(x) Comparative study on the role of organized and unorganized agencies engaged in consumer protections.

BIBLIOGRAPHY

Barksdale, H.C. and Darden, W.R. (1972), "Consumer Attitudes Towards Marketing and Consumerism", *Journal of Marketing*, 36, October, 28-35.

Chaudhary, H.C. (1987), "Emergence of Consumer Movement in India", *Journal of Management Studies*, 2, 137-138.

Darley, W.K. and Johnson, D.M. (1993), "Cross-National Comparison of Consumer Attitudes Towards Consumerism in Four Developing Countries", *The Journal of Consumer Affairs,* 27(1), (1993), 37–54.

Dhyani, A.K., Saklani, A. and Thakur, S. (1990), "Role of Organized and Unorganized Agencies in Consumer Protection", *Consumer Confrontation,* 10 (3), (May-June), 5–9.

Gupta, S.S. (1979), "Consumerism in India and Marketing Responses", *Vidura,* 16 (1), February, 12.

Himachalam, D. (1998), "Consumer Protection and the Law", APH Publishing Corporation, New Delhi, 83-91, 149-155.

Joshi, N.C. (1989), "Creating Consumerism", *Financial Express,* December.

Kaptan, S. (2003), "Nurturing Consumer Activism", Sarup & Sons, New Delhi, 3, 11–15.

Kayank, E. and Wikstrom, S. (1985), "Methodological Framework for a Cross-national Comparison of Consumerism Issues in Multiple Environments", *European Journal of Marketing,* 19 (1), 31-46.

Kumar, S. (1989), "Consumer Movement: Need of in our Era", *Consumer Confrontation,* 9 (3), (May-June).

Malathesh, S. (1981), "Consumerism–An opinion Survey", A Report CERC, (Ahmedabad).

Purohit, H.C. (2004), "Consumer Satisfaction and Complaining Behaviour", Mittal Publication, New Delhi, 1-2.

Sarkar, A. (1989), "Consumer Badly Need Protection. Problems of Consumers in India", Discovery Publishing House, New Delhi, 249.

Seetharaman, P., Sethi, M. (2002), "CBS Publishing & Distributors", New Delhi, 228-229.

Sharma, Chandrakant (1995), "Role of Consumer Organizations in Consumer Protection", Kanishka Publishers, New Delhi.

Sharma, Deepa (2002), "Consumer Grievance Redressal Under Consumer Protection Act", New Century Publications, New Delhi, 4-5. 26-27.

Singh, R. (1990), "Consumer Attitude Towards Consumerism–An Exploratory Study", *Consumer Confrontation,* 10 (1), (January-February), 8–11.

Singh, S.N. (1987), "Consumer Protection Legislation–A Critique", *Journal of the Indian law institute,* 29 (3), (July), 380–385.

Srinivasa, N. (1990), "Role of Government Agencies in Consumer Protection", *Consumer Confrontation,* 4, (July-August), 31–33.

Subramaniyam, D.A.R., Prasad, R. and Kumar, A. (1982), "Need for Consumer Organizations", *Indian Journal of Marketing,* 12 (9-10), (May-June), 17–20.

DIPTI OZA.

16 Gender and Disability

In our multi–cultural, multi–ethnic, multi–religion and multi–linguistic society where persons of all faiths and beliefs live together, however, there are some disparities in services to persons belonging to specific groups. Disabilities is one such area which has experienced low priority in the service sector. India remains a unified country, despite its diversities and a person with disability is not isolated just for the reason that he/she is disabled.

LANDMARK RECOMMENDATIONS ON DISABILITIES

References about the services for persons with disabilities have been made since Independence.

- Article–45–fundamental right of Education (includes disability and women too).
- Report of the Education Commission (1964–66) recommended placement of the child with disability "as far as possible" in ordinary schools.
- National policy on Education (1986) includes a full chapter on "Education of the Handicapped" and formulated guidelines for action. As a result several programmes for the disabled emerged in recent times.
- The period 1983–1992 was declared as the UN Decade of the disabled.
- The world conference on Education for All (EFA) held in Thailand, in 1990 included clause 5 to Article 3 which states that the learning needs of the disabled demand special attention and steps need to be taken to provide equal access to education to every category of the disabled persons as an integral part of the educational system.

India is also a signatory to the recommendations of this world conference and the commitment to services for disabled children was reflected in the policy perspective of the Government of India. The observance of the Decade of the disabled person (1993–2002) is reminding the countries in Asia and Pacific region to make education for all disabled in reality.

The Salamace declaration (1994) and world summit for social development (1995) also provided practical strategies to achieve UEE in case of disabled individual. It very strongly promotes inclusive education or "school for all". It proclaims fundamental right to education. Given the opportunity to achieve and maintain an accepted level of learning. This has created tremendous impact at the Indian scenario too.

In recognition of its concern for the education and rehabilitation of children (individual) with disabilities and also to acknowledge commitment towards the fulfillment of declarations made at the international levels many landmark acts have been introduced in India. The notable development are as under:

1. RCI act 1992 (registration of institutions people working with disability at any level).
2. PWD act 1995 (person with disability act for equal opportunities, protection of rights and full participation).

The act lays emphasis on education, employment, provision of associative device, etc.

INTERNATIONAL CONVENTION ON DISABILITY

Draft Biwako Millennium framework for action towards an inclusive, barrier free and right based society for persons with disabilities in Asia and pacific. The commission, at its 58th session, adopted resolution 58/4 of 22nd May, 2002 promotes this idea, by which it proclaimed the extention of decade of disabled, 1993–2002 for another decades 2003 2012 extended.

RESULT OF DISCRIMINATION

- Low Literacy
- Low Priority in State Agenda
- Poverty

Investment on persons with disabilities should be treated as investment on human capital and services to them must be considered as their human right. About 3% of the total population is individual with disability. Disabled girls constitution 54% of the population. They are not given adequate access to education and rehabilitation services. Moreover, girls with disabilities in rural area are further more deprived due to social conditions.

GENDER SELF–CONCEPT

It is important to note and appreciate how infants and toddlers learn to see themselves as girls and boys in the adult images of women and men in their culture. Equally important is to understand how this process of sex–role identity formation based on differential, often unequal and discriminatory treatment leads to the formation of low/negative self–concept in girls–considering how a low/negative self–concept among girls not only inhibits their self–expression and achievements but is transmitted intergenerationally (from mother to daughters). To study this concept a study was conducted and the result is as follows:

According to the WHO, people with different disabilities constitute approximately ten percent of any population. In India, the number of persons with disabilities is estimated to be approximately 19 million, which form about two percent of the total population (NSSO, 2002). The census 2001 figures, however are an underestimate of the true rates of disability in India which is significantly below the international figure of around ten percent of population of persons with disabilities. There are several reasons for the underestimates in the census figures. Most of the reasons are socio–cultural.

Disability results in exclusion, marginalization and vulnerability. Persons with disability experience discrimination and often excluded from participating in the day-today activities of the family and the community. Most children with disability, as the NSSO report no. 485 also show (NSSO, 2002), receive no formal education and later in life have restricted employment opportunities. Even those who are exploited at large. As a result of their exclusion, people with disability fall in vicious circle of poverty.

Person with disabilities have many of the same needs, feelings and desires as non–disabled persons. Among disabled women and girls are at double disadvantage and face more exploitation and discrimination than their counter part, so comparatively men and boys are attended more on health care, treatment for their impairment, education, family and society at large. Ultimately, often the women and girls suffer from the self–esteem and confidence and poor self–image.

GENDER

Crapo (1996) defines Gender–what role one has in society as 'man' or a 'woman'. It is the social status and roles that people are socialized into based on cultural concepts about sexes. Thus, sex is biologically determined, whereas gender is socially and culturally constructed. People are born with sexual characteristics as male or female, which is a biological fact, it remains the same in any culture or society but gender is something that they learn, nurtured or groomes as per the social and cultural treatment. Therefore gender can be quite different across cultures.

Certain beliefs exist in society about men and women. These beliefs lead to gender norms and rules about how men should behave and how women should behave in society. This leads to discrimination of activities, tasks, division of labour for both man and women. Thus there is differential access to and control over resources, decision making and power. This way the cycle continue and power determines the belief in society. India being male dominated society, follow patriarchy–a social construct. As gender is social construct it can be de and re constructed. It can be changed, improved, modified in the interest of human right. Like non–disabled, every individual with disability has right to dignity, right to family life, right to protection against sexual exploitation, right to employment as mentioned in UN declaration and also reiterated in PWD Act 1995 by Govt. of India. The person with disabilities (Equal opportunities, protection of rights and full participation) Act, 1995, which provides disabled people with protection from discrimination and with rights to access.

DISABILITY

Most of the time the term disability is used as a blanket term for impairment, disability and handicapped but actually each term has very specific meaning. Impairment is a kind of structural body organ loss it could be due to damage, delay or under development of organ or disease. Disability is the functional loss due to the structural loss, while handicapped is the social term that is deprivation of an individual to have socio–cultural access inspite of having abilities to perform.

As a human right advocates the address to an individual who has any disability, never labbled as "disabled person" but he / she is first consider as person and then the condition of which they are victimized, i.e. "person with disability". In June 2003, an international conference in Bangkok made recommendations for a new United Nations Comprehensive and Integral Convention to Promote and protect the rights and dignity to person with disabilities. The Bangkok Recommendations on the elaboration of a comprehensive and integral convention to promote and protect the rights and dignity of persons with disabilities call for a rights based approach to disability by ending discrimination in access to resources.

NOTION OF SELF IN INCAPACITATED INDIVIDUALS

Incapacitated people, persons with loss or reduction in any physiological function which results in a partial or total inability to perform any bodily or mental functions in a manner or within the range considered normal for a human being more often than not evoke indecorous reactions from others. These reactions mostly vary from mere curiosity glances to pity; from the need to protect to shun them; from sympathy to ridicule. It is not some thing unusual for them to be referred by the type of disabilities they have- 'blind', 'mute', 'lame'... than by their respective names. Oftentimes these people are hardly ever recognized for their individuality, their talents or strengths but are perceived with unusual inquisitiveness, scorn and are regarded as burdensome.

As their self-esteem is certainly influenced by perception and reaction to the social contempt towards them as a result most individuals with disabilities often encounter difficulties developing positive self-perception of both their physical and intellectual competencies. In that case, afflictions of disabled persons are not just limited to the physical difficulties like mobility, communication, comprehension, and dependency but also have negative social implications.

A study conducted by Coleman, (1983) showed that mentally retarded students in special education settings evaluated himself or herself significantly higher than peer with mental retardation in regular education. The author suggested that such varying of self-esteem could be because in regular class environments children with mental retardation abilities are likely to appear inadequate in comparison with classmates and special education creates a social comparison group far more homogeneous with regard to ability. On the other hand another study by Wehmeyr (1994) investigated self-esteem of mentally retarded students in special education services and noted that decreased self-esteem is because students with mental retardation do not have opportunities to make decisions on their own and they lack independence.

Sahoo (1991) conducted a comparative study of the behavioral characteristics of the blind, deaf, dumb and the normal children of Orissa. The major finding show that the blind, deaf, dumb children show low self concept then the normal children but among different disabled there is no significant difference with regard to their self concept. Blind children have more problems in maintaining relationship with their peer group while deaf and dumb do not have more problems in having relationship with peer.

These researches suggest that not many studies have been done in the area of disability as far as adolescence is concern and what ever studies have been done are in comparison with the normal children. The other studies are conducted on both boys and girls and there is no exclusive study on adolescent girls. This lays down a further emphasis to explore this area and conduct relevant studies.

Looking at the contemporary Indian Society, the magnitude of the problem becomes all the more grave if the disabled are girls or women as innumerable research studies have gone to show that a large majority of Indian women not only holds a demeaning position both, in the family as well as in the society, but they also happen to be victims of atrocities and violence. Hence for the most Indian women to be born as a girl/ woman is a misfortune. Further, to look physically attractive has been a 'must' for women and under the above circumstances, a physical impairment or disfigurement would be an added severe affliction for them.

IMAGES OF INDIVIDUAL HAVING DISABILITIES

It is important to note that how an infant and toddler learn to see himself or herself as a boy or a girl in the adult images of men and women in their societies and culture. Equally important is to understand how this process of sex–role identity formation based on differential, often unequal and discriminatory treatment leads to the formation of low or negative self-concept in individual specially in case of girls. Considering how a low or negative self–concept among girls not only inhibits their self-expression and achievements but it also transmits intergenerationally (from mother to daughter) reflects in their self–perception and self-esteem, a research study was undertaken by the author.

THE PRESENT STUDY AND ITS SIGNIFICANCE

The present investigation is a phenomenological study conducted with differently incapacitated adolescent girls who are associated with one or the other voluntary organization that provide them opportunities for restoration. The research endeavors to explore the array of encountering of the orthopaedically, visually, hearing and partially mentally incapacitated the adolescent girls with their inadequacies present at the time of survey, their coping mechanism and the emotional experience they undergo. The study also has looked into their interpersonal relationships within family and society, and the changes in their attitude (if any), which can be attributed to the training centres, to which they are affiliated with (during the survey period). The study further has tried to find out their self-esteem and conflict areas.

The deliberation of this study is to bring to foreground the feelings and emotions of the individuals with disabilities and to generate awareness and sensitivity in the society towards these individuals and to encourage more voluntary organization to take up their cause and promote support system for these individuals. As cognized self-esteem and perceived competence is a construct that directly influences a level of self confidence, motivation, self-evaluation and social development, the essential efforts are directed at raising the state of disabled, and indirectly by perception of others about them as disabled. Each of these factors forms development of recognition and conditions formation of self-esteem of these individuals. Keeping this justification a project was carried out.

The title of the project was "A study on self-perception and self-esteem of adolescent girls with different disabilities":

The total sample consists of 60 adolescent girls 15 each in four disabilities namely in hearing, visual, orthopedically and mental retardation. Tools used for data collection were personal information schedules self esteem inventory, self perception questionnaire and case history records. The major research question as kept in mind that, those girls who have got opportunity to come out from their homes, got exposure to certain level of education and could attached to training centre to enhance their skills, have enhanced or improved their self esteem and self perceptions?

The data was collected in July 2004 through personal visits to the different voluntary organization. The girls were given the confidence and confidentiality about the research work. The girls who were willing to participate in the study were administered the different tools.

DEMOGRAPHIC PROFILE OF THE SAMPLE

The sample for the study comprised of 50 differently able adolescent girls from different institutions and special schools. The following data describes the sample.

Table 1
Age Wise Description of the Sample

Disability / Age	*12-14 Years*	*15-17 Years*	*18-20 Years*	*Total*
MR	03	04	06	13
OH	00	02	11	13
VI	04	05	03	12
HI	00	05	07	12
Total	07	16	27	50

Table 2
Orthopedic Disability

Leg Amputation	*Hand and Shoulder Problem*	*Polio*	*Problem in Leg*	*Hunch Beg*	*Total*
1	1	5	2	4	13

The visually impaired were classified as having partial or total impairment.

Table 3
Visually Impairment

Partially Impaired	*Totally Impaired*	*Total*
8	4	12

Similar to visual impairment the hearing impaired can be classified into having partial or total hearing impairment. The categorical classification is as follows:

Table 4
Hearing Impairment

Hearing with Speech Problem	*Only Hearing Problem*	*Total*
9	Partially deaf -1 Totally deaf -2	12

EDUCATION WISE DESCRIPTION OF SAMPLE

From the data obtained it was found that the educational level of the adolescent girls having mental retardation was the lowest and, for the orthopedic disabled adolescent girls it was the highest. The following table shows the educational level of four categories of disabilities.

Table 5

Educational Level Disability	*std 1 to 4*	*std 5-8*	*std 9-12*	*FY BA/BCom*	*other*
MR	04	08	01	–	–
OH	–	–	03	06	02
VI	02	09	–	01	–
HI	–	–	11	01	–
Total	06	17	17	08	02

From the above table it can be seen that the girls with mental retardation did not go beyond std-9 this may be due to the lack of mental ability. Whereas keeping aside the physical disability, the orthopedically disabled girls apart from regular school studies have reached up to college level and two of them even done the courses of office secretary and stenography. Even the visually impaired and the hearing impaired have reached up to first year of college.

INSTITUTIONAL INFORMATION

The adolescent girls whose data has been collected have been going to different institution and special schools. The girls having mental retardation has been selected from 'ARPAN' which is a diagnostic and development centre for the multiply handicapped children mostly catering to the needs of children having mental retardation with speech problems and physical problems. The beneficiaries are mostly from the age of ten days to twenty-six years.

For hearing impairment the girls were selected from Kamalaben Mukhbadhir Shala, which is a special school from KG to std-12 catering to the needs of hearing impaired students.

Blind school run by Lion's blind welfare trust was selected to collect the data for the visually impaired girls. It is a residential cum special school from Std-1 to std-7 wherein apart from regular education, the girls are taught self help skills and skills of being independent.

The orthopedically disabled girls were selected from VRC i.e. the Vocational Rehabilitation Centre especially for the girls and the V-one society, which caters to their vocational needs, and different vocations like tailoring, knitting, computer are being taught here.

Some of the girls who have gone in for college education and have taken some kind of special training have been enrolled with Gujarat Commerce College, Sheth T.C.Kapadia Arts and Commerce college, M.S.University, Sarkari Vinayan Arts college, Pipalia college, Music college (M.S.U) and Dr.B.R.Ambedkar university.

SUMMARY OF PERSONAL PERCEPTIONS OF DIFFERENTLY ABLED ADOLESCENT GIRLS

All the adolescent girls with disabilities have varied interest, but the most common was watching television and films. All of them liked grooming, getting dressed and wearing new clothes and going out. The other interests found were of reading, singing, painting, computer surfing, playing, meeting, people, helping others, learning, dancing, cooking, listening to music, teaching children, tailoring, recording bhajans as one girl is a very good singer.

These girls perceive that they possess certain special qualities like few of them could cook very well, they can be very good assistants, could sing well, could do household work nicely, have competence and patience for teaching children, have confidence to complete any task, one of them is a very good hair stylist, can stitch clothes very well and having computer knowledge.

In spite of perceiving their disability as their weakness and a hurdle in their development they feel that they have got many strengths as well which needs to be strengthened further for their development. These strengths in general for all the girls have quality of mixing with others, can communicate very well, good at painting, being soft and polite, good at working with small children, readiness to learn new things, accomplish new task easily, learning to dance easily, can sing well, can control her anger and no feeling of being jealous of others.

These adolescent girls feel ashamed as they have to be dependent on others, when they cannot express themselves properly, when they have the feeling of being helpless as and when they see a needy person and in spite of an urge to help them they cannot help or when they cannot succeed in any work due to their disability. Finally the most commonly perceived aspect of being ashamed is when people talk about their disability.

When they were asked whether at any time do they have a feeling of being neglected, all of them responded in a negative tone that they never have such a feeling. Due to the problem of disability they have to depend on others for activities of daily living like dressing, grooming, mobility, lifting heavy things, for food and for learning. They also need help from others in the areas of doing household chores, purchase of things of daily use, for going out, for selection of clothes, for solving certain problems, for encouragement, warmth and for company. The parents, siblings, friends and relatives of these girls are rendering this help. This may imply that these girls are quite realistic, they have accepted their disabilities and also accepted that they are dependent on people for one or other things or reasons, so they have to be down to earth and can not be fussy or choosy.

They also get help from the government for bus fare and railways in terms of concession for the girls having disability and also for one of the family members who would be the escort. Their aims are very high and they aspire a lot. These girls aim at getting a good job; become a teacher, to be independent, go for higher education, to become a computer programmer, to start a beauty parlor. Some especially the orthopedically disabled and the hearing impaired wants to get married and settle down, wants to go abroad. It is also found that they have their parents, teachers and other family members as their ideals and they aspire to be like them.

The most happy moments of the adolescent girls are winning prizes, praise by the teachers, director or principal of the institutions which they are enrolled with, they also become happy by appreciation and blessings, they become happy during festive times, taking part in the cultural programmes, getting selected for the special Olympics which is meant for the children having one or the other kind of disability. Finally all of them were happy as they were allowed to go to special schools and study there.

Along with such happy moments they were also felicitated for certain achievements. This being by the parents and others when passed the 10th and 12th examination, medal by the community, by the director and the staff members of the institution, words of appreciation by the Mayor of the city, one of the females was interviewed for her achievement by a local news channel.

These girls are highly indebted to the institutions which they attend on regular basis, as they have won prizes after attending the schools or institutions, they have made good friends on whom they can rely, one of the girls is successfully running her own tuition class, one of the respondents belonged to an orthodox minority family then also she was sent to a special school where she has learnt lot many things. So according to her that is her gain. One of the females has published her own cassette on bhajans.

In spite of all these gains, felicitations and happy moments there is a feeling of disappointment among these girls and that is when they were put in the hostel, failure during their school education, totally being dependent on others, when cannot remember in spite of hard work, when someone discusses about their disability, scolding, people not understanding their feelings.

OBSERVATIONS

The differently abled adolescents girls found themselves most fortunate as their parents has provided them the opportunity to come out of the house for education and training. Education and training has helped them to acquire necessary skills of life. The exposure "out of house" has helped them to have realistic picture of society and their place in this society. They have developed a feeling that they are cared, treated positively; their needs are well accepted and fulfilled by family members. Further they are equally accepted by the special institutions with their abilities and got adequate and relevant training for grooming their natural talents. This opportunity has helped them to gain confidence in them and also gave hope to be economic independent. They feel that such care of parents and teachers/trainers of their special schools have allowed them to grow normally with their peers.

The girls have not faced any serious rejection, ignorance or neglect in society. So far, as most of the time they are in custodial care but there is a fear that when they will be playing their adult roles may face the negative treatment either by the family or by society in general. This fear has made them all the more sensitive to become economic independent. They strongly feel that when an individual is not financially dependent on others, the other dependency are well accepted and face fewer problems.

As girls, have high self-esteem and positive perceptions, whatever ill treatment (Scolding, punishment) today they have received is not because of their disability but it is because of their some fault or inability, which is common for their abled counter parts too.

Another very important understanding these adolescent girls have developed, is that " don't try to have much expectations from others, they also have their own life ", So today whatever facilities, opportunities they have provided us, learn to become independent and be on your own feet. In future one has to keep in mind the short comings of disabilities has to be faced dignifiedly and we have to make our world know our abilities and command respect for the same.

Overall if we try to make observations they will be as follows:

1. Girls with Mental Retardation are having pleasing personality, never complain, and accept life readily with whatever new changes

comes to them. They are highly satisfied when their basic needs are reasonably fulfilled.

2. Girls with Hearing Impairment–They are very eager to socialize and wish to talk and interact with people. They are very happy when people approach them. They are quite aware that they have limited expressive ability especially with new people. They are quite comfortable with family members and people at work/school. They are very talented but they are failing to reach out because of lack of communication. Many times they feel dejection from society. They have a feeling that many a times they are misunderstood and people don't try to cooperate specially during traveling. They love social gathering but either avoid or are not allowed to attend so they feel bad. They have very high aspirations of life.
3. Girls with Visual Impairment: They are quite confident about themselves, happy and more free with their family members while they take long time to make adjustment with outsiders and strangers. They are independent in their daily activities. They are found more festive and try to relish each moment of life. The major problem they face is mobility in new or strange places for which they need support. They aspire for bright and prosperous future. They like to be financially independent. The worst part observed was that they were not trained to walk with stick and have developed negative feeling for using it. This restricts their mobility.
4. Girls with orthopedic disability: Compare to above three categories they were feeling more miserable as they have only physical problems and no other disabilities. They have very high expectations from society and most of the time their level of satisfaction is lower to their expectations. They are highly concerned about their rights and have very strong urge for financial independence. They are very sensitive and have very positive self-perceptions with high self-esteem but at the same time they are engaged in a deep search for their place in society.

Overall the girls have more then average self-perceptions and positive self-esteem. They are also happy with their skills and achievements. They enjoy the life and are ready to make necessary adjustments to make the life more meaningful and purposeful. Most of them feel that the problems whatever they are facing today are the problems not because of the disability but they are life problem which their non-disabled counter part are also facing. All of them are availing all possible Government and NGO's benefits for self and family, quite aware regarding their rights and benefits. The special institutions and training centres have lot of contributions in their development.

SUGGESTIONS

1. The girls should be given training and opportunities, to develop their abilities right from their young age to make them self-reliant and self-confident.
2. There should be social awareness and sensitivity that they are disabled and no one has right to make them handicapped. Keeping in mind this, they should be given due respect in society and provided all what they deserve at the right time.
3. The blind girls should be given training for their mobility using blind sticks, like blind boys. In absence of this training the girls are deprived because of this the girls are not able to move out of their houses and this hinders their coming for the higher education. Their talent is getting wasted because of their immobility.
4. The girls with hearing disability should be provided total communication programme so that they can mix in society and will be able to avail all what they deserve in their life. For these girls, socialization and communication are the major constraints, which should be attended consciously by their family, School and society.
5. They have right to live and right to education, which should be protected with dignity and respect. This is a cooperative, complementing and collaborative efforts of both, the individual having disability and the rest of the people in society. The contributions of all are appreciated in maintaining harmony in the society. This will add to their self worth that is their positive self-perceptions and self-esteem, last word is....

THEY ARE DISABLED.
DON'T MAKE THEM HANDICAPPED.

BIBLIOGRAPHY

Dave P. (2001), *Differently Abled Women,* WSRC, The M.S. University of Baroda, Vadodara.

Pandey, R.N. (1985) *A Study of affect ional Deprivation, ego Strength and Adjustment Pattern Among the Visually Handicapped Children and their Rehabilitation.* Bapu Degree Collage. In Buch, M.B. (1988) Fourth Survey of Research in Education, New Delhi: NCERT.

Pathak, A.B. (1984), *A Study of the Disabled Childrenin Normal Schools.* Ph.D. (ed.) Teachers College., Udaipur. In Buch. M.B. (1988) Fourth Survey of Research in Education, New Delhi: NCERT.

Raghuba, P.C. (1992) *A Study of Adjustment, Aggressiveness, Achievement Motivations and self concept of Physically Handicapped Students as Compare to Normal Students.* Ph.D. (Ed.), Saurashtra Uni. In Buch. M.B. Fifth Survey of Research in Education, New Delhi: NCERT.

Rogers, D. (1962), *The Psychology of Adolescence.* New York : Meredith Publishing Co.

Sahoo, J. (1991) *A Comparative Study of the behavioral Characteristics of the Blind, Deaf, Dumb and the normal Children of Orissa.* In Buch. M.B. Fifth Survey of Research in Education, New Delhi: NCERT.

Websites

National youth policy (2000) www.ncert.nic.in.

WHO Report (1997 and 2002) www.unesocbkk.org.

Adolescents in India–A Profile www.nfpa.org/focus/india/face to face/docs/adolscentsprofile.pdf.2000.

Coping with Limb Loss. www.usinter.net/wasa/contests4g.html.

REENA BHATIA & B. BALAKRISHNAIAH

17 Preservation and Promotion of Crafts: Role of NGOs In Gujarat—Case Studies

PRELUDE

In India, the crafts sector comes second in employment generation, outranked by Agriculture. Gujarat is rich in terms of craftsmanship and heritage. It has been the original home for several crafts and still adding to it is a long list of 'Migratory Crafts' (Those crafts having its origin other than in Gujarat).

In Gujarat, Kutch is one of the richest regions imbued with variety of crafts especially embroidery. Every village has its distinct style and technique. The craft is majorly practiced by the scheduled or the lower castes of the society.

Natural disasters have time and again hit this resilient district of Kutch and still; it springs back to normalcy with or without the government support. Relief and rehabilitation have been the focus of several voluntary agencies, government and even individuals during these disasters. Irrespective of the support of these agencies, the people of Kutch have rebuilt their lives with their discerningly varied skills. This ingenuity of crafts qualifies as the heritage of India which needs to be preserved.

Revival, retention and promotion have been taking place simultaneously for different crafts, in different villages, at different levels by several individuals and organizations. They have tried their bit in the following ways to help the artisan immaterial of its success achieved.

1. Attending to their basic needs and requirements.
2. Fighting for their rights.
3. Helping them in skill development.
4. Generating ways of value-addition and product diversification to enhance market growth.
5. Creating awareness of newer technologies.

Apart from creation and sustenance of craft and craftsmen respectively there is a dire need for the continuity of craft and its preservation. An artisan would live his/her craft only if it finds mass acceptance. What are the means and measures adopted by the non-governmental organizations in achieving this goal?

STATEMENT OF THE PROBLEM

There is a renewed interest in the handicrafts of India; both in domestic urban and international markets. Kutch being the nucleus of most sumptuous, comprehensive and indigenous textile crafts such as Bhujodi shawl weaving, Ajrakh printing, Mirror work, etc. turns to be a living heritage.

With the emergence of new markets and globalization, it becomes imperative to ensure that the artisans are able to integrate contemporary design requirements and their traditional wisdom. The intervention of an external agency has provided the much needed support to the artisans and empowered them for sustainable development leading not only to income generation but retaining it as a living tradition.

With the principal aim to gain an insight of the contribution of NGO's working towards the preservation and promotion of crafts of the region of Kutch, the investigator undertook a descriptive research study.

METHOD AND MATERIALS

The primary data was generated from a case study of two NGO's namely 'SEWA' and 'SHRUJAN', while the secondary data was collected through desk research.

SEWA–A SUCCESS STORY

SEWA–Inspiration

> ***An artisan is the most important member on our premises.***
>
> ***She is not an interruption in our work, she is not an outsider in our business, she is part of it.***
>
> ***We are not doing her a favour by serving her. She is doing us a favour by giving us an opportunity to serve her.***
>
> ***—Mahatma Gandhi***

SEWA–Mission

SEWA–Self Employed Women's Association is both an organization and a movement. SEWA came into existence in December 1971, with the initiative of the leader of women's wing, of Textile Labour Association, Ela Bhatt and its President, Arvind Buch. The endeavours of the women workers helped them cross their first stumbling block of obtaining recognition as a Trade Union in April, 1972.

Since then SEWA has being growing continuously till date. It has always enhanced itself as a confluence of movements, mainly the labour movement, the co-operative movement and the women's movement at state level, national level and international level.

Interestingly SEWA members constantly monitor and evaluate their goal of full employment and self reliance following a yardstick developed by them. Such an effort not only helps them monitor their progress and germane of various activities, but increases the accountability of SEWA's leaders and organizers, to their members.

SEWA is engaged in a wide-spectrum of need based activities of its members. Its member strength comprises of multi-religious, multi-trade sector. Until early nineties, SEWA membership was predominantly urban. SEWA began organizing workers in the villages in 1979. Today the percentage of rural membership is almost double that of its total urban members.

SEWA as a union has remained open for membership to three types of self-employed women workers all over India such as Vendors, Home-based workers and Manual labourers. SEWA comprises of over 11,000 self-help groups, 200 cooperatives and 11 federations throughout India.

The formation of several SEWA Co-operatives (Co-operative consists of group of workers who have contributed share capital to become members of the co-operative. They are collective owners of the co-operative. They elect a managing committee to manage the day-to-day affairs of the co-operative. A member of the managing committee is elected chairperson. The members work in their own co-operative and are their own worker-owners) have resulted in sustained employment and income of its members, while the Gujarat State Women's SEWA Co-operative Federation represents the interest and concerns of the women's co-operatives at the state level with policy makers. Issues including access to raw material, marketing and working capital for production tools/equipment and workspace are raised on behalf of the Federation.

SEWA – Crafts

According to a pre-feasibility report prepared by SEWA researchers, the artisans of the worst hit villages by the tremors in Kutch in 2001 were helped to earn their livelihood through traditional crafts (Times of India, 17-02-01). Since then, there has been no looking back.

Development Design SEWA Centre has been one such cooperative set up by the Federation in 1992 to help artisans meet the demands of design update and link them to global market by upgrading and developing their skills, which would further increase their income generating capabilities. The marketing cell is attached to Design SEWA Centre; where in artisans are their own designers.

Design SEWA located in the heart of Ahmedabad city has housed a museum of traditional and modern designs in the form of catalogues, albums, design books and rare samples. Ideally it is a design library which facilitates the trainers in design innovation and also gives back the artisan their own traditional design and skills which were obscured.

The main objectives of Design SEWA are:

- To identify craft pockets those are relevant and related to the ongoing craft groups and cooperatives.
- To organize the participation of women in craft and cooperatives already formed or those that are at the pre cooperative stage.
- To improve the marketability of products of craftswomen by assisting them to adopt and adapt contemporary market trends through access to Design SEWA.
- To identify the new groups of crafts women who have potential to develop their skills.
- To make artisans into Master craft-women and Master craft-women into designers.

According to Jyotsana Sagra, Co-ordinator, Design SEWA; helps its members on following four fronts:

1. Offer training and up scaling of skills in handicraft designing:The women are trained in different techniques such as block printing, tie and dye, patchwork, aari work, zardosi, crochet, puppetry, etc.
2. Assist in design and product development along with product diversification: Existing designs are transferred on paper; newer designs are created for specific markets and prototype of samples developed to be put into production. Product diversification has been pivotal in adding a flavour to the fading or static product categories.
3. Documentation for reference leading to preservation of designed work: A sample of the vast variety of work created is maintained through photographs, design copies and samplers which serve as a ready reference point for processing future orders and also facilitates linkages with foreign and domestic buyer.
4. Training in photography and screen printing: The outsourcing of all printing jobs, such as printing invitation cards, visiting cards, posters, pamphlets, banners for exhibitions and functions are done in-house. Further, training for the same are conducted in rural areas.

TRAINING

Design SEWA it provides training in design to artisans who need to refine or polish their traditional and sometimes dated art skills. It also gives design training in new skills like zari, tilla, crochet, bead work to help them diversify their capabilities in multiple styles.

The use of computers has been extensive in their design centers/ studio. The women are trained to implement activities like designing, cataloguing and coding through computers. Undoubtedly culture provides concept to the designer while technology gives it the power. Such has been the efforts of SEWA Trade Facilitation Centre (STFC).

STFC–A ROLE MODEL

STFC has been established, owned and managed by the women artisans pursuing craft activities in the drought affected and disaster prone areas of Kutch and Patan, in Gujarat. The promoters of their unique company are SEWA, the Kutch Craft Association and the Banaskantha DWCRA Mahila SEWA Association. It is a commercial venture by the artisan members who have wished to promote access to national and global markets. The main production centre with the state of art technology is housed in Khokhra, Ahmedabad.

The entire embroidery work on the products manufactured on a regular basis is sent to the identified villages in Kutch and Patan in customized packets to the artisan members. The products are segmented into three categories vis-à-vis Home Furnishings, Accessories and Apparels.

STFC has designed a set of training modules for the training of trainers in the area of quality control, supply chain, pricing and costing, sales and marketing, market research and skill up gradation and skill development.

Continuous assessment of the skill levels of women artisans in Nakhtrana (Kutch) and Radhanpur (Patan) are done by STFC. Their existing skills are graded as A, B and C levels. Special training modules prepared for C grade and B grade artisans are administered to upgrade their skills, which serves a requisite to fetch them better economic empowerment.

STFC delivers integrated solutions to bridge the divide between micro-enterprises, poor producer groups in the rural informal sectors and the main stream market systems. These services provide support to the micro-enterprises and grass roots producers' organizations and further help them match their social goals of poverty alleviation through employment with commercial viability, market readiness and greater market opportunities.

PRODUCT DEVELOPMENT AND DIVERSIFICATION

A design studio and resource center at STFC consistently develops a range of products in line with the current trends, fashion forecasts, consumer tastes and preferences employing the traditional skills of artisans. Consistent quality of products is maintained and facilitated by procuring high quality inputs and bulk purchase which yields economies of scale.

Design SEWA sells design samples to member co-operatives as well as small and big corporate. It has created design layouts and samples for companies like Garden Vareli, Bombay Store, Shopper's Stop, Yellow Ridge, Fab India etc. for various instore products. It also, develops prototypes for several exporters.

PROFESSIONAL LINKAGES

Craft sector has the potential for creating jobs and income, together with the need for government to play a coordinating and promotional role within it. The government recognizes the critical importance of remote indigenous craft to the industry and the vital economic, cultural and social role that the Non Government Organizations play in many indigenous communities. The government has a number of schemes for the handicraft sector in its five year plan. However most artisans do not even get to hear about the schemes made for them. If they have heard of a particular scheme, they cannot cope with the complex procedure. Hence Non Government Organizations play a crucial role in assisting their craft groups in accessing government support. The fundamental obstacle to the growth of the craft industry has been the absence of any meaningful interface between producers and markets.

Value added and market development, as well as marketing channels and activities, are key components in the development pathway for many... focusing its partnership programme on collaboration in research with increasing emphasis on systems development and promotion of information dissemination. This needs a wide variety of partnership formats, ranging from bilateral ones, through regional associations and consortia, to global partnerships of academicians, designers, managers, retailers and policy makers. Developing strong partnerships with government is required to lay the foundation for growth. STFC has collaborated with not just design institutes, Professionals, Government and International Agencies, but created a business network to promote the crafts producers to the mainstream global market.

STFC has partnered with NID (National Institute of Design–a premium design institute of the country located in Ahmedabad) to establish a SEWA-NID cell that has empanelled dedicated designers for innovating new product designs, assist in setting of R & D facilities, testing laboratory, and reinforce the best practices of product development and documentation.

STFC has partnered with NIFT (National Institute of Fashion Technology–a premier fashion institute of the country located in New Delhi as well as Gandhinagar and other places in India) to establish a decentralized three-tired production structure with a common production center in Ahmedabad, two district main centres in Radhanpur (District Patan) and Nakhtrana (District Kutch) and fifty common production centres at the village level. The entire production facilities are equipped with State-of-the-Art machines and facilities to implement quality control at all stages and ensure an effective production, packaging warehousing and distribution system.

In order to have greater market penetration, SEWA has tied up with prominent product developers and designers from the US and Europe, who develops a range of products appropriate for niche market.

STFC works with various Government and International agencies to enforce enabling policies for women artisans in the informal sector. To prepare the artisans for the global markets, it has organized three round table conferences on textile, handloom and handicraft issues. These round table conferences have been conducted between the grass root producer women artisans, their micro enterprises with the government and policy maker including World Trade Organization where there was a direct dialogue between micro and macro.

STFC has organized training in association with UNIFEM (UNITED NATIONS DEVELOPMENT FUND FOR WOMEN– mutually beneficial information sharing platforms and create extended market opportunities in the local, regional and global levels. Two important networks that have been initiated by STFC are GRASSNET (network of grassroots producers' organizations in the SAARC member countries) and GTNW–GRASSROOTS TRADING NETWORK FOR WOMEN (model that includes Grassroots Producers Groups (GPO) across three continents, Asia, Latin America and Africa)), New Delhi to several National (Delhi, Andhra Pradesh, Jharkhand, North East in India) and International organizations (Nepal, Bangladesh, Pakistan, Afghanistan, East African countries) which has resulted into better networking to bring poor producers across the world in the mainstream global market.

STFC actively networks with producers groups, government agencies, development organizations, and special subject matter experts.

Market Approach

'Banascraft' and 'Kutchcraft' set up in 1989 and 1995 respectively support the local women in their efforts to preserve and promote their traditional craft skills. The strength of these marketing efforts lie in the fact that the grass root level craftsperson have gradually become the manager-owner, of her enterprise through local groups which are federated into district level co-operatives. Banascraft the main retail outlet in Ahmedabad, at a premium shopping area is managed by the local women. The collection includes a wide range of contemporary product design–

Apparels, Accessories and Home furnishings embellished with traditional hand embroidery in exquisite and intricate finesse.

Nandika–a boutique is an up market store that caters to a niche market of upper class business travellers and tourists, located in a shopping arcade of a high end Hotel in Ahmedabad.

STFC has a well designed marketing strategy that has a range of channels to expand market opportunities; bridge this disconnects. Exhibitions in various metropolitan and mega cities of India are a regular feature of STFC. This further provides them an opportunity to undertake market research, pilot testing of new products and allows market linkages to large section of population. International exhibitions have been successfully organized by STFC in Spain, South Africa, Germany and Washington DC.

It extends its marketing network through marketing links established with a number of national and international institutions, for example its participation in various trade fairs such as Indian Handicrafts and Gifts Fair, New York International Gift Fair, Tendence, Ambeinte. SFTC presently exports the products of its member artisans to USA, UK, Belgium, France, Spain, Germany and South Africa.

SEWA Gram Mahila Haat (SGMH) an apex local, national and international fair trade organization provides marketing facilities and other market related support to the rural producer groups towards their empowerment and economic self-reliance. To build local marketing network SGMH has established 'RUDI' Bazaar presently which not only generates rural employment but brings assured market for the producers, since it is built on the smallest consumer with a purchasing power of only Rs. 50/- to Rs. 100/- a month.

SEWA Kalakruti a common label used by the artisans co-operatives lends an identity and credibility to their products exhibited in solo exhibitions held in Mumbai, Hyderabad and Chennai and even Paris and America. The entire responsibility of publicity to sale is handled by the Federation's team.

'Kalakruti' is a concept of collective marketing to mainstream the products of women artisan's cooperatives eliminating the middle man. The premise has display facilities, exhibition arrangements and has effectively laid out counters with customers' service.

It also serves as a meeting centre for artisans and their customers to negotiate and formalize orders, linking them with varied marketing possibilities. Local, national and international exhibitions are also organized by the marketing cell. Such exposures help the artisan women get attuned to new markets, new trends and new techniques and they learn to predict the consumer behaviour and product acceptance.

Marketing through order catalogues is another salient feature which is introduced recently. Also, managed is selling of hand crafted items to several national and international retailers and wholesalers.

Impact of STFCs' Services

- Fifteen thousand artisans are the shareholders and suppliers of the company.
- Artisans have become the owners and managers of their enterprise.
- Increased employment.
- Influence the prevailing local wages.
- Ensure a wage of rupees one thousand five hundred to each artisan. (One USD = Rs. 46).
- Develop high value added products.
- Develop products with high wage component.
- Increase bargaining power of artisans.
- Reduce forced migration.
- Empowering the rural communities.
- Provide sustainable livelihood strategies.

STFC's activities initiate a virtuous cycle which is preserving indigenous skills and leading to greater livelihood security i.e. vulnerability reduction, health security, food security, childcare facility, and asset building for rural households with a specific focus on the economic organization and empowerment of women.

Final word

Both the urban and rural self employed women workers of SEWA today have been brought into the main stream; have access to technology, new techniques and new markets. In addition they are self-reliant managers and decision makers of their own co-operatives.

Since, women are the center of all development. SEWA not just promotes employment but goes beyond to bring about all round progress in family, community and nation in larger perspective.

SHRUJAN–AN ACCOMPLISHMENT

SHRUJAN–Inspiration

As followers of the Sri Ramakrishna Mission, the teachings of Ramakrishna and Swami Vivekananda are observed:

> *'Religion is not for empty bellies... it is futile to preach religion... without first trying to remove their poverty'.*

To make this philosophical ideal into a practical reality, they believe that rural communities are best served by maximizing local, available resources, situations and skills; that all forms of useful work are equal; and that the unnatural divides of caste and communities can be overcome.

SHRUJAN-Mission

SHRUJAN was initiated by the Shroff Family under the guidance of Swami Armasthanan of the Ramakrishna Mission in 1969, as a part of famine relief operations in Kutch in 1969. Its overall mission:

1. Developing economic self-reliance among rural women.
2. Providing training for skill formation and entrepreneurship development.
3. Creating wealth generating opportunities for artisans.

SHRUJAN serves as a vital source of supplementary income, generating employment for craftswomen in their own homes, restoring their pride in their crafts and in being self sufficient, helping to build a society of creative, productive, and honest people. It organizes craftswomen and teaches them how to deal with people, handle money and keep accounts etc.

After its early beginning–in 1969 SHRUJAN has greatly expanded its role to encompass not just a wide range of activities but to bring more and more people within its fold. It has gone beyond the embroidery and textile crafts to bring the other crafts of Kutch within its fore view. These include weaving, wood carving, block printing, tie and dye, patola, leather cutting, metal work and lacquer work, most of them done absolutely by the men. The artisans are paid a decided price for each piece they prepare.

SHRUJAN works for the people, by the people and of the people. It operates within a number of clearly defined objectives:

- To create employment for as many women as possible.
- To develop a system for this employment that does not disrupt family, village, and community life.
- To train the women to become self sufficient business people with the ability to develop their own market opportunities.
- To train the women to the highest standards of embroidery skills.
- To introduce new design options and information to village women without the means for travel or outside education.
- To restore the embroidery of Kutch to the highest possible level and to revive embroidery styles in danger of extinction.
- To encourage skill sharing between women of castes and communities who, traditionally, would not have sat and worked together.

SHRUJAN–Crafts

In the absence of Flora and Fauna, a fine kind of mathematics manifests itself in geometric designs, creating an artistry which is quite indigenous to this area. The expressions of embroidery differ from village to village.

TRAINING

The training programme is firmly committed to creating skills and upgrading existing ones. The two kinds of training undertaken are:

1. Initiating completely new craftswomen.
2. Upgrading the skills of old crafts women.

New craftswomen work with master craftswomen for 6-12 months, learning basic embroidery techniques, colourways, selection of fabric, etc. Old, traditional craftswomen who have been out of touch are brought to update with the latest market trends, new colour combinations, newer stitches, etc.

At the training stage itself, those with the potential to be entrepreneurs are identified and taken on wages. After having learnt managerial skills, they are promoted as Commission Agents and then as Entrepreneurs; the whole process takes 2-5 years. Once they have successfully established themselves as entrepreneurs, SHRUJAN encourages them to supply embroidered goods and crafts ware to other customers, apart from SHRUJAN.

SHRUJAN runs training programmes both in small business management, and embroidery, at which both teachers and students are paid a stipend. Since 1969, SHRUJAN has provided training to over 18,000 women. In recent years, women from the traditional embroidery communities have voluntarily chosen to share their knowledge and have run classes outside of their communities.

The women though working for generations did not use their skills for commercial purposes. Until SHRUJAN came in with the following goals:

1. Boosting rural skills and creativity.
2. Safe guarding dignity and skills of the craftswomen.
3. Improving quality of life.

Training facilities from teaching crafts to managerial skills are offered. Assistance with making project reports obtaining bank loans and other related matters is also made possible.

PRODUCT DEVELOPMENT AND DIVERSIFICATION

With the main aim of preservation of the craft heritage, the women have organized themselves and developed a range of home furnishing articles, accessories and apparels, using traditional motifs but with a contemporary look (i.e. the colours, fabrics, size, placement of design may be changed);

SHRUJAN provides fabrics and other raw materials (procured from either local traders and/or Mumbai) to the women workers. The designs and the motifs used in the embroidery are traditional, which is worked in association with in house designers and visiting designers. A mobile van goes from village to village distributing and selling raw material (cloth, designs, and threads). It also provides 'market cover' by purchasing the finished goods back from them against immediate payment. All this in turn helped preserve the rich traditional skills and craft.

Over the last few years, Shrujan is slowly spreading its wings to source handloom fabrics from Orissa, Andhra Pradesh, Tamil Nadu, Karnataka to synthesize Kutchi embroidery with other traditional styles and to increase its value, boost demand and create a new look.

PROFESSIONAL LINKAGES

SHRUJAN invites persons in the fields of arts and craft, designing, management, fashion technology, marketing, human resource development and rural development, who can help in the training and workshops, and by identifying and implementing programmes. It also invites funding for infrastructure development of new projects.

The Director of SHRUJAN plans to settle in Baroda and wishes to build a liaison with different Design institutes in Baroda and further strengthen and develop relation for benefit of craftsmen/women.

MARKET APPROACH

It retails a vast variety of high end products with the brand name 'SHRUJAN' from its shops in Kutch and Mumbai. In addition regular exhibitions are held nationally and sometimes internationally.

Selling through E-Marketing is also achieved. In addition it facilitates sales directly to national and international, retailers and wholesalers too.

MUSEUM PLAN

SHRUJAN plans to set up a museum and reference library in Kutch which will be partially funded by TATA. The work is in progress. The museum will have on display huge panels each with a number of embroidery stitches covering a total of fourteen embroideries of Kutch and Banaskantha. There will be two collections, each consisting of traditional and contemporary designs. One collection will be for exhibition in cities around the world and the other will be maintained in Kutch for research by overseas designers and academics, and most importantly, as a mechanism of professional development for the local craftswomen. The design studio, staffed with illustrators, skilled demonstrators and coordinators will include raw material bank, design bank and sample making for the benefit of all. A Guest House for visiting designers and buyers from India and overseas is also in the offing.

The Design Centre on Wheels is an extensive and ambitious project to preserve, document and rejuvenate Kutchi embroidery. The crucial, underlying principal behind the project is that the embroidery shall match, and even surpass, the levels of exquisite skill practiced before the more recent pressures of commercialism took over. SHRUJAN has deployed and trained 400 of its best craftswomen to work on this project, all of whom have benefited from the increased income that the project provides.

SALIENT FEATURES

Analyzing the two and reviewing the available literature, it was observed that both SEWA and SHRUJAN are there, to help the rural and the tribal families. SEWA exists with broader perspective and approach. Also, it is extremely huge in size as compared to SHRUJAN. However, SEWA has concentrated more on the embroidery crafts, while the other crafts of Kutch remain neglected. There is lot of media attention given to the SHRUJAN Trust and it caters to the problems of artisan primarily in Kutch. SEWA can be simulated to an art film, wherein a lot of efforts are put in and whatever the outcome; it only fetches a small viewer ship, whereas SHRUJAN is like a commercial film appealing the masses or say reaching out to masses.

The truth–both the organizations have been successful in fulfilling their objectives of self employment for women and in the process are contributing to the preservation and promotion of the living traditions of Kutch, in India.

A Critical Analysis

An analysis of the production process brings to light the issues and lacunae of the NGOs, which deserve attention.

The organization does not compromise for quality. Any unsatisfactory work is not accepted, which further has to be sold in local market at lower price or otherwise is sold to other NGO's at cheaper prices. Also, if the material is provided by the organization then the worker is paid less than the fixed price. Alternatively this could help crafts women to strive for the best. On the other hand since, it is quality work; it is often high priced and therefore caters only to a selected segment of the society and this needs reconsideration. It may uproot the function of gainful employment.

The exhibitions are held quite often, i.e. at regular intervals in all metro cities of India and hence wider market penetration. The effort at least extends the probability of visual craft appreciation if not economic gains.

Exporters have approached the organizations from Europe, France, England, for their quality work, but fruitful results are distanced since the specifications of the buyer cannot be met, in absence of State–of–the–art technology in SHRUJAN. It is difficult to maintain uniformity/standardization of work.

SEWA Vs SHRUJAN: a quick glimpse

	SEWA		SHRUJAN
1.	SEWA (Self Employed Women's Association)	Name	SHRUJAN
2.	Ahmedabad	Origin	Kutch
3.	Full employment and Self Reliance	Goal	Rural Development
4.	600 women More than 2,05,985 (Gujarat) and 3,18,527 (All India)	Initial Membership Now	20 Women Above 2,500 Women spread across 85 villages
5.	Well-organized	Structure	Entrepreneurs (Village women), sub-entrepre neurs–unstructured
6.	Rural areas of Kutch and urban areas of Ahmedabad, Lucknow City of India	Organizing	Only Kutch
7.	Tied up with prominent product developers and designers from US and Europe for Niche market	Market Penetration	With advise from Excel Industries (Shroff family Business)
8.	New York International Gift Fair (NYIGF)	Market Testing	–
9.	Collaborated with– –NCAER –National Level –GIDR-State Level –WIEGO-International Level	Research Activities	In-house
10.	Magsaysay Award and Economic Times Award - for Elaben Bhatt	Awards	–
11.	'BANASCRAFT', 'KUTCHCRAFT' and 'KALAKRUTI'	Brand name	'SHRUJAN'
	www.sewahousing.org www.sewamart.com www.banascraft.org www.kutchcraft.org www.sewabank.org www.sewa.org/giss www.sewa.org/smm www.sewa.org/gsmcf www.sewa.org/insurance www.ansooya.org www.earthquake.sewa.org.	Links	www.shrujan.com shrujan-at google search

Be it the Design services of SEWA or Design Centre on Wheels of SHRUJAN, they provide a variety of services to both craftswomen and customers. Lot of pre-planning is done and extra effort involved by the organization to consider fashion. Since each item takes at least three months to complete and if the goods not delivered right in time (a remote chance) than it does not serve the very purpose of being in fashion.

An Observation Made

A 4' x 4' design area filled with chain stitch (done by hand) with a stitch density of twelve stitches per inch would take minimum of two days to complete just the frame work i.e. the outline of the design.

On an average it would be 4-5 hours of work in a day. One cannot devote a continuous time period. The work is accomplished in breaks/ intervals. Since Ariwork is done using a frame, delicate fabrics are damaged due to excessive stretching (loss to be borne by the organization i.e. at the end of the whole [intricate] work the fabric tears .....)

A heavily embroidered piece (5 yards of width 24") would take as much as 1½ year. When the Artisan is paid per piece, there are chances of injustice (5000-6000/ 1½ year would approximate to 6/- per day). The work done is on a regular basis, in an unhygienic condition, which leads to the soiling of the piece (lot of handling for long periods).Again the loss if any to be borne by the organization.

The artisan does not realize the importance of a piece of work. They further sell it to others at price they like. Also, handling of the piece is casual–give reasons as–child used it as a play item; the goat ate away, etc. Spoiling or loosing of items is a common feature/problem faced for which the compensations are not made and the organization again has to bear the loss. Moreover, they do not maintain a storing place for different items. The segregated articles are bundled and kept.

Also, storing and managing of smaller pieces is painful and therefore they are not made. The smaller pieces as bands, yokes, strips and patches are used mostly for personal consumption only. The concentration therefore is more on making dresses, saris, accessories and home furnishings–which has a greater market.

CONCLUDING REMARKS

The attempts of these NGOs have made craftsmen a self-motivated and successful entrepreneur and they no longer remain picturesque exhibits of our past. The other Voluntary Organizations can follow the footsteps of these NGOs. Additionally, other aspects like heritage conservation and professional linkages which are the right way forward can be reflected on.

Commitment, competencies and skills of people working in the Non-Government Organizations has significant impact on sector performance and its reform process. However, the NGOs need to invest progressively and in a proactive manner towards improving the professional linkages, to improve and sustain the motivation of its beneficiaries. Improving motivation for the craftsmen also involves issues related to, continuous craft education and training, and prioritization and synchronization of short term achievable goals and long-term research based actions.

In order to hold good our traditional treasures few initiatives need to be put in practice, such as develop taste and refinement through craft education. Expand preservation technology. However, even the common man needs be sensitized towards conservation of craft heritage.

National curriculum of the schools and design institutes need to include craft education as one of the ancillary subjects if not the principal to equip the young Indians to face the challenges of the changing global market while safeguarding their own craft heritage. In addition, it shall result into inculcating the value of art appreciation amongst the young. Crafts projects and interactions could be a means of linking rural and urban youth. The IIMs too have contained community welfare projects in their curriculum, which helps them understand the social compulsions of their country along with the nitty-gritty of business administration. NID is another example where design is used as a device to solve problems specifically in a societal context. Its International Centre for Indian Crafts in collaboration with Development Commissioner of Handicrafts works towards capacity building, design technology and skill up-gradation of craftsmen. There are several faculties in The Maharaja Sayajirao University of Baroda whose internship programmes have not only build linkages with the NGOs but sensitized the student community to rural crafts and needs of the craftsmen.

Such kind of integration will strengthen the Indian economy since one in every 200 Indian is an artisan. A linkage between professionals, design institutes, local organizations, corporate sector, industry, Government Organizations and Non-Government Organizations is the need of the hour. It is understood that a hierarchy of institutions satisfies a hierarchy of local demands ranging from skills to new technologies. It is thus the networking amongst each of these institutions which shall help in creating better opportunities for market penetration and sustenance of craft and craftsmen along with heritage conservation and preservation. The linkages will not only provide support to the craft sector but also assist in dissemination of the outcomes of the several inputs through its vast network.

Primary Source of Information

Field visits to the respective Organizations and regional exhibitions. Conversation with SHRUJAN'S Designer/Marketing executive Jai Singh and SEWA Design Centre's Co-ordinator Jyotsana Sagara and the Crafts women.

Secondary Sources

- Indian Express, March 15, 1999 and February 05, 2001
- Times of India, February 17 and February 19, 2001

- Baroda Times, Times of India, August 21, 1999
- Sunday Times of India, Ahmedabad, February 05, 2006
- Indias' Artisans–A status report, SRUTI (Society for Rural, Urban and Tribal Initiative), Hauz Khaz, New Delhi, Sponsored by Capart, 1995.
- Co-operatives are Strength–10 years of Gujarat State Womens' Sewa Co-operative Federation Ltd. 1992-2002.
- http://www.humanscape.net.
- http://www.undp.org
- http://www.indiaseminar/2003/523/523maggiebaxter.htm
- http://www.craftsindia.com

D. Paul Chowdhry

18 NEO–NGOs

In the earlier days, voluntary workers used to manage and run field based child welfare agencies themselves. The paid staff consisted of only domestic and office aids. Head of an orphanage, most of the time, secretary/superintendent used to stay at the premises to look after the children. Availability of grants–in–aid, introduction of concept of training in social work and men and women from affluent middle class heading voluntary agencies brought in the practice of hiring social workers. With the advancement of medical and social sciences, child development agencies appointed either whole–time or part–time professionals or consultants. However, as compared to other fields there are very few activities in the field of activists of child welfare.

The funding for child welfare was basically in the form of community contributions as their main sources, gradually got replaced by government grants, the sources of which are the Central Social Welfare Board, Department of Women and Child Development, Ministry of Social Justice and Empowerment, Labour, Health and Family Welfare.

Some of the enlightened agencies also drew on foreign funds utilizing the provisions of Foreign Contribution Regulation Act (FCRA) but bulk of these foreign funds went to community development agencies. This completely changed the scenario of voluntary action. Business and management culture entered in this brand of voluntary sector. First of all, business like designation replaced the Honorary Secretary by paid Executive Director. This change attracted educated, professionals and retired bureaucrats to either start new or work with existing NGOs. They drew fat salaries, some times enjoying corporate life style and having computerized offices and /or residence in high rent areas. The old school of thought or old breed of voluntary workers is not very happy with this trend. The new corporate style jargons such as 'project report', 'action plan', 'strategies', blue print, irksome monitoring, fax, e–mail, website, etc., sometime became some for genuine grass–roots voluntary workers who are still struggling to take care of community need with particular reference to child welfare and development but with poor resources and old infrastructure. We have, therefore, to see how far the NGOs working with children are influenced by impending socio–cultural, political and international influences and how they adjust to the further changes in this century.

NGOs AND THE GLOBALIZED ECONOMY

The NGOs have to work within the social, political and economic frame–work. In India, voluntary agencies have been supplementing and complementing governments', efforts within this system. Some of the educated and smart voluntary workers built up contacts with foreign funding agencies and developed new projects with their assistance. This lead to enactment of Foreign Contribution Regulation Act (FCRA) which seeks to regulate foreign funding. During the last two decades, there have been rapid changes in the scenario which is quite different from what it was 50 years ago. These changes are reflected in the following areas.

(i) Technological changes resulting in global village concept.

(ii) Explosion of knowledge.

(iii) Rapid progress in information technology, completely changing the communication system world–wide.

(iv) Effects of this 'progress' on our education and health, system, erosion of social values through money economy resulting in child labour etc.

(v) Religious fundamentalism taking the place of secularism, narrow ethnicity, creating violence, hatred and violation of human rights.

(vi) Changes in the economic structure resulting in consumerism, price rise, inflation, devaluation, unemployment, improverishment, social disintegration, and migration resulting in problems like, child abuse, prostitution, dowry deaths and violation of human rights.

Child welfare agencies in India were funded by CASP Plan, Save the Children Fund, U.K. and Canada, SOS Children's Village of Austria, CIDA, SIDA, Foreign Christian Mission etc. So far, the foreign funding agencies had a remote control on the aided agencies in India. With the establishment of multi–national companies, there is going to be closeness with the Indian NGOs and multi–nationals. In their anxiety to tap foreign funding, there is possibility of closer connivance of donor and donee agencies, which may jeopardize national interests, resulting in likely erosion of social values and national security. This is also, likely to adversely affect our traditional virtues like dedication, human–touch, nearness to community, social commitment etc.

In India NGOs as in other countries, commercial and government establishment, have to use new office gadgets as part information technology such as VCRs, fax, computers, attachments of telephones, word–processors, dicta–phone as part of professionalization of the new age, they would not only need foreign funding but it will also adversely affect direct contacts with the community.

Globalization and market economy with all its accompanying ill–effects may help in physical development but how far it will control poverty and affect human development is yet to be seen, with particular reference to the establishment of crèches, pre–school and day care centres, institutional support to children deprived of families, small family norm, family welfare services, child recreation, juvenile delinquency, etc.

Therefore, the future NGOs have to remain in preparedness to work in the changed circumstances. NIPCCD as a training and research institution in voluntary action should take a lead and evolve new methods of training and management of NGOs to be able to face the challenges of religious fundamentalism, market economy. Free enterprise, and globalization, which include orientation to new methods and techniques of child survival, growth, development and welfare in order to build up the first generation of adults of the 21st Century.

NETWORKING

In a country like India which has the largest child population–200 million in pre–school age alone with limited resources and with mush-rooming of agencies particularly because of government assistance, a need was felt for bringing about closer working relationship between agencies for working in different fields of child welfare and development particularly since the time we accepted integrated approach to child development. For instance any pre–school children centre–nursery school, Balwadi, Anganwadi or a crèche also needs inputs of health and nutrition. Moreover, child welfare agencies working in a given geographical area say village, block or district could with advantage share their infrastructure and services not only with governmental but non–governmental organizations also. This relates to buildings, staff, equipment, funding, public relations, etc. A school which closes at 3:00 p.m. could allow its building being used for other child development programme such as play, dramatics, special coaching, etc. Similarly, a children home establishing their own school could instead send their children to schools in the community or admit children from outside in their school in order to save no costs and create an atmosphere of interaction of neglected children with those living with their families.

This calls for a need for coordinating councils wherever necessary and possible at the district and state levels. The constitution of the

Central Social Welfare Board and the Indian Council for Child Welfare and NIPCCD provide for this mechanism but over the years, these NGOs have hardly been able to net–work among their own state or district units much less with other agencies. Even with our 50 years of experience we are still not clear as to how to go about in this aspects of our work.

AGING NGOs

As an author of book on 'Aging and the Aged' and with around fifty years of association with voluntary agencies particularly those engaged in child development, I have developed a theory that like human beings, institutions also go through aging process and thus also suffer from aging problems. I have seen growth, development and decline of NGOs, particularly losing luster of their youth. I have been associated with NGOs like the Central Social Welfare Board, the National Institute of Public Cooperation and Child Development; Indian Council of Social Welfare as also the Ministry of Community Development, Public Cooperation Division of the Planning Commission and several child welfare institutions at the local level. I have observed these agencies aims and objects, contributions and standing in the national life and/or the community have shown signs of deterioration as these grow older. The purpose of this personal observation is to draw the attention of the professionals and NGOs to this process of aging. Their old buildings, without funds for their periodical repairs, old disgruntled staff, frustrad because of lower wages with no sign of increase and absence of work satisfaction, inadequate government grants, drying of community contributions, resulting below standard services and neglected of beneficiaries, squabbles among members of management committees and ultimately government not showing sufficient interest in the programme of the agency are the signs of aging process. As it is difficult, if not impossible to rejuvenate an old person, same phenomenon appeals to institutions and agencies.

This aspect of NGOs and voluntary and other agencies has unfortunately not been taken note of by those who are involved in community and voluntary action. All effects of aging are visibly felt in children's institution, some of which are even a century old but majority of these have at least worked for around 50 years. Management consisting of older people, old building with no funds for repairs, increase in number of beneficiaries depleted budget, and above all lack of attitudinal changes with fixed ideas based on old philosophy of 'charity' for those who suffer from curse of God are some of the facts which prevent either closing down or bringing about changes in the agencies because of which children suffer. Today what we call 'development of pre–school child' is the process of pre–poning primary education at the age of three by old timer child welfare workers having not been exposed to modern psychology and processes of child development. There are also a variety of aging institutions for the disabled carrying on with out–moded practices. Unfortunately, neither there has been any study of such agencies nor any surveillance. NIPCCD could take a lead in this venture and undertake research on the concept of aging institutions.

PIONEERS

Our experience of working with the National Children Fund and Public Cooperation reveals that there are no takers of innovative projects by voluntary agencies because of their long association with structure grant–in–aid schemes for the last 50 years. However, my close working relationship with voluntary agencies since in 1951 have indicated that there have been seeds of pioneering work in relation to different aspects of child development in the voluntary sector, some of which have sprouted into institutions during the last 50 years. There have been experiments in MCH services, child health and nutrition, family planning, children's institutions, pre–school services, crèches, child recreation such as play centres and Bal Bhawans, adoption, sponsorship, foster care. An illustrative list of pioneering agencies and names of their founder promoters are mentioned below:

1. Central Social Welfare Board–Dr. (Mrs.) Durga Bai Deshmukh
2. National Institute of Public Cooperation (and now) Child Development–John Bernabas
3. Indian Council for Child Welfare–Mrs. Indira Gandhi and Raj Kumar Amrit Kaur
4. Kasturba Gandhi National Memorial Trust–Smt. Pai
5. Planned Parenthood Association–Lady Rama Roa
6. Family Planning Association of India–Mrs. Avabai Wadia
7. Balkanji Bari–Dada Shewak Bhoj Raj
8. Mobile Creches–Mrs. Mahadevan
9. Andhra Mahila Sabha, Madras and Hyderabad– Dr. (Mrs.) Durgabai Deshmukh
10. Delhi Maternity Hospital–Dr. B.L. Kapoor
11. Sitabaldi Maternity Home, Nagpur–Kamlabai Hospet
12. Comprehensive Rural Health Project, Jamkhed–Dr. Arolay's
13. CINI, Calcutta–Dr. Chaudhry
14. Manipur Children Home–Mrs. Aka
15. SOS Children Hoems–(ICCW)–Mrs. Achamma John Mathai and Tara Ali Baig.

16. Andhra Balananda Sangham, Madras/Hyderabad–
    Mrs. & Mr. Raghav Rao.
17. Nanhi Dunya, Dehradun–Mrs. & Mr. Lekh Raj Ulfat
18. CASP Plan, Mumbai/Pune–Dr. Sharad Gokhle
19. Children Aid Society, Mumbai–Kulkarni and Gokhe
20. The Hari Prasad Institute for the Mentally Handicapped, Hyderabad–Shri Hari Prasad.
21. Bal Bhawan, Rajkot–Kanubhai Acharya
22. Dakshmi Murti
23. Arya Kumar Asharam, Thiruvanatapuram–Krishnanad Acharya
24. Bal Mandir Madras–Manju Kashmiri
25. Nutan Bal Shikshan Sangha, Mumbai–Tara Bai Modak
26. Grameen Shikshan Sangha, Kosbad–Anu Tai
27. Bal Niketan Sangha, Indore–Shalini Moghe
28. Indo–Dutch Project, Hyderabad–Dr. Butt

CHILD RELATED LAWS

The Indian constitution has laid down a legal base for children welfare and development. Under the directive principles of state policy the state has to provide for free and compulsory elementary education and forbids the employment of children in hazardous occupations. The provisions for women also ultimately help in child development. Some of the laws enacted for child welfare are listed below:

1. Supreme Court guidelines on Adoption
2. Hindu Adoptions and Maintenance Act 1956
3. Hindu Minority and Guardianship Act
4. Guardianship and Wards Act 1890
5. Child Labour Act 1986
6. Bonded Labour System (Abolition) Act
7. Juvenile Justice Act 1987
8. Children institutions related laws are
   (a) Societies' Registration Act, 1860
   (b) Indian Trust Act
   (c) Foreign Contributions Regulation Act
   (d) Orphanages and other Charitable Institutions (Supervision and regulation) Act, 1956.

The National Children Policy lays down directive principles of child development and involvement of voluntary agencies. However, there has been no occasion to review the impact of this document and the need for amending it based on our experience of 25 years. This matter needs the attention of the National Children Board. The latest legal document is the UN Convention on the Rights of the Child which though ratified by India has not been taken seriously, perhaps because of several constraints. There is a need for reviewing the National Children Policy on the basis of the provisions of the UN Convention on the Rights of Child. It is also time now to have a second look at various laws concerning children and women so as to make these more relevant keeping in view the above documents and the Perspective Plan for Child Development, 1992. In doing so, there should be wide consultations with NGOs.

NGOs RELATIONSHIP WITH GOVERNMENT

At the central level, the following organizations assist, guide and coordinate with the voluntary agencies engaged in child development. These are:

1. Department of Women and Child Development
2. Central Social Welfare Board
3. National Institute of Public Cooperation and Child Development
4. National Children Board
5. National Children Fund
6. Ministry of Health and Family Welfare
7. National Institute of Health and Family Welfare
8. All India Institute of Medical Sciences
9. Department of Education (Ministry of Human Resource Development)
10. National Council for Educational, Research and Training
11. Ministry of Labour
12. National Labour Institute

A beginning was made in 1953 to guide, assist, promote, strengthen and bring up coordination between the voluntary agencies themselves and the government. The Board also initiated new programmes of child welfare such as crèches, balwadis, holiday camps, Bal Sevika training, foster care etc. Thus the Board contributed in expanding the network of child welfare agencies, and covering gaps in programme contents. Today, there are around 10000 agencies of different types on the Brand's list of assistance.

In 1966, the Public Cooperation Division of the Planning Commission initiated the establishment of the Central Institute of Research and Training in Public Cooperation with a view to strengthen voluntary action. The Institute have for one third of a century organized a large number of seminars, workshops, and orientation programmes in addition to publishing research studies on voluntary action in different aspects of social welfare. During the last two decades in its new incarnation called NIPCCD, its charter specially coveres child development. Thus the two disciplines 'voluntary action' and 'child development' had an opportunity of performing supplementary and effective role. Because of lack of emphasis on child development in the first decade and diversion of its programmes, activities and infrastructure towards ICDS related child development, ironically, it could not make much headway on promotion and strengthening of voluntary action in child development. Moreover, there is no documentation on this total effort. It is a pity that although community participation was an important method in promoting ICDS, yet precious little was done by the Public Cooperation Wing in this area. Therefore, there is a need for a review of public cooperation effort of the institute so as to decide its future thrust in view of changing scenario in social welfare and development and institutes thrust on child development. Their fragmented efforts now needs consolidation.

In addition to funding ICDS the Department of Women and Child Development and the Ministry of Welfare have now larger allocations for assisting programmes of child development. The other Ministries and autonomous institutions listed above have, however played marginal role in child development, particularly in areas such as child health, nutrition, preschool education, child labour, etc.

Thus despite different structures in the government meant for child development, voluntary effort in child development has found a place in the budgetary provisions of these departments, although some of them had also contributed in training effort. Lack of close working relationship between these governmental organizations on the one hand and voluntary sector on the other have stood in the way of better utilization of resources and delivery of effective child development programmes.

It was, however, expected that the formation of the National Children Board with the Prime Minister as its chairman would help in brining closer and effective working relationship for the cause of children but here one could not see perceptible and effective change, because of a variety of constraints such as absence of an effective secretariat of the National Children Board and marginal interest among the member of the Board.

CONCLUSION AND SUGGESTIONS

Community participation has taken several forms and nomenclatures. A study of voluntary action in child development indicate that although some of the organizations are more then a century old, yet voluntary agencies came into action during the last fifty years gathering impetus and support from the Government as a part of Five–years Plans. Today, there may be around 10,000 voluntary agencies of different hues and colours with a variety of programmes for children. They first began with purely welfare services for vulnerable child population but since mid–seventees child development initiated by official agencies contributed a great deal in this field. In fact one can see and feel voluntary action, in all aspects of basic needs and problems of children. Despite various efforts made during the last five decades, voluntary action for child development needs to be strengthened from the point of view of their organization, management, methods, programme contents, coverage of fields of child development and quality of services. This calls for a closer working relationship between the Central Social Welfare Board as a funding agency and the National Institute of Child Development and Public Cooperation as a training and research agency after evaluation of their work of more than three decades.

GAPS IN SERVICES

It has also been felt since long that both government and voluntary agencies together have not been able to cover growing child population with their programmes resulting in overlapping in some areas and gaps in others with particular reference to different social needs of different categories, age–groups and areas (village or city segments). Concentrated efforts have to be made to fill in these patches with particular reference to the needs of first generation of the 21st century. While doing so, family involvement has to be given greater emphasis as it is the basic child development institution. A mechanism of networking between voluntary agencies, families, local bodies and government agencies, therefore becomes necessary.

The implementation of the National Children Policy, the National Children Fund and working of the National Children Board need to be reviewed after 25 years of their creation, with particular reference to the UN Convention on the Rights of the Child.

Research, training and academic institutions concerned with child development may be motivated to have closer collaboration with voluntary agencies in child welfare and development to begin with at the national level and then at the state level down wards.

In collaboration with voluntary agencies our education system has to be revamped with particular reference to meeting the special needs of the following:

1. Slow learners and children with scholastic backwardness but with normal IQ.

2. Identifying and helping gifted children in the specific fields of their interest.
3. Indepth review of pre–school education/service so that children can be allowed to grow mentally at their own speed and interest rather that being pushed into the system because of competition at the higher education level.
4. Bringing larger number of girls under education system.

Nutrition programmes for pre–school children and women through ICDS, Balwadis and crèches have made them very expensive because of expenditure on distribution machinery. Moreover, areas which are not yet covered by any child development schemes show a signs of higher malnutrition rates. Till these areas are provided with nutrition component, local voluntary agencies and Mahila Mandals could be associated with this work. In fact since the source of supply of food for nutrition programmes is primarily the Food Cooperation of India and official machinery has been created for its cooking and distribution among families of malnourished children be supplied food by Public Distribution System through local voluntary agencies who should be approached to prepare foods cards for such families and ensure that food reaches the child.

Bias against girl child is a part of our culture and is born in the families. Therefore, it calls for an extensive social awareness effort. This could be done by voluntary agencies alone.

INNOVATIVE PROGRAMMES

The voluntary agencies worked mostly on the structured and tailor-made government programmes with standard budgets, had over the years lost their virtues of innovation and initiative as their hands were always tied. Therefore, they failed to work on innovative child development programmes when opportunities were given to them. The National Children Fund and the Public Cooperation Division of the Ministry of Rural Development where the author had association could not achieve their laudable objectives because of this weakness. This aspect has to be seen critically and voluntary agencies be motivated and assisted to work in newer areas. Some of these are suggested below for being funded by the National Children Fund:

1. Review of programmes and institutions for pre–school which unfortunately has become the first phase of child education, rather than a programme of child development doing more harm to the pre–school child for giving it a new orientation after delinking it from education system.
2. Project of special services for the slow learners and children with normal IQ suffering from scholastic backwardness.

3. A study of family background and personal qualities of those who made a mark particularly in the nineteenth century as poets, initiators of arts, music, cinema, sportsman, scientific inventions like electricity, bulb, rail engine, aircraft, watch, computer, telephone and those who made special contribution to religion and culture like Swami Vivekananda, Swami Dayanand, etc.
4. Projects of identifying children with potentials of giftedness in art, science technology, culture, etc. and giving them special inputs based on our studies so as to.

As compared to the last century, we are entering the 21st century with a large percentage of children and with support of governmental and non–governmental infrastructure, funds and experience, backed by knowledge generated by several national institutes and the UNICEF. It should help us in generating effective voluntary action for child development in some of the newer areas thus resulting in promotion of innovations among NGO's to develop a modules of promoting giftedness among children.

A study of child welfare and development programmes indicates that pioneering work in several child related fields/aspects was done by voluntary workers. The relationship with government was mainly through a large–scale grant–in–aid system and partly through legislation on child welfare and training through NIPCCD. However, net–working aspect of child development has been rather weak and needs a closer look. Effective methods of closer co–operation between voluntary agencies themselves and the government have to be adapted.

Whereas new breed of voluntary agencies has come, innovation and activisim among child welfare agencies. On the one hand, NGO's have to be in the state of preparedness to face new challenges in the changing social, political and economic scenario, particularly in the context of free market economy of globalization on the other, we have to create an awareness about aging institutions and their problems.

CASE STUDY

NANHI DUNYA DEHRADUN

Selection of Nanhi Dunya for a case study is motivated by the following factors:

1. It came into being just before India's independence
2. Its track record is different from other agencies of its age
3. Its founder promoter Sh. Lekh Raj Ulfat was not only a lovable and fascinating person but a worker who was not a stereotype of social workers

4. Unlike many other social workers involved in a variety of social and political activities, Ulfat was fully devoted to child development.
5. The author has known very closely this fascinating agency and its founder promoter for last 45 years.

Nanhi Dunya in Urdu means a world of small (children). It was founded by Late Prof. Lekh Raj Ulfat after an intensive period of studies and discussion. On November 17, 1946, six tiny tots gathered for the first time on an old blanket under a tree in Dehradun. They were virtually the founder members (not as much beneficiaries) of Nanhi Dunya's children club, which because of pressing demands developed into a school later. From the very beginning Nanhi Dunya was a calling to a vocation in social work which Ulfat felt throughout his life. In 1951, he was jointed by his wife Smt. Sadhana Ulfat and later by his two children Alok and Kiran who are themselves products of Nanhi Dunya culture.

Shri Lekh Raj Ulfat refused offer of State Civil Service but joined freedom movement. While he was being chased as a revolutionary by the British Government there, he migrated to Dehradun in 1944–45. He felt slavery was a curse and every self respecting person must revolt against the foreign rule. At Dehradun, Ulfat came in contact with socialist leader Mr. M.N. Roy. There was a change in his attitude towards life from nationalism to humanism. Perhaps creation of Nanhi Dunya was an answer to his strong desire as a member of "Family of Man" as he termed it. He felt very strongly that in order to build a society he had in mind, one should begin with children. Therefore, in Nanhi Dunya he found reflection of his thoughts.

AIMS

The main aim of Nanhi Dunya is to awaken a deeper interest in the education and development of child through:

1. Offering possibilities of artistic and spiritual growth of an individual.
2. Equality of opportunity of all children–rich or poor, normal or handicapped.
3. Community education for development of intellectual, social and manual capacity in work culture.
4. Integration of development and education of the disabled children into the mainstream.
5. Linking parent, family and the community with particular reference to their social and economic situation with child development.

ACTIVITIES

From a humble beginning Nanhi Dunya has grown into a movement. It has support of thousands of its former children (now grown–ups), parents, teachers and social workers. In a beautiful city of Dehradun, Nanhi Dunya is still a well–known organization among the middle class, although it has admirers both in India and abroad. Briefly, the following are some of the activities /centres of Nanhi Dunya:

(a) Rural Balwadis

(b) Urban Preschool Centres

(c) Primary School for Children in the age–groups of 6–14 years

(d) Teacher's Training Courses

(e) Children Libraries

(f) Natyashala

(g) Monthly Children's Magazine

(h) Children Hoby clubs and recreation centres

(i) Creches for children of working mothers

(j) Mother and child health programme

(k) Child guidance centre

(l) Supplementary nutrition programme

These programmes and activities are spread in more than around twenty locations both in rural and urban areas. Nanhi Dunya has adopted innovative methods in child development. Though small in size it has adopted methods, such as training and deployment of teachers, close working relationship between them and the parents, special education for the disabled, emphasis on play, painting, music, modeling with waste material, etc. According to Mrs. Ellen Roy' "Nanhi Dunya" is more than a school. It helps in opening the mental windows of children to the whole wide world, breaking down artificial barriers..."

COMMUNITY PARTICIPATION

Although Nanhi Dunya does receive some state assistance, yet it believes in solving their problems with local means and material and total involvement of beneficiaries who are motivated to contribute in cash, kind and voluntary services. Collection of one rupee in an empty match box was a drive started by Ulfat as a symbolic of people's participation on birth day of Nanhi Dunya on 17 November. In the words of Ulfat 'we must generate richness within us to dispel poverty. We need millions but we must not lose sight of the penny...' We all have to learn to respect the CHILD and realize its importance in the evolution of a new world order–peace loving, just and free'.

STAFF

The annual average number of children served by Nanhi Dunya varies from eight to ten thousand. It has a strength of around 100 workers who are essentially voluntary, drawing some honorarium. However, emphasis is on a degree of their awareness and attitude and development of skills through training on the job.

FINANCES

The average annual expenditure in Nanhi Dunya has been around Rs. Five Lakh including grants from the UP State government and the Central Social Welfare Board.

Although Nanhi Dunya does suffer from financial constraints, yet it always tries to stand on its own, Ulfat had curious ways of raising funds. He says 'God–in each one of us. Awake him and the fellow says Ulfat'. His faith works. Thus each project of Nanhi Dunya has a story to tell. Nanhi Dunya never starts a project to collect a grant. If there is no money to run the kitchen, Nanhi Dunya's good will bring grossaries on credit from the neighbouring store. More than funds and its not so good financial position, Nanhi Dunya takes pride in its pioneering and innovative work, since it has rendered to needy children and the community and demonstration of dedication, commitment and human–touch which are fast disappearing from the voluntary agencies elsewhere.

SIMPLE LIVING

Unlike many social workers Nanhi Dunya is lead by a couple who had accepted to lead a simple life with complete devotion to child development. Smt. Sadhana Ulfat had sold all her jewellery for purchasing a building for the organization. Both being busy in their work their domestic help used to be Chintu and Mintu–two mentally retarded children who grew with Nanhi Duniya. We have seen devotion and love of these two not only towards children but also for the Ulfats.

FOREIGN TRAINING

Ulfat had many facets of his work. In the late fortees, he led a number of trade unions, particularly among tea gardens. Labour welfare and sound industrial relations to him were the basic needs of a healthy and democratic society. Problems of juvenile delinquents and prisoner's were subjects as dear to him as Nanhi Dunya. His quest for knowledge never stopped. He once quoted the parting words of his teacher Dr. S. M. Abdullah of Punjab University, Lahore who said 'Be a student throughout your life and never allow sincerity to leave you'. Despite heavy responsibilities at home and late in his life Ulfat embarked upon a long journey visiting 15 European countries. He met Dr. Rudolph Steiver an educationist and philosopher. He also met Mr. Francies Edmunds who arranged a scholarship for him at the Emerson College England. In England, he got opportunities to work with children and young people. He also visited several institutions. This helped him to widen his vision, enhance his skills and enriched his thought – process about child development.

CONCLUSION

Nanhi Dunya represents the hard work, dedication, commitment and devotion of a freedom fighter Prof. Lekh Raj Ulfat during the last 54 years backed by his wife Sadhana and now his daughter Kiran who wants the candle lighted by her father going despite several difficulties faced by them. Along side growth of Nanhi Dunya Prof. Ulfat also grew mentally and intellectually and ultimately reached the highest position at the national level from grass–roots and also at the global level. Although experience has shown that after half a century older institutions get degenerated because of mere process of aging but this has not been the case with Nanhi Dunya which has growth in leaps and bounds and is still going strong. During the last fifty years, Nanhi Dunya under the leadership of Prof. Ulfat has served thousand tiny tots of Dehradun sincerely and honestly without any ulterior motive. Long live Nanhi Dunya and the royal faqir Ulfat.

BIBLIOGRAPHY

Chowdhry, D. Paul (1995), Child Welfare and Development, Atma Ram & Sons, Delhi–4th Ed.

Chowdhry, D. Paul (1993), Handbook of Social Welfare, Atma Ram & Sons, Delhi.

Chowdhry, D. Paul (1988), Inter–country Adoption. ICCW, New Delhi.

Chowdhry, D. Paul (1990), Voluntary Effort in Social Welfare and Development, Siddharth Publishers, New Delhi.

CSWB–Annual Report 1998–99.

GOI – Child related Laws.

a. Juvenile Justice Act 1986.
b. Child Labour Act 1986.
c. Hindu Adoptions and Maintenance Act 1956.
d. Orphanages and other Institutions Supervisions and Control Act 1962.
e. Foreign Contributions Regulation Act.

GOI – Indian Constitution.

GOI–Ministry of Social Welfare–National Children Policy–1974.

NIPCCD–Reports and Publications.

UN–Convention on the Rights of Child.

NEERJA JAISWAL & AMI SHAH

19 Empowering Consumer Through Consumer Organisations

INTRODUCTION

The consumer is the forgotten man of the modern Indian economy. He is the least organized and the most centrifugal element in the circle of investment, production, sale and consumption, and is generally taken for granted as one who has to any-how buy in order to live.

Adulteration, variation in the contents of the pack, use of deceptive or fractional weights are all the ways and means by which the consumer is exploited to the maximum extent possible. The absence of perfect competition makes the things worse for the consumer. In fact adulteration of goods, poor quality, failure to give fair measure, lack of service and courtesy to the consumer, misleading or dishonest advertising are all examples of violation by a business enterprise of its' obligations towards the consumer of it's products.

As a result consumer criticism of the business community is often echoed in respect of factors like price, quality, advertising, packing, distribution, after-sales service etc. In view of the enormity of problems being faced by the consumers, the proportion of supportive agencies for it is quite insignificant. The apathy of Indian Consumer is clearly reflected in the fact that for a population of one billion, there are just about 500 consumer organizations in the country (Gulshan, 1996).

There is an urgent need to develop a new consumer culture for which consumer education has become a necessity. Supportive role can be played by many agencies, consumer organizations could be one of them. The consumers can be made more alert, vigilant and intelligent by the developmental and continuous effort being made by the supportive agencies. Voluntary Consumer Organizations can play a crucial role for championing the cause of consumers.

How many voluntary consumer organizations existed in the metropolitan city of Mumbai, Maharashtra? What proactive role were they playing for the consumers at Mumbai? and What were the different ways being adopted by them to educate and empower consumers? were the queries to be answered, which motivated to conceptualize some of the present study with the following objectives:

OBJECTIVES OF THE STUDY

1. To identify the existing voluntary consumer organizations in the metropolitan city of Mumbai, Maharashtra.
2. To explore the functioning pattern, the activities were being carried and the educational programs being undertaken by them to empower consumers.

DELIMITATION

The study was limited to 8 non-governmental consumer organizations of Mumbai Metropolitan City only.

METHODOLOGY

The present descriptive study was carried at Mumbai Metropolitan city of Maharshtra State. Consumer organizations for the present study were operationally defined as the registered voluntary consumer groups. The list of the consumer organizations (14 in number) was procured from the directory of one of the consumer organization. The samples were selected on the basis of set criteria i.e. (a) those functioning at the time of data collection, (b) those were non–governmental in nature, (c) those who were willing to share information about their organization, and (d) those were in existence for 3 or more number of years. Of the enlisted consumer organizations, only eight were found to be eligible to be included in the present study. These were (i) Consumer Guidance Society of India, (ii) Mumbai Grahak Panchayat, (iii) All India Bank Depositors Association, (iv) Mumbai Grahak Sanstha Manch, (v) Bombay Telephone Users Association, (vi) Women's Graduate Union, (vii) Association for Consumer Actions on Safety and Health, and (viii) The Passengers And Traffic Relief Association.

Pre-validated interview schedule was utilized as a tool to collect data from the heads of the consumer organizations. The investigators collected the data personally. The tool comprised of open and close ended questions. An in–depth information collected, assisted in developing case studies for the selected non-governmental consumer organizations. The data were further categorized, tabulated and analyzed in terms of the descriptive statistics.

FINDINGS OF THE STUDY

The detailed information about the consumer organizations was gathered in terms of their establishment, functioning pattern, publications, activities and educational programs undertaken by them. Let us discuss about each case study in detail.

Case 1: Consumer Guidance Society of India (CGSI)

In 1996 CGSI pioneered the consumer movement in the country. It was born out of melting pot of food adulteration and harmful food additives, spurious and hazardous drugs, quality defects and quantity deficiencies of consumer goods, shady services, rising prices coupled with acute shortages, black marketing and its after ego, profiteering.

The Consumer Guidance Society of India was the first consumer organization to be set up in India. It was non-profit making, non-political voluntary body. It depended on consumers to keep it going. It was supported solely by membership subscriptions and grants from public interest groups or charitable trusts. It did not accept commercial donations or advertising.

CGSI although not very old had successfully accomplished its objectives and had served thousands of consumers. The prime objective of this organization was to get redressal for consumers. The total membership of the organization was more than 2153 including yearly, life patrons, institutions and corporate bodies as members. There were eight employees working in the organization. It served to rural as well as urban population.

Redressal to consumer was one of the most important activity of CGSI. In the past three years the consumer organization had received around 700 complaints out of which 70 per cent of them had got redressal. The organization was also involved in the counseling activity. Every Saturday volunteer Lawyers served to consumers by giving them advice and directions on filing the complaints, writing the complaint and following it.

The organization mainly served to urban population but also organized Camps and Shibirs for rural population. They also undertook awareness campaigns about consumer rights and activities in rural areas. The organization had training programs for their staff so that they can educate rural consumers effectively.

The organization was also involved in organizing competitions like painting, essay, and eloqual, quiz contest and so on. Income generating activities like candle making and soap making were also demonstrated by the organization. CGSI arranged talks and seminars on consumers awareness and rights and responsibilities for school and college students.

The food adulteration kit was produced by the organization, which was sold at very nominal cost for the consumers. There was no laboratory facility available in the organization but for testing of samples CGSI send the sample to S.N.D.T. laboratory.

CGSI's Education committee members had been working with other like minded educationists to formally introduce consumer education in the school curriculum. After nearly two years of meeting and discussions, efforts were fruitful. The Maharashtra education board introduced consumer education at 9th standard level in 1994 progressively covering students from the 4th standard onwards.

CGSI started rural projects in the villages of Thane and Raigad districts in 1997 with funding from ACTION AID and with a staff of six.

Consumer training was given to people of 21 villages in 1997-98 and this was extended to 90 villages in 1998-99. Over 32,300 people were given consumer education through 750 talks and demonstration in the two years duration of the project. Till date 107 training programs were organized and 5767 potential activists had been given special training in consumer activism by the organization.

The consumers themselves had set up five local consumer groups in different areas and these were now actively organizing exhibitions, given talks and redressing complaints. More were expected to come up soon.

CGSI was the first consumer organization to demand special consumer courts for redressal of consumer's complaints. In 1975, CGSI led a delegation of five consumer organizations from different parts of India to meet the then minister for food and civil supplies, Mr. T.A. Pai, to demand a comprehensive consumer protection Act, special consumer courts and a directorate for implementation of the Act. The first two had now become a reality.

The CGSI aimed at making consumers conscious of their rights and responsibilities and strives to ensure, that the consumer gets his money's worth, that the goods sold are up-to the national and recognized standards, that producers and manufacturers abide by such standards as are necessary for the health and safety of the users.

CGSI received the 'National award' in its silver jubilee year in 1991 for services to consumers. CGSI was a 'FULL' member of the international organization, consumers international, London (formerly known as the international organization of consumers Union IOCU). CGSI had been appointed member of both state and central consumer protection councils under the consumer protection act, 1986. It was a member of the governing council of the apex coalition body, consumer co-ordination council, New Delhi. It was a member of the development council set up under the industrial development and regulation Act, New Delhi. CGSI's technical experts members were nominated as members of several sectional committees of the Bureau of Indian standards.

Keemat was a monthly journal published by CGSI for the members. It was now in its 29th year of publication, the only consumer magazine in India to be published regularly every month. The main objective of their publication was to predict the rights and interest of consumers, provide them with information and counsel, take up their complaints with the offending party and/or the authorities and help them to select goods and services which were a fair return for the money they spend.

CGSI had printed eight educational booklets to its credit to help the consumer, which are for sale in their office.

1. Buying Guides for (a) Electrical appliances, (b) Edible oils, and (c) Pesticides & You.
2. Nutritional recipes booklets (Marathi/Hindi/English)
3. Apali Shakti (Marathi). (Grahak Suraksha Kayda, 1986)
4. Food Adulteration (Marathi/Hindi)
   Misleading Advertisement (Marathi)
5. Samarthya Ashok Chalavaliche (Consumer movement)
6. Safety at home
7. Safe blood and you.

In order to create consumer awareness and educate consumers they were utilizing medias like video-films, lectures, workshops, exhibitions, camps and seminar.

CGSI also owned educational program developed by its committee to educate consumers on topics like adulteration, rights and responsibility, misleading advertisement. Media used were posters, kit, video-films, and invited lectures.

In order to manage, work effectively and timely many committees were appointed by the organization like managing committee, testing committee, legal aid committee, complaints committee, media complaints panel, consumer education committee, publications committee and press and public relations committee.

Case 2: Mumbai Grahak Panchayat (MGP)

Mumbai Grahak Panchayat, a non-governmental organization was established in 1976. The prime objective of the organization was to provide pure and proper weighed products to its members at a reasonable rate. The organization also aimed in giving redressal and legal guidance to consumers.

Although MGP was involved in many activities, there were only 6 paid employees working in the office. Volunteers working in the fields were reimbursed only conveyance. MGP had committees Like Organization Committee, Education Committee, Purchase Committee, Grahak Path Committee And Managing Committee for the efficient working of the organization.

On invitation, MGP sent its trained staff to deliver lectures on related topic. They also organized different competitions in college and school to create awareness among students about various consumer concepts. The organization had six complaint center where even non-members could also register their complaints.

Minimum 11 families in the same locality or building could form a Grahak Sangh and register it with MGP. The Grahak Sangh was given a code number. The registered sangh only got the benefit of the doorstep distribution system. All essential household commodities were supplied to members on 'No Profit, No Loss' basis.

There were more than 18,315 families as members of the MGP in Mumbai. It meant, it caters to the needs of more than 97,700 consumers. The distribution of goods monthly to these families was an important facet of MGP's working.

MGP had created some regional committees also. This had decentralized the activities effectively. These regional committees perform the functions like distribution of essential commodities, educating the consumers, giving fellowship and redressing their disputes. These regional committees successfully operated: "Consumer Disputes Redressal Cell" in their respective regions. This work was supervised and assisted by the study and research of the MGP. These cells undertook an in-depth study of consumer problems, contacted the concerned government departments and acted on consumer problems and complaints and mediated between the consumers, manufacturers and government departments.

The MGP used to advise to the aggrieved consumer to make a complaint personally and pursue the matter in the district forum or state commission or the national commission. MGP had created a unique distribution system in Mumbai and Thane.

Other noteworthy activities of MGP were:

(a) MGP arranged four Grahak pathos at Dadar, Vile-Parle, Borivli, and Thane before Diwali for the benefit of consumers.

(b) MGP publishes its monthly Newsletter 'GRAHAK' since 1976. It gave information about the distribution scheme. It educated the consumers and provided a platform to have a frank and free dialogue. Varied subjects were handled through the Newsletter to develop consumer awareness.

(c) MGP activists write articles regularly in some leading newspaper in Maharashtra.

(d) MGP volunteers use Doordarshan and Akashvani for furthering consumer awareness and education. Doordarshan had its own programmer 'Grahakshi Hitguj'.

(e) MGP activists had enacted dozens of street plays for the benefit of consumers.

(f) MGP had published a number of information Booklets such as:

1. Consumer Complaints Guide
2. Takrar
3. Grahak Hitachi Gurukilli
4. Consumer Protection Act and Consumer, and
5. Medical Negligence And Consumer Protection Act

(g) It had also published buying guides, leaflets on bank services and Consumer Protection Act. The publication was mainly in English, Marathi and Hindi languages.

(h) MGP ran consumer guidance centers at Borivili, Dadar, Gurgaon and Chembur in Mumbai.

(i) MGP had its fully equipped study and research wing.

(j) MGP arranged seminars for people, workshop for college students and workshop for its active members and volunteers.

(k) MGP arranged annual get together for its members regularly.

There was no laboratory facility in MGP. Hence, samples to be tested were sent to S.N.D.T. laboratory or activists sent it to the reliable and convenient laboratories. MGP was also a recognized member of Co-ordination Council, Consumer Protection Council Set-up, and Consumer International. The funds were raised only through membership fees. Future planned activity of M.G.P. was to develop a laboratory and to start National Institute Of Consumer Education.

Case 3: Mumbai Grahak Sanstha Manch

Mumbai Grahak Sanstha Manch was a 31 years old organization established in 1969. The organization had 131 members from urban area in the form of Consumer Co-operative Society registered under Consumer Co-Operative Act. Fifteen honorary workers were giving their services to the organization.

It's main objective was to establish consumers co-operative society for consumers and assist them to run properly. The activity of the organization involved handling of consumer complaints and legal counseling. Only 3 to 4 complaints were received every year by the organization, probably because it deals with complaints related to only consumer co-operative society. Non-member consumers were allowed to attend lectures organized by Mumbai Grahak Sanstha Manch.

It also organized training program on subjects like "How to run Consumer Co-operative Society". The funds were gathered through membership fees and through the sale of publications like 'Manch Patrika'.

Journal called 'Manch Patrika' was published every year by the organization for Consumer Co-Operative Society in Marathi and English. Its circulation was about 500 copies every month. It included issues and highlighting problems of consumers co-operative, new laws introduced and any other current issues. The organization was also planning to publish "Panch Patrika" in near future with the same objective.

The organization also conducted lecturers, workshops, discussions, exhibitions, camps and seminars for the benefit of consumer co-operative societies. Lectures and seminars were also organized on the topics like "how to purchase", "sales management", "how to run a retail shop and dealing with employees". It was a member of organizations like Consumer Protection Council Set-up and State Level Federations.

Case 4: All Indian Bank Depositors Association

32 year old All Indian Bank Depositors Association was a voluntary organization serving to the masses at national level. The bank employees were restricted to become the member of the organization. There were no paid employees in the organization, fifteen employees worked voluntarily for the organization.

The main objective of the organization was to serve interest of depositors and healthy banking industry. The organization had credited banks like State Bank of India, Union Bank of India and Bank of Punjab by awarding them.

The organization was involved only in handling banking related problems for consumers, and educating people about banking problems. It received around five complaints everyday and solved most of them as well. The funds were raised through their sale of published booklets.

Publications of the organization included booklets like 'Coin shortage and Soiled Note', 'Depositor rights and customer service in Banks', 'Bank Scam and Safety of Depositors Funds' and 'Bank Strikes and Public Interest'. Besides these print media, the organization conducted workshop, seminars, lecturers and discussions in order to create awareness among consumers about the bank services.

Case 5: Bombay Telephone Users' Association

Bombay Telephone Users Association was a young organization established in 1985. There were fifteen volunteers serving to the organization, three in the office and the other twelve in the fields. The current membership status was 260 consumers; all of them were individuals from urban areas. Only in past, the Corporate, Co-operative societies, schools and so on constituted 7 to 8 per cent of the membership of the organization. The organization was very active at its initial years but after few years it had reduced it's activities. From 1998 it had picked up its activities again.

The main objective of the organization was to fight for the betterment of telephone subscribers on issues related to all telecom policy, which affects them in case of tariff, quality, laws and rules, services etc. It also aimed in educating people on various telecom issues and took up fighting individual issues with MTNL or mobiles and cases, which camp up in the consumer court.

The organization was also involved in the handling of telephone related consumer complaints. There were around 1700 complaints received every year by the organization out of which around 5 per cent of them got solved. It was also involved in providing legal counseling to the consumers, creating awareness about consumer rights and responsibility and educating consumers. It took up issues with the government with Telecom Regularity Authority of India (TRAI) and also conducted comparative study between performances of the telecom equipments manufactured by different companies.

The organization was planning to publish a monthly letter booklet, which would focus on the main issues, activities of the association, and deal with consumer grievances and their redressal. The language of the planned publication was English.

There were two committees working for the organization namely (a) Complaints Committee, and (b) Counseling Committee. To perform various activities, funds were raised only through membership fees. Future planned activities of the organization were to hold seminars on telecom related issues for members, produce a newsletter, form a committee to study in detail about the matters of costing of telecom services and get recognition as national organization.

Case 6: Association for Consumer Action on Safety and Health (acash)

"acash" was an independent non-profit voluntary organization formed to conduct research, assist and deal with health related consumer issues and to protect the rights of the consumers and the general public. "acash" was founded by a group of doctors, lawyers and other concerned individuals in 1986. The organization was open for membership to all except where there was any conflict of interest like pharmaceuticals companies. There were total 250 registered members in "acash" in the form of individuals and institutions. Majority of them were from urban area. There were total five employees working for the organization in the office as well as in the fields.

For the accomplishment of objectives and activities various committees were framed by "acash" like fund raising committee, young child and infant feeding practice committee, tobacco control committee, medical negligence and patients rights committee, and drug issue committee. The prime objective of the organization was to secure, protect and preserve consumer interest and assert their rights as consumer of goods and services pertaining to health and safety. Members were not the only beneficiaries but they helped the organization to run through membership fees. Funds were also collected from other organizations except from any pharmaceutical companies.

The organization handled complaints related to medical negligence. Every year around seventy complaints were received by the organization. For legal guidance and counseling "acash" had network with Consumer Guidance Society of India and Mumbai Grahak Panchayat. It was also involved in creating awareness and educating young consumers about their rights and responsibilities related to health.

"acash" worked actively for health awareness activities like anti drug campaigns, bottle feeding, child care and vaccination, anti tobacco campaigns, health and hygiene, and trained rural health workers for physical health centers, aayas, nurses etc. It also organized campaigns against Cigarette, Bidis, Aids and prostitution. Competitions for school children were organized by the organization. "acash" was strongly against the advertisements of tobacco. It publicized "anti tobacco" advertisement with the support from film stars. The organization had no testing facility but the samples for testing were sent to Consumer Guidance Society of India.

"acash" was a member of organizations like Bureau of India Standards, Consumer International, International Lactation Consultants Association (ILCA), Baby Friendly Hospital Initiative (BFHI), Breastfeeding Promotion Network Of India (BPNI), All India Drug Action Network (AIDAN), Voluntary Health Association Of India(VHAI), Medico Friend Circle (MFC), Health Action International (HAI)M International Breast Feeding Promotion Organization World Alliance For Breast Feeding Action (WABA)M International Baby Food Action Network (IBFAN) and International Network of Women against Tobacco(INWAT), "acash" also had close contacts with UNICEF and WHO. "acash" served as an information center to educate, guide and disseminate information in the field of health and safety issues.

"acash" also had representation on various government committees like Central Pollution Control Board (Ecomark technical sub committee), Bureau of Indian Standards (Sub committee on soaps and detergents)and Maharashtra Breast Feeding Promotion Initiative (MBPI).

"acash" had been appointed by the Government of India, Ministry of Human Resource Development, Department of Women and Child Development as per gazette notification GSR 540 (E) to monitor and report violations of the "Infant Milk Substitutes, Feeding Bottles and Infant foods (Regulations of Production supply and Distribution) Act, 1992".

The projects and campaigns undertaken by "acash" were:

1. To collect and provide information about the hazardous drugs and adverse drug reaction, to campaign for a national drug policy, to provide essential drugs at low cost, and to bring out publications on drug information.
2. On maternal infant health and nutrition:
   - To study and recommend appropriate health care facilities and nutritional requirements for expectant and nursing mothers and infants.
   - To protect, promote and support breast feeding.
   - To train health professionals for "Human Lactation Management Training (HLMT)" and counseling for successful breast feeding.
   - To foster and form 'Mother to Mother support groups.
   - To co-ordinate the effort of doctors, nurses, health workers, primary health care centers and voluntary organization in the field or infant feeding practices at the state and national level.
   - To monitor and work for the implementation of the infant milk substitutes, feeding bottles and infant foods under Regulation Of Production, Supply and Distribution Act, 1992, through out the country.
   - To lobby for infant friendly health policies.
3. For tobacco control:
   - To create awareness among different groups about the risk of tobacco hazards.
   - To mobilize mass support against tobacco company tactics.
   - To lobby with the government tobacco control policies and legislations.
   - To build conditions and co-ordinate tobacco control networks at city, state, national and South Asia level.
   - To conduct research on the socio–economic implication of tobacco production, use and marketing.
   - To network with International Tobacco Control Organization and movements.
4. On Health Rights: To provide education and training in relation to rights and responsibilities of consumers and patients regarding safety and health.

5. On legal Cell: To process consumer complaints in relation to safety and health i.e. issues dealing with marketing of banned and hazardous drugs, false claims of food and drug companies and medical negligence.
6. On Environmental Safety: To collect and disseminate information in relation to environment pollution, and chemically harmful products.

   "acash" had the following publications to its credit on the topics:

   - Helping mothers to breastfeed (English/Marathi)
   - Maternity home practices and breastfeeding.
   - The infant milk substitutes, feeding bottles and infant foods (Regulations of Production, Supply and Distribution Act 1992).
   - Five steps for healthy living (Hindi/English).
   - Questions and Answers on Breastfeeding (English, Gujarati, Marathi, Hindi).
   - Healthy living leaflet.
   - Patients rights and responsibilities (English).
   - Maternity Home practices (English).
   - Guidelines for breast feeding (English, Hindi, Marathi).

Besides these publications, in order to create awareness among consumers "acash" had developed a video cassette on healthy living and healthy food habits. Available in Hindi/English it had also developed advertisement on "anti tobacco" and "ill effects of bottle feeding".

"acash" also contributed articles in news papers and magazines, organized puppet shows, skits, slide shows, lectures, workshops, exhibitions, discussion etc for educating the consumers.

It borrowed training manual on "Breast Feeding And Human Lactation Management" from UNICEF.

Case 7: Women's Graduate Union (WGU)

As early in 1915, when the WGU was founded, women with vision recognized the imperative need to encourage the empowerment of women through education and career enhancing activities. Now, eighty five years down the line, WGU not only grew strong but also expanded. 225 members from urban areas were registered with WGU. For the functioning of the organization it had recruited ten employees.

The objective of the organization was to look after the interest of women and children. One of the most daring ventures, perhaps the first of its kind in India, was the construction and management of the Seth Purshottamdas Thakurdas Hostel for working women, which opened in 1974. The project struck out for the independence of women providing safe and comfortable living facilities for women from anywhere in India who wished to be in Mumbai to avail themselves of the better job opportunities offered by the city.

The increasing pressure of urban living and the impact of the diverse conflicting cultures have created stresses and strains in daily life, resulting in the need for emotional support and psychiatric advice. To help such individuals with their mental and emotional problems, WGU had set up a counseling and guidance center which had been able to fulfill the felt need of the society.

The problems of the poor have escalated beyond the belief. Our predecessors did not have to confront the problem of the present day, fostering slums, where hundreds of thousands of deprived children cry out for a healthier environment and some education. To help at least a minuscule proportion of these, a study center was set up in 1985. This center, which is one of its kind, offered municipal school children a quiet and comfortable place away from their dingy and chaotic homes, providing them a facility to study after school hours under qualified supervision.

The Behramjee Lalkaka Nursery School was started about five years ago to provide pre school education for the children of the poorest of the poor, who otherwise would never know the luxury of a nursery school. Nourishing snacks were provided to the children daily, regular health checks were arranged, and they had the opportunity to become socially aware and happy individuals. WGU's late endeavor was to arrange for a study class to help senior students of the municipal schools.

WGU had a consumer and civic affairs cell, which contributed to making life more livable in the city. Consumer awareness workshops and seminars were held regularly to tackle issues while complaints were dealt speedily and satisfactorily.

As in the past, individual donors and public trusts continued to response their faith in WGU's ability to administer scholarships. Almost every year, people who wished to donate a scholarships entrusted their money to the WGU to set up a new endowment. Scholarships amounting to over Rupees 11/2 lakhs were given every year to about a hundred women who were found promising by the scholarship committee. The ideas and concerns of members were given effective voice through a monthly newsletter "The University Women" which created awareness and knowledge. As in the past, affiliation to the international and Indian Federations of University Women had enabled the WGU to forge links with thinking women all over the world.

Over the years, the programs and Fund Raising committee had made strenuous and imaginative efforts to raise funds and arrange programs for the varied WGU activities to enrich and empower its members. It would not have been possible for the Women Graduates Union to accomplish as much as it did without the continued support of many generous donors, advertisers, experts and dedicated members, who volunteered their time, talent and energy. Experts were invited by WGU for seminars and symposium open to all on current issues. It did not have any laboratory facility but had collaboration with S.N.D.T laboratory and also Mumbai Grahak Panchayat.

It held the membership of 'Bureau of Indian Standards', 'Consumer protection Council Set-up', 'Ministry Consumer Affair Government of India', 'State Level Federation'. It was also affiliated to 'Indian Federations of University of Women Association' and 'International Federation of University of Women'.

The publication of the organization included handouts titled 'Consumer Counseling Guidance', 'History of Women's Graduate Union' and 'Consumer Power' in English, Marathi, Gujarati and Hindi languages. Also a newsletter was brought our every month for its members, comprising of information on activities of various committees and global activities. In order to accomplish the objective of the organization, WGU organized seminars, discussions, workshops, skits, lectures and exhibitions. The future planned activity of WGU was to start a computer class for unprivileged girls, candle making and sewing classes and adult literacy class for parents of study center children.

Case 8: The Passengers and Traffic Relief Association

Established in 1915 the Passengers and Traffic Relief Association was one of the oldest consumer organization. There were one skilled and other unskilled personnel working in the organization's office. The membership strength of the organization was 623 members, most of them from urban areas.

The objective of the organization was to reduce the problem of commuting public by road, rail and air. The organization received around 60 complaints every year out of which around 50 per cent got redressal, which was the main activity of the organization. Besides, the organization was also involved in imparting education and giving legal guidance to consumers. It handled complaints, which were related to consumers utilizing the services of railways, buses, taxis, auto rickshaws, airplanes etc. Even a non-member consumer could avail the facility offered by the organization. The organization was a member of Consumer Protection Council Set-up. Along with the membership fees it also collected funds through donations, functions and fund collecting drives.

Earlier a Journal called "Rail news" was published by the organization in English, the publication of which was stopped since 1990. It highlighted topics like "Guidelines to passengers", and included articles that made public aware about latest development in any mode of transportation. Besides this, the organization was also involved in organizing awareness camps for the consumers. For the systematic working of the organization, it had appointed committees like executive committee and sub-committees under different heads like Railways, Roadways, Airways, and River ways.

The detailed case studies of the consumer organizations brought into light certain revelations that are presented as follows:

Age and Size of Consumer Organizations: Majority of the consumer organization were aged 35 years or less. One-fourth of them were in existence since 15 years or less and the same percentage were found running for more than 55 years. The organizations were small as well as large in their size. The paid employees strength ranged from 2 to 215.

Type of Consumer Organization: All the eight consumer organization studied were Non-Governmental organization and were functioning independently.

Membership Status and Pattern: The cases studied reveals that all the consumer organizations were offering life and yearly membership to the consumers. Consumer organization's life and yearly members ranged from 31 to more than 2000 and 15 to more than 17,000 members respectively. Viewing the pattern of membership of the consumer organizations it was found that their members on the basis of place were proportionately distributed. One-half of them comprised members from rural as well as urban population. The other one-half had members from urban population only. Most of them (66.66 per cent offered membership to Individual members. Only one of them had members in the form of institution, and corporate companies.

Membership Fees: The members of all the consumer organization were required to pay membership fees. Membership fees was one of the main source of funds for all the consumer organizations. Besides this, some of the organizations were found receiving funds from public interest groups, and charitable trusts.

Publications: As evident from the cases studied, that more than three-fourth (77.77 per cent) of the consumer organizations had publications of their own in the form of journals, books, handouts, booklets and newsletters. The topics covered by them in their publications included "Rights and responsibilities", "Consumer Protection Act, 1986", "Advantages of Breast Feeding", "Patients Rights", "Maternity Home Practices", "Available Bank Service and Rights of Consumers", "Protection of Consumer Laws" and "Food Adulterations", "Consumer Counseling Guidance", "Standardized products", "Health Awareness", Misleading Advertisements", "Consumer Movement", etc.

Educational Programs: More than one-half (55.55 per cent) of the consumer organizations were found possessing educational program for imparting education and creating awareness on consumer related issues. The main purpose of any educational program was to empower consumers to fight apathy, get redressal, become intelligent consumers, sensitive to the prevalent malpractices. As highlighted through the cases studies, that slightly more than one-tenth (11.11 per cent) of the consumer organizations possessed educational programs on the topics like "Adulteration", "Rights and Responsibility", "Misleading advertisements", "Breast feeding", and "III effects of Tobacco, Drugs", "Healthy living and Healthy food habits".

Media and Teaching Methods used by consumer organizations to impart education: The analysis of case-studies made it evident that there was a wide range of media and teaching methods being used by consumer organizations. The consumer organizations were found using medias like print (news paper, magazines, journals, booklets), radio, dramatized experiences (street play and skits) and video tapes. Teaching methods like lecture, discussion, demonstration, seminar, camps, workshops, puppet shows, slide shows, exhibitions were also used by consumer organizations to educate consumers.

Activities of Consumer Organizations: Data showed (Table 1) that all the consumer organization were involved in redressal activity. Redressal activity involved fighting for the better services to consumers, fighting individual issues, and solving consumer complaints. It includes protection of overall consumer interest. One-half of the consumer organization dealt with all types of complaints. But the other organizations dealt with issues and complaints of specific subjects like bank, medical negligence, telephone, traveling by railway, bus, taxi, auto-rickshaw, and air etc.

Table 1
Distribution of Consumer Organizations by their Activities

(n=8)

Activities	*f*	%
Redressal Activities	8	100
Legal Counseling	7	87.50
Awareness campaigns	3	37.50
Educational campaigns	7	87.50
Income Generation activities	4	50.00
Production of educative kit	1	12.50
Lab testing facility	0	0
Fund collection activity	7	87.50
Training program	5	62.50

Multiple responses.

Legal counseling comprised of activities like assisting people to file complaints, following them and seeking redressal. It also involved increasing awareness among people about legal rights and responsibilities. Majority of the consumer organizations were involved in legal counseling and guidance too.

Slightly more than one-third of the organizations were involved in awareness campaigns. This broad category included specific topics like social responsibilities, on dowry, hassled women, child care, health awareness regarding aids, drugs, tobacco, cigarettes, and awareness of rights and responsibilities.

Majority of consumers organizations were found being involved in organizing educational campaigns to empower consumers. The focus of their educational motive was to disseminate information on "Rights and Responsibilities of Consumers". "Ways and Methods of tackling Banking Problems", "Telecommunication Service Problems", "Medical Service Negligence Problems", and "Transport Problems". Of the eight consumer organizations, only one was found arranging demonstrations on income generating activities like candle making, soap and detergent making, handicrafts, cent stick making, and flower making.

Adulteration kit was produced by only one of the consumer organizations. None of the organizations had any laboratory facility for testing of the product, but more than one-half of the consumer organizations were found sending samples to other laboratories for testing them. Another one-half of the organization expected members to get it tested from outside on their own.

The main purpose of membership fees of all consumer organization was to collect funds. Fund raising was one of the important activities for members of the consumer organizations. Funds were collected by majority of the organizations from various sources like by organizing cultural functions, and other organizational aids. Other organizations gathered funds through membership fees only.

In order to ensure that the objectives of the consumer organizations are met efficiently the staff of the consumer organization whether voluntary or paid need to be trained properly. Nearly two-third of the consumer organization (62.50 per cent) were conducting training programs for their staff on subjects like "Development of effective communication skills, language development, demonstration of the activity concerned, exposure to the masses and leadership.

CONCLUSION

The developmental activities being undertaken by the selected consumer organizations to empower consumers were:

- Distributing brochures, journals, books, leaflet and monographs highlighting the rights and responsibilities of consumers based on the researches conducted.

- Empowering consumers by accelerating consumer awareness and educating masses.
- Collecting data on different products, testing them and informing the findings to consumers and business.
- Arranging talks, seminars, workshops and conferences for the purpose of focusing the problems of consumers and finding solutions thereof.
- Encouraging consumers for boycotting goods, which are defective and poor in quality by putting up confrontation and resistance.
- Filing suits, complaints and writ petitions on behalf of consumers before the courts.
- Investigating into problems of consumers.
- Resisting price rigging, preventing adulteration, hoarding and black-marketeering, and checking underweight selling.
- Educating the consumers to help themselves.
- Educating the women regarding consumerism.
- Organizing exhibitions concerning spurious, adulterated products etc, to create awareness.

Presently there is an urgent need of more number of well-organized, non-violent, strong, steady, vigilant, widespread network of consumer associations to empower consumers by promoting and protecting the consumer welfare, and preventing the malpractices of unscrupulous retailers, quick profit-seeking peddlers and unethical manufacturers. There is also a need to popularize their existence so that maximum number of urban and rural consumers could avail their services. Special efforts need to be initiated for rural consumers.

BIBLIOGRAPHY

Agrawal, A.D. (1989), A Practice Handbook for Consumers. Bombay. India Book and Course.

Azami, S.S.H. (1992), Sale Goods and Consumer Protection in India. New Delhi. Deep and Deep Publications.

Ghosh, A. (1992), The Theory of Consumer Behaviour and Welfare in Classical Paradigm. Bombay. Himalaya Publishing House.

Gulshan (1996), Consumer Protection and Satisfaction: Legal and Managerial Dimensions. New Delhi. New Age International Limited.

Himachalam, D. (1998), Consumer Protection and the Law. New Delhi. APH Publishing Corporation.

Jajie, M. (1977), The Indian Market Place: Guidance to Consumer Education. New Delhi. Brindavan Publishing House.

Loudon, D.L. and Della Bitta, A.J. (1993), Consumer Behaviour: Concepts and Applications. New York. McGraw Hill. Inc.

Mehta, S.C. (1993), Indian Consumer: Studies and Cases for Marketing Decisions. New Delhi. Tata McGraw Hill Publishing.

Seetharam, P. & Sethi, M. (2001), Consumerism: Strategies and Tactics. New Delhi. CBS Publishers.

Sethi, M. & Seetharam, P. (1994), Consumerism: A Growing Concept. New Delhi. Phoenix Publishers.

Sherlekar, S.A. (1984), Trade Practice and Consumer. Mumbai. Himalaya Publishing House.

Shah, Ami (2001), Development and Impact Assessment of Educational Program on Wise Buying, Unpublished Master's Dissertation, Dept. of Home Management, Faculty of Home Science, The M.S. Univ. of Baroda, Vadodara.

Sharma, C. (1995), Role of Consumer Organizations in Consumer Protection. New Delhi. Kanishka Publishing Distributors.

Singh, M.P. (1995), Consumer Protection Digest. New Delhi. Bharat Publishing House.

Sirkar, A. (1989), Problems of Consumers in Modern India. Delhi. Discovery Publishing House.

Sundram, S.I. (1985), Consumer Protection in India. New Delhi. B.R. Publishing Corporation.

Bibliography

"Contradictions Between Development and Environment", New Quest, September–October 1992.

"ECOSOC', Open Door Policies", Transnational Associations, No. 6, 1993, pp. 335–37.

"NGOs and conflict: three views", Humanitarian Monitor, 2, February 1995, pp.32–33.

"Non–Governmental Development Organization: From Development Aid to Development Co–operation", World Development, Vol. 15, Autumn 1987, pp. 69–77.

"People's Convergence: Shaping Our Future", Sagarmatha Declaration, Kathmandu, Nepal, 1996, Asian Action, Vol. 100, April–June, 1996.

"Social Crises and Transformative Politics", New Quest, November–December 1993.

A.S. Altekar, Education in Ancient India, Manohar Prakashan, Varanasi, 2000, pp. 19–20.

A.P.J. Abdul kalam and Y.S. Rajan. A Vision for the New Millennium, Penguin Books, India, 1998.

Abha, Vijal and Prakash. Voluntary Organizations and Social Welfare, ABD Publishers, Jaipur, India, 2000.

Agarwal, B., "Women, Poverty and Agricultural Growth in India". Journal of Peasant Studies, 1986.

Ahmed, I., "Technology and Rural Women in the Third World", International Labour Review, 1983.

All India Democratic Women's Association and Other (AIDWA). "National Perspective Plan for Women (1988–2000 AD). A Perspective from Women's Movement, Report of a Debate, August 22nd to 23rd, New Delhi.

Amitai, Etzioni. Modern Organizations, Prentice Hall of India Pvt. Ltd., New Delhi, 1965.

Ammu Menon, Muzumdar. Social Welfare in India, Asia Publishing House, Bombay, 1964.

Antonio Donini, "Missions impossibles',Le monde des debats, July–August, 1994.

Apffel, Marglin F. and Marglin, S.A. (eds.), Dominating Knowledge: Development, Culture, Resistance, Oxford: Clarendon Press, 1990.

Aruna Asaf Ali, 'An Agenda for National Renewal', IASSI Quarterly, Vol. 14, January–June, 1990.

Aurora, Shashikala Gayatri, et.al., "New Economic Policy, Voluntary Organisation and Rural Poor", Economic and Political Weekly, April 2, 1994.

Banerjee, N., Unorganized Women Workers: The Calcutta Experience, Calcutta: Centre for Studies in Social Sciences, 1982.

Bangia H. Administration of Project in Voluntary Organization. Social Welfare, Vol. 47 No. 11 Feb 2000, pp. 31–32.

Barbara Crossette, "UN Leader to Call for Changes in Peacekeeping", New York Times, 3 January 1995, A3.

Bardhan, P., Land, Labour and Rural Poverty: Essays in Development Economics, New York: Columbia University Press, 1984.

Baroda Citizens Council Project on Urban Community Development to Raise Levels of Living of Disadvantaged Groups in Baroda, 1976 (Cyclostyled Report).

Baroda Municipal Corporation, A Report on the slums of Baroda, 1976.

Barton, Morgan and et al., Methods in Adult Education. Interstate Publishers, Inc. Illinois, 1960.

Bauer, P.T., Equality, the Third World and Economic Delusion, Cambridge, Mass: Harvard University Press, 1981.

Bazwa Z. The Non–Profit Sector Non–Government Agencies and Entrepreneurship in Pakistan, Dissertation Abstract International, Vol. 52, No. 12, June 1992, 4483–4484.

Benedict Anderson, Imagined Communities: Reflections on the Origins and Spread of Nationalism. London: Verso, 1991.

Bertrand Schneider, The Barefoot Revolution, London: IT Publishers, 1988; and Alan Durning, "People power and development", Foreign Policy, 76, Fall 1989, pp. 62–82.

Beteille, A., Distributive Justice and Institutional Well–Being, text of V.T. Krishnamachari Lecture, mimeo., Delhi School of Economics, 1990.

Bhagwat P. "Evaluation of Condensed Courses of Education for Adult Women" Indian Journal of Adult Education Vol. 42; No. 10; Oct. 1981 pp.17–20.

Bhandari J. "Factors Affecting Persistency and Dropout of Adult Literacy Classes in Udaipur District" Ph.D. 1974 (Abstracted in Buch M.B. ed. A Survey of Research in Education, CASE M. S. University of Baroda 1974).

Bhasin, K. Ed. Towards Empowerment, Report of F.A.D., FFHC / AD, South Asia Training for Women Development Workers, 2004.

Bhatia A. Women's Development and NGOs. Rawat Publications, Jaipur and New Delhi, 2000.

Bhatt Usha. The Physically Handicapped in India–A Growing National Problems. Poona Oriental, Waterman Publishing House, 1963.

Bikram K. Pattanaik. "Empowerment of Women and Rural Development" Yojana, October 1997, p. 26.

Bottomore, T.B. Sociology: A Guide to Problems and Literature, George Allen and Unwin Ltd., London, 1982.

Brahmbhatt, U. Study of marriage counseling service provided by Karelibaug Bhagini Samaj Trust, Dissertation (M.S.W.).... M.S. University, Baroda, 1996.

Britto, G.A.A., Participation, Draft paper presented in the Ph.D./M.Phil. seminar held at the Tata Institute of Social Sciences, Bombay on Octrober 26, 1981.

Chakravorty S. Ed. "Rural Women's Claim to Priority: A Policy Debate", Selected Documents from International and Indian Archieves, 1975–85, Centre for Women's Development Studies, New Delhi.

Chandra Mouli, Role of Voluntary Organization in Social Development, Sterling Publication, New Delhi, 1990.

Chandra Subhash, "An Evaluation of Urban Community Development in India. Community Development Journal Vol. 9 No. 3. Oct. 1974 pp.191–202.

Chandra, S. NGOs Structure Relevance and Function, Kanishka Publishers, Distributor, New Delhi, 2001.

Chatterji, J. Ed. The Women's Decade 1975–85. An Assessment, "Published by ISPCK, Delhi, for WCSRC–CISRS–JWP, New Delhi, 1986.

Chaudhari Paul D. Voluntary Effect ın Social Welfare and Development, Sidhartha Publications, New Delhi, 1988.

Chaudhary, D. Paul Voluntary Social Welfare in India, Sterling Publication (P) Ltd. New Delhi, 1971.

Cohen, Lillian, Statistical Methods for Social Scientist, Prentice Hall of India Pvt. Ltd., New Delhi, 1983.

Collins, Randall, Sociological Insight: An Introduction to Non–Obvious Sociology, New York: Oxford University Press, 1982.

Copley, Brent Herbert, "Canadian NGOs: Past Trends, Future Challenges", World Development, Vol. 15, Autumn 1987.

D. Bandyopadyay, "Voluntary Organisations and Panchayats". Mainstream March 25, 1997, p. 12.

D.R. Sachdeva. "Social Welfare Administration in India" Kitab Mahal Distributions, New Delhi, 2002.

Dandekar V.M. and Rath N. "Poverty in India"–(Indian School of Politics and Economics, 1970) Indian Behavioural Science Abstract Vol. 2, No. 2, June 1971.

David Cooperrider & William Pasmore, "The organization dimension of global change', Human Relations, 44 (8), 1991, p. 764.

Dayal R, Ed. Resource Book on Women's Development, Cooperation with Government Donars and Voluntary Organizations, SIDA and Dept. of Women and Child Human Resource Development, Government of India, 1984.

Decen D.A. & Robbins S.P. Personnel/Human Resource Management, New Delhi, 1989.

Desai A.N. "Helping the Handicapped" Problem and Prospects Ashish Publication, 1990.

Desai N. and Krishna Raj. M. Women and Society in India", Ajantha Publications, New Delhi, 2003.

Desai N. Report of the World Conference to Review and Appraise the Achievements of U.N. Decade for Women. Equality, Development and Peace, Nairobi, July, 15th to 26th 1986.

Deshpande, Vasant, Developing Voluntarism, Pune, Gramayan, 1981, (mimeo.).

Dhama, O.P. Education and Communication for Development, Oxford Publication; New Delhi, 1985.

Directorate of Non–formal (Adult). Ministry of Education and Social Welfare Government of India, New Delhi. Non–formal Education; Directions and Responsibilities. 1975.

Discussion of the literature about NGOs in the context of teaching international relations, international law and international organizations, see Lawrence T Woods, 'Nongovernmental organizations and the United Nations system: reflecting upon the Earth Summit experience', Research Note, 18(1), 1993, pp. 9–15.

Dixon, R., "Mobilizing Women for Rural Employment in South Asia: Issues of Class, Caste and Patronage", Economic Development and Cultural Change, 30, 1982.

Drabek, Anne Gordon, "Development Alternatives: The Challenge for NGOs: An Overview of the Issues", World Development, Vol. 15, Autumn 1987.

Dreze, J. and Sen, A., The Political Economy of Hunger, 3 Vols., Oxford: Clarendon Press, 1990.

Dror, Yehezkel, "Request for helpwith preparation of a Club of Rome report on Governance for the 21st Century", Transnational Associations, N.I. 1992.

Dubey, Muchkund (ed.), Indian Society Today: Challenges of Equality, Integration and Empowerment, New Delhi: Har Anand Publishers, 1995.

Economic Times (The), NGOs blame IBRD for ignoring $68–meco projects in India', Mumbai, October 23, 1996.

Eliott, Charles, "Some Aspects of Relations Between the North and the South in the NGO Sector", World Development, Vol. 15, Autmun 1987.

Ellien Young Husband: "Social Work and Social Change", Published by National Institute for Social Work Training, London, 1964.

Encyclopedia of Social Work in India issued by Director, Publications Division, Ministry of Information and Broadcasting, 1972.

Encyclopedia of Social Work in India, Vol. 1.

Encyclopedia of Social Work in India, Vol. 2.

Etzioni, A. The Modern Organization, Prentice Hall, New Delhi, 1981.

Evelyn W. Hersey, The Future of Voluntary and Private Welfare Agencies in India T.C.M. American Embassy, New Delhi: 1990.

Evelyn W. Hersey. "The Future of Voluntary and Private Welfare Agencies in India", Published by American Embassey, 2002.

Farquhar J.N.; Religious Movements in India; Munshiram Manoharlal, Naisarak, New Delhi, 1999.

Ferreira, J.V., "The Therapy of Methodological Reversal' in A.M. Shah, B.S. Baviskar and E.A. Ramaswamy (eds.), Social Structure and Change, New Delhi: Sage, 2004.

Fishkin, J.S., "Can There Be a Neutral Theory of Justice?", Ethics, 93, 1983.

For detail see Proceedings of the All India Conference of Voluntary Social Agencies and Workers held on 20–21 March, 1995, Association of Voluntary Social Agencies and Workers (India), New Delhi.

Fox, Thomas H., "NGOs from the U.S.", World Development, Vol. 15, Autumn 1987.

G.R. Madan, 'Indian Social Problems', Social Work, Vol. II, New Delhi: Allied, p. 79, 1994.

G.R. Madan, 'Welfare Organisations and Foreign Funds', Voluntary Welfare Periodical, Vol. I No. 5, August, pp. 1–2, 1992.

G.R. Madan, 'Welfare Services for the Slum Dwellers of Delhi', India's Social Transformation, Vol. II: Problems of Welfare and Planning, New Delhi: Allied, pp. 317–397, 1996.

G.R. Madan, A Guide for Voluntary Social Workers in India, New Delhi: Allied, pp. 16–34, 1989.

G.R. Madan, Cooperative Movement in India: A Critical Appraisal, New Delhi: Mittal Publications, p. 449, 1994.

Gajerndragadkar S.N. "Disabled in India" Bombay Somaiya Publication (P) Ltd., 2000.

Gaonkar, R. Role of SHGs in Empowerment of Women, Zuarinagar, Goa. Mimeographed paper read as ISTR Sixth International Conference, Contesting Citizenship and Civil Society in a divided world, Toronto. Canada, 11–14 July, 2004. (www.jhu.edu/nistr/conferences/toronto/abstracts/gaonkar.pdf)

Garfinkel, H., 'The Origin of the Term 'Ethnomethodology' in Roy Turner (ed.), Ethnomethodology: Selected Readings, England: Penguin Education, 1974.

Gomes, I. Role of Voluntary and Other Organizations in Development, Yojana, Vol. 33, No. 23, pp. 28–31, 1989.

GOMES, LAWRENCE Role of Voluntary and Other Organisations in Development. Yojana, Vol. 33, No. 23, pp. 28–31, 1989.

Gore, M.S. Social Work and Social Work Education, Asia Publishing House, Bombay, 1985.

Gore, M.S., Social Policy and The Sociologist, Presidential Address, XVI All India Sociological Conference, 1982 at Annamalai University, Annamalainagar, December 29–31, 1982.

Government of India, Literacy Mission Report, 1990.

Gulhati R., Gulhati K., Mehra A., Ranjan J. Strengthening Voluntary Action in India, Ashish Publication, New Delhi, 1995.

H.M.S.O., Report of the Working Party on Social Workers in the Local Authority, Health and Welfare Services; 1998.

Hall, Anthony and James Midgley (eds.), Development Policies: Sociological Perspectives, Manchester: Manchester University Press, 1988.

Harshad R. Trivedi. NGO: An Omnibus Myth. Paper presented at the meeting of members of Acharyakul, Gujarat Vidhyapith, Ahemdabad, 1999.

Helan Witmer. "Social Work" An Analysis of a Social Institutions, Published by Rinchart & Co., Inc., New York, 1962.

Heresy Erelyn. The Future of Voluntary and Private Welfare Agency in India, American Embassy, New Delhi, India, 1990.

Hirsch, F., Social Limits to Growth, London: Routledge, 1977.

Hirschman, Albert O., "Reactionary Rhetoric", The Atlantic Monthly, May 1989.

Hobman David; A Guide to Voluntary Service; H.M.S.O., London, 1969.

I. David Brown. 'Bridging organizations and sustainable development', Human Relations, 44 (8), 1991, pp.807–831. Brown argues that 'development sustainability depends in part on institutional factors–effective local organizations, horizontal linkages that enable intersectoral cooperation, and vertical linkages that enable grassroots influence on policy–making–that can be influenced by bridging organizations'. Ibid, p. 825.

I. Satya Sundaram (1986) Voluntary Agencies and Rural Development, B.R. Publishing Corporation, New Delhi p. 264.

I. Satya Sundaram. Voluntarism in the New Millennium. Social Welfare Vol. 46. No. 11. Feb 2000 p.11–14.

Ibid, Also see A.F.C. Bourdilon (ed.), Voluntary Social Services: Their Place in Modern state, London: Methuen; and William Beveridge, 1979, Voluntary Action in a Changing World, London: Bedford Square Press, 1975.

India Papers (The), Aspects of NGO Participation in Social Forestry, Bangalore, September, 1986.

India, Department of Women and Child Development. Ministry of Human Resource Development. National Perspective plan for Women 1988–2000 A.D. Government of India, 1988.

Indian Adult Education Association "Handbook for Adult Education Instructors" New Delhi, 1980.

Indian Council of Social Welfare; Role of Volunteers in Social Work (Report of the Seminar; March 1964).

International Conference of Social Work; Mobilising Resources for Social Needs; Tokyo 1978.

International Conference of Social Work; Social Work in a changing World–Its Functions and Responsibilities; Rome, 1981.

Jackie Smith, Ron Pagnucco & Winnie Romeril, "Transnational social movement organizations in the global political arena", Voluntas, 5 (2), 1994, p. 1077.

Jacob, K.K. Social Development Perspectives, Himanshu Publication, New Delhi, 1997.

Jain, D. and Banerjee, N., Tyranny of the Household: Investigative Essays on Women's Work, New Delhi: Vikas, 1985.

Janie Leatherman, Ron Pagnucco & Jackie Smith, International Institutions and Transnational Social Movement Organizations: Challenging the State in a Three–level Game of Global Transformation, Working Paper Series, South Bend, IN.: Kroe Institute, October 1993, p. 4.

Jencks, Christopher, Rethinking Social Policy, Cambridge: Harvard University Press, 1992.

Jhamtani, A., Bhat C.M., and Singh, P., Role of Women Panchayat Members, Project Report (unpublished), New Delhi IARI, 1995.

Johan Kaufmann & Nico Schrijver, Changing Global Needs: Expanding Roles of the United Nations System, Hanover, NH: Academic Council on the United Nations System, 1990, pp. 40–45.

Johnson, M. Harry., Sociology: A Systematic Introduction, Allied Publication Pvt. Ltd., Bombay, 1966.

Joshi, M. Women's Empowerment Experience from Watershed Project. Social Welfare, Vol. 51, No. 4, July 2004, pp. 32–37.

K.A. Suresh, 'Role of Non Governmental Organizations in Development" Kurukshetra, October 1998 p. 59.

K.K. Mukherjee. 'Voluntary Organizations in Rural Development'. Voluntary Action, July–August, 1979. Section II p. 3.

Kalpana Sharma 'How Free are the Rural Women' The Hindu Sept. 19, 1997.

Karat, Prakash, "Action Groups/Voluntary Organizations: A Factor in Imperialist Strategy", The Marxist, Vol. 2, April–June 1984.

Kaul, A. Educational, Economic and Social Impact of Voluntary Training Agencies offering Income Generating Programmes on Low Socio Economic Status Women of Baroda City. Ph.D. (Thesis)....., M. S. University, Baroda, 1990.

Khinsuka, S.K. Social Work in India, Sarvodaya Sahitya Samaj, Jaipur, 1962.

Kothari, Rajni, "The Non–Party Political Process", Economic and Political Weekly, February 4, 1984.

Kripa, A.P., "Ratiha Sangha's Political Dilemma", Economic and Political Weekly, January 21, 1995.

Krishnaji, N., "Poverty and the Sex Ratio: Some Data and Speculations", Economic and Political Weekly, 22, 1987.

Kulkarni, Sharad, Social Mobilisation Groups: A Review, 1981 (mimeo.).

Kumar A. Human Resource Development An Interdisciplinary Approach Volume 1 & 2, New Delhi: Anmol Publications, 1991.

Kumar J. A Study of Voluntary Welfare Org. in the city of Baroda. Unpublished Master's Dissertation, Faculty of Social Work, M. S. U., Baroda, 1967.

Lalitha B.T. NGOs in Development, Rawat Publication, Jaipur and New Delhi, 1997.

Lalitha N.V. Voluntary Work in India, A Study of Volunteers In Welfare. National Institute of Public Co–operations and Child Development, New Delhi, 1975.

Latitha, N.V. and Kohli, M. Status of Voluntary Effort in Social Welfare, NIPCCD, New Delhi, 1982.

Lawani, B.T., NGOs in Development, Rawat Publication, Jaipur and New Delhi, 1999.

Lester M. Salamon & Helmut K. Anheier, The Emerging Sector: An Overivew, Baltimore, MD: Johns Hopkins University Institute for Policy Studies, 1994.

Lipton, M., "Poverty, Undernutrition and Hunger", World Bank Staff Working Paper, Washington, DC: The World Bank, 1983.

Lucy T.V. Social Reforms to Voluntarism in India, Legal News and Views, December 1993. pp. 42–424.

M.L. Datwa, Harsh Sethi, Pravin Visaria. Social Change through Voluntary Action edited by Sage Publications, New Delhi, 1998.

M.A. Muttalib, 'Voluntarism and Development: Theoretical Perspectives', Indian Journal of Public Administration, Vol. XXXIII No. 3, July–September, p. 400, 1987.

Macmillan and Max Siporin. Introduction to Social Work Practice, New York, 1975.

Madan, GI.G.R., Indian Social Problems, Vol. I Allied Publishers Pvt. Ltd., Bombay, 1966.

Maithani, B.P. Voluntary Organisations as Partners in Promoting Participatory Development, Kurukshetra, Vol. XLIII, No. 5, pp. 3–5, 1995.

Mangesh Kulkarani, The Political Discourse of Voluntarism in India. New Quest Jan–February 1998 p. 26.

Maria Garner, "Transnational alignment of nongovernmental organizations for global environmental action'. Vanderbilt Journal of Transnational Law, 23 (5), 1991, p. 1077.

Mazhar Ali Sabri 'Ensure Rural Women's Participatory Power', Social Welfare October 1998, p. 10.

Mazumdar, Haridas T., Grammar of Sociology: Man in Society, Bombay: Asia Publishing House, 1966.

Mazumdar, V., Emergence of Women's Questions in India and the Role of Women's Studies, New Delhi: Centre for Women's Development Studies, 1985.

Meher C. Nanavatty & P.D. Kullarni. NGOs in the Changing Scenario, Uppal Publishing House, New Delhi, 1998.

Mehrotra F.P. & Khanna Kailesh "A Model for Teaching Girl–dropouts in City slums" Indian Journal of Adult Education Vol. 44; No.7; July 1983; pp.11–17.

Mehta and Das, NGOs and Women Empowerment in Pandya R.M., and Mathu, A.A. (Eds.), Imbibing value education–various perspectives, Kalpaz Publications, Gyan Book House, 2003, pp. 163–167.

Ministry of External Affairs, "India National Report" for World Summit on Social Development, Government of India Publication, 1995.

Ministry of Finance, Government of India. Economic Survey 1998–99 p. 144.

Mohsini, S.R. "Eradication of Illiteracy: Towards a Comprehensive Programme. "Indian Journal of Adult Education Vol. 43: No. 8–9. Aug–Sept, 1982.

Morris Mary; Voluntary Work in Welfare State; International Library of Sociology and Social Reconstruction; London, Routledge & Kagan Paul, 1990.

Munshi, K.M.; British Paramountcy and Indian Renaissance (Part II); Bombay, Bharatiya Vidya Bhavan.

Muzaffar, Chandra, A Letter to NGOs in Asia, (12 August 1992), circulated on the eve of a World Conference on Human Rights organized by the UN Centre for Human Rights in Vienna, Austria in June 1993. The Heads of Government were to assemble in this meeting (Bayan Baru, Penang, Malaysia).

Muzumdar Ammu Menon; Social Welfare in India–Mahatma Gandhi's Contribution: Bombay. Asia Publishing House, 1964.

Naik J.P., 'Non Formal Education in India: A Retrospect and a Prospect", in 'Non–Formal Education and the NAEP', Shah and Bhan (Eds) Delhi Oxford University Press, 1980.

Narain, U.A., Social History of Modern India; Meenakshi Prakashan, 1972.

Narayan E.A., Voluntary Organization and Rural Development in India. Uppal Publishing House, New Delhi, 1990.

Natarahab S., A Century of Social Reform in India, Asia Publishing House, Bombay, 1962.

Natarajan, S., Century of Social Reform; Bombay, Asia Publishing House, 1980.

National Council of Social Service & National Institute for Social Work Training; Voluntary Worker in the Social Services; London, Allen & Unwin Ltd., 1969.

Nayar D.P. 'Urbanisation and Adult Education' Indian J. of Adult Education Vol. XXXV No. 4–5 April/May 1974. pp.13–17.

Naylor N. Harriet; Volunteers Today–Finding, Training & Working with them; New York. Association Press, 1967.

Non–Governmental Voluntary Organizations: The True Mission, Kollam, Kerala: Mass Line Publications, 1995.

Norman Johnson Basit Blackwell and Mortin Robertson Voluntary Social Services, Oxford Publication, Delhi, 1981.

Novak, Michael (ed.), Democracy and Mediating Structures, Washington, DC: American Enterprise Institute, 1980. See especially Novak's Changing the Paradigms: The Cultural Deficiencies of Capitalism', pp. 180–200.

Oomen, T.K., 'Analysing rural Social Change: A Perspective' in M.N. Srinivas and S. Seshaiah (eds.), Dimensions of Social Change in India, New Delhi: Allied Publishers Pvt. Ltd., 1977.

Padron, Mario, "NGOs and Grassroots Development in Latin America", Paper presented at the XIII International Congress of the Latin American Studies Association (LASA), Boston, October, 1986.

Pandya, R.M. NGOs–Towards Self–Reliance. Social Welfare. Vol. 43, No. 5, August 1996, pp. 22–24.

Parmar B.A. A study of Voluntary Welfare Org. in the City of Baroda. Unpublished Master's Dissertation, Faculty of Social Work, M.S.U., Baroda, 1967.

Patel C. (Edu.). Social Work Practice, Religion, Philosophical Foundations, Rawat Publications, Jaipur, 1999.

Peter Spiro, "New Global Communities: Nongovernmental Organizations in International Decision Making Institutions". Washington Quarterly, 18 (1) 1995, p. 48.

Pilling, Geoffrey, The Crisis of Keynesian Economics: A Marxist View, London: Croom Helm, 1986.

Planning Commission, Government of India (Ed.) Plan and Prospects of Social Welfare in India, New Delhi, 1955.

Planning Commission, Government of India (Ed.), Social Welfare in India, New Delhi, 1963.

Planning Commission, Government of India. Ninth Five Year Plan, 1997–2000 Vol. II p. 123.

Pran Chopra 'Dilemmas of Voluntary Agencies' Indian Express, April 23 and 24, 1981.

Pruthi, R.K. Manual of NGOs How to Manage? Crest Publishing House, New Delhi, 2000.

Punalekar, S.P., "Poverty, Management and Politics", Economic and Political Weekly, November 24, 1990.

R. Sooryamorthy 'NGOs Need for a Code of Ethics'. The Hindu January 19, 1999.

R. Sorryamorthy: Have NGOs Lost the Spirit of Voluntarism". The Hindu October 27, 1998.

R.C. Majumdar, 'Social Work in Ancient and Medieval India' in A.R. Wadia (Ed.), History and Philosophy of Social Work p. 22, 1961.

Rakiya Omaar & Alex de Waal, Humanitarianism Unbound? Discussion Paper No. 5, London: African Rights, November 1994, p. 6.

Ram, N., "An Independent Press and Anti–Hunger Strategies: The Indian Experience", in Dreze and Sen (1990), Vol. I.

Ramachandran, K.N., "Ambedkarism: Ideology for a New Ruling Class Alternative", Red Star, Thrissur, June and July 1994.

Ramani, M.N. Communication in Home Science Extension. New Indian Press. New Delhi, 1968.

Ramesh C. Shrivastava. Securing People's Partnership for Progress. Social Welfare Vol. 46, No. 11, Feb–2000 p. 15–18.

Rana K. People's Participation and Voluntary Action, Dimension, Roles and Strategies, Kanishk Published, Distributors, New Delhi, 2001.

Rana, K., People's Participation and Voluntary Action. Dimension, Roles and Strategies. Kanishka Published, Distributed, New Delhi, 2001.

Rino J. Patti. The Hand Book of Social Welfare Management, Sage Publications, New Delhi, 2000.

Robert D. Hermen and David O Renz. Non Profit Organizational Effectiveness, New Delhi, 1998.

Robson, Lacke and Dawson, User Involvement in the Control of Voluntary Organizations, 1997 (www.irf.org.uk).

S.R. Maheshwari, 'Voluntary Action in Rural Development in India', Indian Journal of Public Administration, July–September, p. 566, 1987.

Sangave, Vilas, Dakshin Bharat Jain Sabhecha Itihas, 1976, pp. 9–30.

Sarma, Nandita "Preparation of Adult Education Teachers: Methods and contents" Indian Journal of Adult Education Vol. 43, No. 5 May 1982 pp. 18 to 20.

See Francesco Mezzalama & Siegfried Schumm, Working with NGOs: Operational Activities of the United Nations System with Non–governmental Organizations and Governments at the Grassroots and National Levels, Geneva: Joint Inspection Unit, 1993, document Jiu/REP/93/1.

Sen, A. and Williams, B. (eds.), Utilitarianism and Beyond, Cambridge: Cambridge University Press, 1982.

Sen, Amartya, Inequailty Reexamined, Cambridge: Harvard University Press, 1992.

Sen, S. Voluntary Organisations and Women Development. Dissertation (MSW)..., M. S. University, 1994.

Shah Dinesh. "Voluntary Agencies in the Seventh Plan". Voluntary Action. March–April, 1985, Vol. 27.

Shah Ghanshyam. Economic Differentiation and Tribal Identity. Ajanta Publications, Delhi, India, 1984.

Shah Ghanshyam. Economic Differentiations and Tribal Identity, Ajanta Publications, Delhi, India, 1984.

Shah, A.M., B.S. Baviskar and E.A. Ramaswamy (eds.), Social Structure and Change (Vol. 1: Theory and Method: An Evaluation of the Works of M.N. Srinivas), New Delhi: Sage, 1996.

Shakuntala Balaraman and Visa Rarindran. 'Changing Face of Voluntarism' The Hindu (Magazine Section) November 29, 1998.

Shan, H.R. Voluntary Action in Environmental Awareness Programmes, Paper Presented in UGC National Seminar on Environment: Problems and Issues for Education. Oct. 16–18, 1999 Shimla Department of Education, H.P.U., Shimla.

Sharma, U., Women, Work and Property in North–West India, London: Tavistock, 1980.

Shashi Ranjan Pandey. Community Action for Social Justice, Grass Roots Organizations in India, Sage Publications, New Delhi, New Bury Park, London, 1980.

Shiva, Vandana, "Democracy in the Age of Globalization", Asian Action, Vol. 100, April–June 1996.

Singhal, C.S. Assam: Survey of NGO activities. Social Welfare, Vol. 45, No. 10, January 1998, pp. 24–29.

Siwach, R.K. Perspective Role of VOs in Tenth Plan. Social Welfare, Vol. 50, No. 11, February 2003, pp. 13–15.

Sondhi G.D. "A Plan for Youth Welfare" Ministry of Education and Youth Welfare, New Delhi, 1968.

Srinivasan, T.N. and Bardhan, P. (eds.), Poverty and Income Distribution in India, Calcutta: Statistical Publishing Society, 1974.

Stephen P. Marks, "Forgetting "The policies and practices of the past": Impunity in Cambodia', The Fietcher Forum of World Affairs, 18 (2), 1994, pp. 17-43; and Jarat Chopra, United Nations Authority in Cambodia, Occasional Paper #15, Providence, RI: Watson Institute, 1994.

Subramanian, S., "The Liberal Paradox with Fuzzy Preferences", Social Choice and Welfare, 4, 1987.

Sundaram I.S. Voluntary Agencies and Rural Development, B.R. Publishing Corporation, Delhi, 1980.

Suresh, K.A. Participation of beneficiaries in the Developmental Programmes of NGO in Kerala. Journal of Rural Development, Vol. 9, No. 5, September 1990, pp. 911–915.

The First Five Year Plan issued by Director Publications Division, Ministry of Information and Broadcasting, New Delhi.

The National Association for Public School Adult Education "A Treasury of Techniques for Teaching Adults." Washington D.C. 1964.

The Second Five Year Plan issued by Director Publications Division, Ministry of Information and Broadcasting, New Delhi.

The Third Five Year Plan issued by Director Publications Division, Ministry of Information and Broadcasting, New Delhi.

Thomas, William V., "Voluntarism in the Eighties", Congressional Quarterly, Inc. Vol. II, No. 22.

Thorner, Alice, "Nehru, Albert Mayer and Origin of Community Development Projects", Economic and Political Weekly, January 24, 1981.

Turner, Roy (ed.), Ethnomethodology: Selected Readings, England: Penguin Education, 1974.

UN, Economic and Social Council, Open–Ended Group on the Review of Arrangements for Consultations with Non–Governmental Organizations,

'General review of arrangements for consultations with non–governmental organizations', UN Doc. E/AC.70/1994/5 (26 May 1994), p. 18. Hereafter cited by document number.

UNESCO, Regional Office for Education in Asia–Reviews, Reports and Notes,– The Growing Interest in Non–Formal Education', No. 9, March 1976, pp. 15 to 26.

United Nations, Department of Public Information, "NGO/DPI List, Information for NGO Representatives", New York, July 1980.

V. Umathe 'Bhadrabharati', Small Life Sketch of Pujya Samantbhadra Maharaj (Marathi), December, 1991.

Vaidyanathan, A., "Food Consumption and the Size of People: Some Indian Evidence", Economic and Political Weekly, 20, 1985.

Vidyathi L.P. Rai B.K. The Tribal Culture of India, Concept Publishing Company, New Delhi, 1987.

Vyasulu, Vinod, Crisis and Response: An Assessment of Economic Reforms, Delhi: Madhyam Books, 1996.

Wadia A.R. (Ed.), History and Philosophy of Social Work in India, Allied Publishers Bombay, 1992.

Wadiwale, Role of SHGs in empowerment of women, Social Welfare, April 2004, Vol. 54, No. 11, pp. 20–25.

Windey, M.A. "A Rural Reconciliation Movement in India". Voluntary Action, March April, 176. Vol. XVII pp. 55–56 Times of India dated, 6th March, 1995.

Yadav, V. Role of NGOs in Improving Environment: A Study of SOCLEEN Activities" a paper presented in Annual Conference on Management and Environment: Challenges and Strategies Conducted by Gujarat Council for Educational Administration and Management (Jan. 11–12, 1998) Vadodara: Tejas Vidyalaya.

Appendix

APPENDIX - A

LIST OF NGOs WORKING IN BARODA

1. Adarsh Education Society
2. Akshar Trust
3. AKSHARA
4. Ambalal Sarabhai Foundation
5. Anand Bal Marg Darshan Kendra
6. ARogya Pracharak Mandal
7. Arpan Charitable Trust
8. Asha Special Education Centre
9. Association of Relations of the Chronically Mentally Ill Patients
10. B.M. Parikh Foundation Trust
11. Bal Bhavan Society
12. Baroda Citizens Council
13. Bhasha Research & Publication Center
14. Bhulka Bhavan
15. Bosco Snehalaya
16. Centre for Rural Care
17. Community Science Centre
18. Deepak Charitable Trust
19. Disha Charitable Trust
20. Friends Society
21. GSFC Science Foundation
22. Gujarat Nature Conservation Society
23. Gujarat Safety Council

24. Hariom Seva Trust
25. Helping Hands
26. Heritage Trust
27. I Create
28. International Society of Naturalists
29. Jagrut Grahak
30. Jeevan Akshay Charitable Trust
31. Jummadada Vyayam Mandir
32. Kamubala Sahakari Audyogik Vikas Mandir Ltd.
33. Kareilbaug Bhagini Samaj Trust
34. Lifeline Foundation
35. Maharani Chimnabai Stree Udyogalay
36. Mamasaheb Ghorpade Memorial Trust
37. Mangalam Shikshan Sanskar Bhavan
38. Mook badhir Mandal
39. Naisargi
40. NEEDS
41. Nutan Bal Shikshan Sangh
42. Olakh
43. Prem Trust
44. Premdas Jalaram Hospital
45. Quality Circle Forum of India
46. Sahaj Shishu Milap
47. Sahiyar
48. Sahyog Charitable Trust
49. Sankalp Foundation
50. SEVATIRTH
51. Shishu Palak Vrund
52. Shram Mandir Trust
53. Shree Laxminath Vyayam Mandir
54. Shri Laxmi Mahila Credit Co. Op. Society
55. Shroff Foundation Trust
56. Sindhu Sevak Sangh
57. Smt. Kamlaben Badhir Vidhyalaya
58. Sneh Setu Foundation
59. Snehdeep
60. Society for the Physically Handicapped
61. SOCLEEN

62. SVADES
63. Tree Lover's Edu. & Res. Foundation
64. Vadodara District Aids Control Society
65. Vadodara Society for Prevention of Cruelty to Animals
66. VCARE
67. Vikas Jyot Trust
68. Vivekanand Gramudyog Society
69. V–ONE Society

APPENDIX - B

DETAILS OF THE NGO'S WORKING IN BARODA

1. Community Science Centre
2. Karelibaug Bhagaini Samaj Trust
3. Kamubala Sahakari Audyogik Vikas Mandir
4. Shree Maharani Chimnabai Stree Samaj
5. World Vision
6. United Way of Baroda
7. Friends Society
8. Shramik Vidyapeth
9. Vikas Jyot
10. Baroda Citizen Council
11. BHASA
12. Jamuna Sanskruti
13. Shree Seva Tirth
14. Vadodara District AIDS Control Society
15. Nayee Roshnee
16. Olakh
17. Shayiar
18. Shri Jalaram Seva Samaj Trust
19. DISHA
20. ARPAN
21. Shroff Foundation

1
COMMUNITY SCIENCE CENTRE

Year of Establishment

1983.

Address

Community Science Centre
Institute of Engineers (1) Building,
Nandanvan, DDE ORG Building,
Sarabhai Chemical Premises,
Near Race Course, WadiWadi,
Vadodara–(0265) 321577, 381334.

INTRODUCTION

Community Science Centre (CSC) Vadodara was founded in the year 1983 with a view to promote and popularize Science and Technology among various sections of the Communities. It has been registered both as charitable trust and as Society. It is being governed by Governing Council, comprising of six founder members, donors, patrons and associate members and the invitees.

OBJECTIVE

- Development of Science Culture
- Inculcate an interest in Science
- Thinking of Science all around
- Informal Education
- Active Interaction

ACTIVITIES

During the last decade and a half, CSC has been carrying out number of extension programmes with the help of Models, Scientific Toys, Video Cassettes, Slides, Posters and Books and other Teaching Aids. Some of the activities carried out are given below:

- Science Fairs and Science Exhibitions are organized in association with member Industries and Institutions in and around Baroda on various topics of interest. Large number of students, teachers and members of public visit these exhibitions.
- Orientation programmes for Science Teachers for starting science promotion activities and science clubs in their schools.
- Workshops for Science Teachers and Students on "Making Low–cost Teaching Aids" using easily available material and explaining basic principles of Science.
- Organization of science fair and science exhibition on various topics such as 'Water', 'Transport', 'Environment', 'Communication Plans', 'Processes',

'Use of Modern Technology in Human Life', etc. there fairs and exhibitions have invited considerable interest among people, particularly the youths.

- Quiz programs, essay competitions, drawing competition, elocution competitions on science subject are conducted regularly.
- Publication of "Vigyan Jyot"–a quarterly magazine devoted to popularizing science with articles from students and experts in a regular features.
- Organization of popular science lectures on current topic of scientific importance.
- Conducting weekend science lessons.
- Science education trips and field visits.
- Proxy teaching in schools.
- National science day celebration.
- Vacations programs.
- Special programs for ladies, senior citizens, etc.
- Publication of "Vignan Jyot"–a quarterly magazine devoted to promotion of Science, since 1991.
- Display of popular science books, other exhibits and use of posters, video cassettes at various schools on number of subjects.
- Essay competitions, drawing competitions on topics such as energy conservation, modes of transport, science in daily life, etc.
- Vignan Kasoti–competition based on popular science books.
- Showing video cassettes, slides and posters on popular science subjects at the activity centre and also loaned to interested institutions.
- Special programmes on "Activity Oriented Science Teaching" in schools.
- CSC has established a "Science Activity Centre" at Anand Balwadi Campus, Gotri Road and another centre in collaboration with Bal Bhavan Society, located near Sayajibaug.

ADMINISTRATIVE STRUCTURE

President
(Shri. Ramanbhai B. Patel

↓

Chairman
(Dr. M. H. Mehta)

↓

Honorary Secretary
(Shri V. B. Desai)

↓

Joint Honorary Secretary
(Shri M. V. Naik)

FUNDS

Fund obtained from Government, institutions, individuals as donations, grants, sponsoring of specific activities and programmes, membership and subscriptions.

HIGHLIGHTS OF THE INSTITUTE

- In the year 1995 Governor of Gujarat gave 6.5 Lakhs to this institute and from this it came up Anand Balwadi at Gotri Road. They started with green house and Groeta Chamber.
- Live Tree Museum has been constructed by this institute which is sponsored by GSFC science foundation at fertilizer nagar, Vadodara.
- This institute has conducted a children play park with funds from Bal Bhavan society for children to understand science through games.
- They have planned several programmes for environment in collaboration with university students to promote science culture in the community.

2
KARELIBAUG BHAGINI SAMAJ TRUST

Year of Establishment

15th August, 1971.

Address

Karelibaug Bhagini Samaj Trust,
"DHIBA BHAVAN",
Near Adhyapak Nagar Society,
Water Tank Road,
Opp. Jain Mandir,
Karelibaug,
Vadodara–390 018.
Phone No. (0265) 2415848.
Email: bhaginisamaj@yahoo.com

INTRODUCTION

"Karelibaug Bhagini Samaj Trust" an organization which was instituted on 15th August, 1971, with the main aim and objective of physical, mental, intellectual, social and economical development of both women and children of Baroda city in Gujarat State of India. It aims at arousing in themselves the feeling of mutual love and cooperation and interest in them in Indian civilization in order to establish the society based on the principles of equal right and equal opportunity. Since last three decades it is observed that slowly and steadily the intensive theme for the betterment of women has figured up under one shadow of a large tree with the most healthy shelter of unity, still progressing ahead upto the present times.

OBJECTIVES

- The main objective is physical, mental, intellectual, social and economic development of women and children.

ACTIVITIES

1. *Health*

- Child Health Care and Mother's Advisory Centre: With the help of Baroda Municipal Corporation every Friday all kind of children vaccination are being administered free of cost. Appropriate advice on food nutrition and proper diet of children is given by highly qualified doctors at mother advisory centre.
- Homeopathic Clinic: The homeopathic treatment and medicine is provide free of cost with the cooperation of Divyajivan Sangh three days a week.

2. *Income Generation Activities*

- Industrial Cooperative Society: Women's are trained in household commodities like soap, detergent, phenyl, brooms, doormats, cleaning powder, etc.
- Mahila Udhyog Kendra: Domestic commodities like hand pulverized spcies, papad, pickle, dry snacks, etc. are prepared and sold at reasonable prices.
- Credit Cooperative Society: Concept of savings is encouraged among women and credits are provided to the needy members.

3. *Educational Activities*

- Computer Education: Short term certificate courses as well as diploma courses of computer programming and training on modern method of computer systems are provided at lower fees.
- English Speaking Classes: Practice for fluents command over vocabulary and language and grammatical guidance are given.
- Sewing and Embroidery Classes: The institute is running a government recognized CGM diploma courses in sewing and general courses in sewing course of tailoring and embroidery is run through Gujarat state women Economic development corporation. Sewing machines are also provided through Bank loan facilities. Leather and retain training centre is also running with the grant in aid from Gujarat Mahila Arthic Vikas Nigam, Gandhinagar.
- Beautician Training Course: Short term professional diploma courses in training in beauty parlour treatment, skin test and skin care are conducted. Mahendi design, fabric painting, nib painting, ceramic pot painting, glass painting, flower making, soft toys making are also conducted at the lowest fees.

4. *Social Activities*

- Family Counselling Centre: With the financial assistance of central social welfare board it provides necessary guidance, advice and aid into the family problems.

- Cultural Activities: Mahila mandal has been formed and various types of competitions and other festival and cultural programs like organizing picnics, tours, outings, funfairs, etc. are being carried out. This mahila mandal group is also ahead in lending helping hand to those needy who are victims of natural calamities and disasters.

ADMINISTRATIVE STRUCTURE

Trusties (11 Trusties)

↓

General Manager

↓

Manager

↓

Accountant

↓

Staff (32 persons)

FUNDS

Trust is registered under Public Trust Act, 1950 wide Vadodara E–2201 dated 3–4–73 according to the regulation of charity commissioner of Gujarat Government. Its PAN No. is AAATK–2365G dated 11–9–1999. Donations are exempted under sec 80G (5) of Income Tax Act, 1961.

HIGHLIGHTS OF THE INSTITUTION

- It was awarded a shield (Late Shri L. M. Patel Shield) in 1988 for giving impetus to women's activities in the district.
- It was recognized as best organisation for Best Women oriented activities by Baroda Citizens Council.

3
KAMUBALA SAHAKARI AUDYOGIK VIKAS MANDIR

Year of Establishment

1940.

Address

Saint Kabir Road,
Baranpura,
Baroda.
Phone No. (0265) 2427474, 2421474.

INTRODUCTION

Kamubala Shakari Audhyogik Vikas Mandal was started by Shri Baniya Chaganlal Zaveri in 1940. His wife's name was Kamuben. After her death he again married. His second wife's name was Baluben. Unfortunately she also died. Hence Shri Chaganlal Zaveri decided to indulge in social work, which would be for the upliftment of women. The basic purpose was that women should become independent. He sold his wives jewellery and got Rs. 500 out of it. From that money he started a small institution in the name of his late wives. In this way the Kamubala institution came into existence.

This institution was first started at Sadhana Talkies, near Tarkeshavari Mandir with machinery course at the cost of 25 paise. After that, this institution was registered by government in 1950. It started with two departments.

When this institution came to know that the same type of machinery institution is running at Bombay, they sent two women from the institution to gather more information about tailoring. After that in 1953, this institution started the embroidery classes along with tailoring classes. In 1955, the certificate training classes were started.

OBJECTIVES

- To develop the skill of women in tailoring so that they can be independent and can help their families in raising their standard of living.
- To make self employed women by increasing skill in stitching garments.

ACTIVITIES

- Sewing Course
- Embroidery Classes
- Tailoring Classes
- Beauty Parlour Course
- Mehendi Course
- Cooking Course
- Book Binding
- Training classes for job opportunity in Govt. offices
- Medical Health center for Women
- TTAC Course [Teacher's Training Adult Craft]

Alongwith learners the teachers of this institution are also given training. The examination is taken for teachers by the Gandhinagar Center, which than issues certificates.

COURSES

1. *Examination Courses*

In this type of courses there is a great job opportunity, because at the end of the year, they have to appear for the exam for which they get government certificate.

2. *Non–Examination Courses*

In this type of course, learners are not provided with any certificate by the government. The learners work for their interest. Here, learners do not require any fixed qualification. They only have practical work.

For, embroidery course there are three types of embroidery course.

- Hand Embroidery
- Simple Machine Embroidery
- Fancy Embroidery

3. *Training Courses*

The teachers teach the students both, the theory as well as practical work. The teachers take help of some of the books available in the market and also with the help of their own knowledge. For teaching they take help of their own knowledge. For teaching they take help of Machines, Black Board, Books, Pamphlets, etc.

Attendance is also taken regularly and those who remain absent for longer time, for them action is taken. The paper is of 100 marks.

This institution also formed a Mahila Mandali. Once a week the women of this mandali gather and conduct some activities like demonstration, some cultural activities, organizing picnics, etc.

AGE AND QUALIFICATION

For the training courses of tailoring and embroidery, the students should be minimum of 14 years old and should be 7th class passed. In these courses, women having different problems like marriage problems, low income groups, divorcee or widow, unemployed women can come for training in this institute.

TTAC COURSE [Teacher's Training in Adult Craft]

Along with learners the teachers of this institute are also given training. The examination is taken for the teachers by the Gandhinagar Center, which then gives certificates to them.

FUNDS

This institution gets finance from collection of fees and also from the Baroda Municipal Corporation [BMC] gives grant of rupees [2000–5000]. The accountant has to keep record of accounts, which then is submitted to the government for getting grants for the next year.

HIGHLIGHTS OF THE INSTITUTION

- This institution is non–Government institution but the examination of tailoring and embroidery course is taken by the Gujarat board of Gandhinagar.
- This institution also helps in buying a machine at subsided rate and give loans to economically poor women.
- There are 50–60 machines provided by the government worth Rs. 2200 each. There are fancy machines also of Rs. 5000 each. The women who

work in this institution have to bring their own cloth and sewing kit. Only the machines are provided to them by the institute.

4
SHREE MAHARANI CHIMNABAI STREE SAMAJ

Year of Establishment

1915.

Address

Maharani Chimnabai Stree Samaj
12, Sanstha Vasahat
Mir Bakar Vlivado, Raopura
Pratap Road, Vadodara.

INTRODUCTION

Chimnabai Stree Samaj is 75 years old. Dr. Chandrabadha and Maharani Chimnabai had started this institution in Jubilee Baug with one Small room. The rent of the room was Rs. 75/-. They get the money or financial help from the donors.

This institute was earlier on rent. But, afterwards they bought a new place of work. The place has the area of approximately 400 sq. feet and it is two storyed building which was bought by Sreemati Kamlaben, Todarmal, Seth Shamad Bechar and Shaikh Shree Rajmitra, Chimanlal. They also run one another unit which is also a part of this sanstha. This unit is called Gangaba Samaj. It is a working women's hostel. Gangaba Mutu Shree Banuben Jadiya is the Director of the institute. She comes every Friday for visit. 12 ladies forum a committee and conduct meeting. These ladies are chosen by the members through voting. This institution were offered government aid, but they refused as they don't prefer to take. This Sanstha handles and maintains things by itself. It is an independent kind of Sanstha. Earlier they had 2 machines but slowly as the number of trainees increased the number of machines also increased. They bought more and now [at present] they have 22 machines. This Sanstha has main working hours from morning 8 A.M. to 5 P.M.

OBJECTIVES

- To provide knowledge along with creativity.
- To provide self employment training.
- To help the females in raising their standard of living.
- It is voluntarily open for all the females.

ACTIVITIES

This institution provides a diploma course of 1 year, it also provides health awareness to the woman:

- Embroidery classes (with 52 stitching hand embroidery).

- Knitting (with thread and wool)
- Amprapalli dolls
- Stuff toys
- Kashmiri dolls
- Fabric painting
- Ceramic painting
- Paper Craft
- Fancy work

ADMINISTRATIVE STRUCTURE

Key Person.
(Smt. Banuben Jadiya)

↓

Teachers

↓

Accountant

↓

Helper

FUNDS

Donation from the donors.

HIGHLIGHTS OF THE INSTITUTE

Different recreational activities like Games, Navratries, Rangoli competitions are organized by the Institution.

Prizes are also given to the participants. Every Friday they play cards, have ice cream parties, picnics, undhiya party, etc.

The contribution of money is done half from the ladies themselves and half from the Sanstha. There are some dormant members who actively do not participate but they do give donations or funds and come only for their recreational purpose.

The girls coming here are generally SSC and HSC passed. And even graduate students also come over here but the number of widow ladies is more. Right now there are 24 diploma girls working and 30 general courses are present.

5
WORLD VISION

Year of Establishment

1962

Address

"Saleel Bunglow"
Opp Sonalika Apts.,
Fatehgunj Main Road,
Vadodara–390002.
Phone: (0265) 2792867.

INTRODUCTION

World Vision of India had started it's work in 1962 and was registered under the Tamil Nadu Society Act in March 1976. Today they help to meet the Educational, Health and other basic needs of 100,00 children spread over 480 projects, through its childcare and Community Development program in India. Under WEST ZONE, presently work is going on in Gujarat, Maharastra and Karnataka States through 23 Area Development Programs [ADPs] and 40 Traditional Projects.

OBJECTIVES

- To develop good relation with GO's and NGO's to facilitate integration of their efforts in rural development.
- To strengthen agriculture, the farmers are equipped with necessary skills and training.
- To improve general health of people and eradicate T.B. to make them aware about HIV / AIDS.
- To improve living conditions of poor people, so as to make their life meaningful and simple.
- Develop capabilities of the poor in their development process through leadership building on the principles of community participation and sustainable development approach.
- Create interest about education in children in order to reduce school dropouts.
- Street children of Vadodara to be assisted, so that they can live a dignified life with self esteem.

ACTIVITIES

- The main activity of the institute is related to street children.
- They provide saving credit scheme to the target group and have Rs. 20/– saving per month.
- Training in sewing and other area keeping in mind the need and interest of the target group.

Water Resource Development

- Installation and repairing of Handpumps.
- Installation of submersible pump.
- Facilitate water tank construction.

Agriculture

- Fertilizer distribution to needy farmers.
- Vermicomposting.
- Agriculture Training and field exposure.
- Demonstration plot.

Leadership Development

- Formation of youth groups
- Formation of village development committees.
- Sports competitions.
- Strengthening Local Governments at Panchayat level.

Education

- Education material and school uniforms to children.
- Pre–primary schools (Balwadis).
- Inter–School Sports competitions.

Community Health

- All diseases diagnostic camps for identification of diseases.
- Providing medicines as a part of follow up.
- Eye check–up camps and specks distributions.
- Medical treatment of needy children.
- T.B. identification camp.
- Nutritive food of T.B. patients along with regular monitoring for the doses of Dot, Prescribed by Government and WHO.

Women Development

- Women's awareness meetings.
- Training on animal husbandry and storage of grains through field exposure trips.
- Field exposure for Income Generation programs of women.

Networking

- Relationship building GO's / NGO's for possible resource tapping.
- Assisting community in creating awareness on availing Government Schemes/Loans.

Highlights of the Institute

- Till now they have given several sewing machines to the women for income generation.
- They provide 50% loan to the women for sewing machine.
- They distribute seeds for kitchen gardening.
- At Waghodia Taluka in Vasvel village they have provided training for sewing and stitching to the target group.
- Area development programme (Baroda) has been initiated in October 1996 poor and needy people of 23 villages øf Waghodia are being assisted through, various development activities.
- The main tribes in this area are Vasava and Baria.
- They organize area development programme to achieve a wider impact over area covering a larger population.
- They give education to the street children for self–development and also health in which attention is given to health programme.
- They also carry out emergency relief and rehabilitation in which several thousand of children and their families who have been rehabilitated and helped to find a new meaning in life.

6
UNITED WAY OF BARODA

Year of Establishment

1986

Address

Federation of Gujarat Industries building,
R.C. Dutt Road, Vadodara–5.
Ph. 0265–328091,320944.
Email: bcc.uwb@wbbs.net

INTRODUCTION

United Way is a global movement with a track record of more than 100 years. It has presence in 30 countries spread over 6 continents. The United Way of Baroda was started in 1986, with tripartite participation of Baroda. Citizens Council, United Way International and UNICEF for the initial period of five years. Since than it has emerged as a useful "Support Organization" in the city helping various health and Human care institution through the process of need based funds, pooled common services, dissemination of useful information, training and management assistance. Today a modest but critical assistance offered by the United Way of Baroda is appreciated by most NGOs which are its members.

Over the years, United Way of Baroda has given need–based assistance to the extent of Rs. 150 lakhs to support a wide range of much needed programmes and services in the city. Although all the programmes and services have their own importance, United Way of Baroda has chosen to allocate funds according to the priority and needs of the time, set upon it as an upfront service organization. This is the philosophy of need–based allocation that has served the United Way movement so well since its inception.

OBJECTIVES

- To assess and analyze the health and human care needs of the city.
- To provide financial as well as management assistance to the local voluntary health and human–care institutions of the city.
- To create spirit of sharing and caring amongst the citizens of Baroda.
- To set up volunteer based system of raising resources and distribution.
- To support voluntary development work and volunteerism.
- To promote partnership approach to city–level issues.
- To develop city affiliation.
- To spread the united way concept in other cities.

ACTIVITIES

- Health and Medicare
- Services for Disabled
- NFE & Recreation
- Women's organizations
- Animal Welfare
- Consumer Protection
- Center for Senior Citizens
- Literacy Group
- Center for Young Child
- Youth Organization

TRAINING PROGRAMMES

The following training programmes have been organized for the functionaries of NGO's:

- Fund raising.
- Project formulation.
- Use of audio visual aids.
- Use of computers in the development sector.
- Programme planning for NGO's.
- Low cost group media skills.
- How to bring out effective publication.
- Account writing and presentation.

- Effectiveness of voluntary organization.
- Enlarging the voluntary blood donation movement.
- Sale of medicines at subsidized rates to poor patients.
- Surgery, physiotherapy, aids and appliances and special education for disabled children.
- Informal science education.
- Garbage management.
- Consumers education and protection.
- Income generation, saving and credit associations for needy women.
- Animal welfare.

HIGHLIGHT OF THE INSTITUTION

Health and Human Care

- Drug Abuse and Alcoholism rehabilitation.
- Training of mentally retarded children.
- Medical rehabilitation, social integration and education of crippled, blind, deaf and dumb–children.
- Day care centres for young children and senior citizens.
- Sports and cricket camps for students.
- Housing, training, income generating activities and legal aid for needy women.
- Rehabilitation of street and working children.
- Meaningful vocational training, leprosy detection, treatment of Tuberculosis and Diabetes.
- Free medicine and treatment for the poor and needy.
- Science and computer training for young students and women.
- Animal welfare rescue, treatment and adoption.

7
FRIENDS SOCIETY

Year of Establishment

August, 1969

Address

Petit Library,
Opposite Parsi Agiyari,
Fatehgunj, Baroda–390002.
Gujarat, India.
Phone: 0265–2328629.

INTRODUCTION

Friends Society is a voluntary youth organization actively functioning since August 1969. The society is registered under Public Trusts Act 1950 (Regn. No. BARODA/F–109). Friends Society stands for the mobilization of voluntary efforts of young persons, especially University students, for conducting need based community service projects and developing their personality. Friends Society is a voluntary city level non–political organization run by the students of Maharaja Sayajirao University (M.S.U.) of Baroda. Its source of funds are: membership fees, fund raising programmes, monthly contributions from past members and well wishers, donations from individuals, trusts and other organisations. Friends Society has a band of volunteers who do everything possible to keep its overhead administrative cost to a bare minimum. Hence, almost all the money raised is used directly for service and developmental projects.

A BIT OF HISTORY... One day in August 1969, a group of students from the M. S. University of Baroda, decided to spend their spare time constructively. Gradually others joined and thus Friends Society was born. From modest beginnings, Friends Society has expanded in its concept and widened its range of beneficiaries.

PROJECTS... Friends Society carries out community service projects catering to five groups of beneficiaries:

1. The Handicapped
   Cheer–up
   Sunday School
2. The Poor And Needy Patients
   Blood Donation Programme
   Sheth Kushalchand Charitable Medical Centre
   Eye Donation
   Thalassaemia Patient Support Group
3. The School Children
   Programmes for Future Leaders
4. The Fatehgunj Community
   Public Reading Room and Library
   Child Health Care Centre
   Youth Club
   Integrated Balwadi
   Income Generation Programme
5. The University Youth
   Programme for the University Youth

MEMBERSHIP

Only persons who can devote a minimum of 2 hours a week for a service project can become members. Others enroll as Associate members, life members or paid patrons.

FEES

		Rs. / Year
Members & Students		20
Associate Members Non – students		30
Life Members	within India	400
	Outside Indian	1000
Patrons	within India	5000
Outside India		10000

HIGHLIGHTS

Friends Society publishes an annual newsletter – 'INVOLVE'.
An audio – visual about Friends Society and its projects has been prepared.

HOW YOU CAN HELP

You can help us, The Friends Society by becoming a life member or a paid patron. Can also help us through donations, releasing advertisements in our annual publication 'INVOLVE', donating blood, buying our greeting cards and sponsoring the education of a needy child. Donations to the Society are exempted under Section 80G (5) of the Income Tax Act, 1961. Cheques should be issued in favour of 'FRIENDS SOCIETY, BARODA'.

8
SHREE SHRAMIK VIDYAPEETH

Year of Establishment

April, 1984

Address

20, Gurukrupa Society,
Jalaram Mandir Marg,
Karelibaug, Vadodara–18.
Phone: 0265–2541067.

INTRODUCTION

Shramik Vidyapeeth, Baroda, is an autonomous organisation, registered under the Indian Society Registration Act 1980 [Gujarat 610, Vadodara, dated: 21–4–84]. Its activities are financed and monitored by the Ministry of Human Resource Development, Government of India, New Delhi.

OBJECTIVES

- To further the polyvalent education among the illiterate and economically deprived in urban areas.

- To conduct a wide range of training programmes.
- To develop skill that can help target group to earn additional income.
- To improve their technical skills and increase their productive ability.

ACTIVITIES

There are 33 training programmes in the Shramik Vidyapeeth. They are:

- Tailoring Training
- Hand Embroidery
- Patch Work
- Fabric Painting
- Nib Painting
- Soft Toys Making
- Glass Painting
- Chinese Dishes
- Bakery Products
- Farsan Making
- Scooter Repairing
- Computing Accounts Package
- First Aid Training
- Doormat Making
- Yoga
- T.V. Repairing
- Wireman Training
- Fancy Dress
- Machinery Embroidery
- Rakhi Making
- Ceramic Work
- Mehandi Application
- Raxine Article Making
- Punjabi Dishes
- South Indian Dishes
- Ice Cream
- Sweets Making
- Self Beautification and Hair Styles
- Sewing Machine Repairing
- Candle, Aggarbatti, Detergent, Powder Making
- Repairing of Electrical Appliances
- Screen Painting

HOW SHRAMIK VIDYAPEETH WORKS

The training programmes organized by the Vidyapeeth are specially tailored for a harmonious polyvalent approach to meet the various inter–related needs of target groups in an integrated manner. The approach is based on the principle that such target groups in an integrated manner. The approach is based on the principle that such target groups must have continued access to education and training that addresses their specific needs for the programmes to be worth while for the participants, their technical skills, social and cultural inputs, functional literacy, other educational and personal enrichment components such as health, family welfare, social education, etc... managerial inputs for running small businesses profitably and so on.

There is no age bar or educational restriction. The programmes are organized at centres that are convenient to the participants, only a nominal fee is charged, and the focus is constantly on actual practice orientation rather than theoretical training, deserving candidates are awarded certificates and recruits placed in fields according to the syllabus of the training programmes laid down by the institution.

OTHER MAJOR PROJECTS

Shramik Vidyapeeth, Vadodara, also offers Management's Training to unemployed educated youths to set up small business / training / industrial service units under the Prime Minister Rojgar Yogana sponsored by the District Industries Centre.

Under the International programmes an Elimination of Child Labour [IPEC] to be implemented over one year in Vadodara city. Shramik Vidyapeeth will conduct programmes at Woolen Carpet Weaving Center [Urban & Rural Unit], Furniture & polishing center [Urban Unit]. The entire infrastructural grant for this programme will be provided by the International Labour Organization.

The Shramik co–operative society managed by the Vidyapeeth is formed by, of and for the trainers who were the former participants of the Vidyapeeth's various training programmes.

THE SHRAMIK CO–OPERATIVE SOCIETY

The Shramik Co–Operative Society was formed as a formal sales outlets for products of the Shramik Vidyapeeth Beneficiaries. The society encourages the efforts of the members channelising their creative and idealistic energies towards constructive and result oriented activities. The society provides skilled members on contract for Building Maintenances and Domestic Wiring Job work also.

The co–operative society has a regular stock of materials like stitched and embroidered needle work items such as bed sheets, bed covers, pillow cases, cushion covers, dining table sets, handkerchiefs, wall hangings, carry bags, jewellary boxes, file–folders, spectacles cases, jackets, washing powder, candles, chalks, balms, doormats, kites, canned food products like pickles, jams, papads, dry snacks, rakhee, etc.

The society also accepts large–scale orders for specific items. Such intervention encourages the beneficiaries to give their best to experiment with newer ideas, invest in modest machinery to increase output and improve quality.

PRODUCTION CUM SALES AND SERVICE CENTRE

After undergoing vocational training, trained beneficiaries who may want to produce different articles for self–employment or for income generation can approach the Vidyapeeth for a sales outlet. Accordingly, the Vidyapeeth assists the beneficiaries through the sale of finished foods through the registered Baroda district Shramik Utpadak Sahakari Mandali Ltd. Hence, it plays a unique role in order to provide marketing facilities as well as technical support to the beneficiaries.

COLLABORATIVE AGENCIES AND HOW THEY CAN HELP

Shramik Vidyapeeth believe that non–formal education for the deprived classes is an on going process that needs to be sustained at different levels by the community as a whole. The Vidyapeeth therefore is always open to suggestion, co–operative effort and help from different organization, institution and socially – conscious individuals to promote the Vidyapeeth's programmes and continue to gainfully help participants to have positive and self–reliant lives.

9
VIKAS JYOT

Year of Establishment

1970

Address

Vikas Jyot
Near Nagarwada Char Rasta,
Vadodara – 390001.
Phone No. 0265–2412530, 2436032.

INTRODUCTION

Vikas Jyot had a modest beginning unlike quite a few voluntary service organisation. Its social service activities started under the banner of Shri Lalitadevi Stree Sahayak Audhyogik Co–operative Society as early as 1970 and Vikas Jyot came into existence with prime motive of providing legal counsel to distressed women and also with an idea to undertake supportive income activity geared towards economic uplift of needy women.

OBJECTIVES

- To educate women and children for their over all personality development.
- To help them seek independent identity through self–supporting earning and inject in them a sense of their usefulness to the society.
- To remove fear complex from them and make them aware and capable to fight against social injustice and inequality in marital life.
- To offer income oriented training courses to help needy and distressed women with independent source of income and establish them as important and earning member in the family with a status and respect.

ACTIVITIES

1. Family Advice Center

Counseling of the different problems such as: money management, childcare, husband wife relationship, family planning, etc.

2. Legal Advice Center

Under this legal guidance/advice is provided in different areas: divorce, property, land, theft, dowry.

3. Bakery Industry

This includes production and sale of biscuits, buns, cake, pastry.

4. Cattering Service

Providing service for the orders placed during occasions, marriages, festivals, etc.

5. *Tiffin Services*

Tiffins are supplied at different places like offices, hostels, homes and many other places.

6. *Bag Making*

A large scale production of the bags was started since the institution was started. Cloth and Jute bags are produced according to the orders placed.

7. *Stitching*

Under this cutting stitching and of different clothes is taught. Patch work and embroidery work is also taught.

8. *Educational Activities*

Includes personality development classes, vocational courses etc. it also organizes seminars.

9. *Awareness Camps*

This institution organizes awareness camps on different subject for bringing awareness among women regarding their important role in the family, child care, health of women, etc.

10. *Dry Nasta Making*

Food packets and nasta is supplied to the offices, institutions and factories.

11. *Food for Children*

Nutritious food which is liked by the children is supplied to different anganwadi working under ICDS scheme.

12. *Day Care Centre*

Women are trained to start & work in the day care centers.

13. *Educational Activities*

Includes personality development classes, Vocational courses, etc... Seminars are organized from time to time covering different topics.

Recently, this institution has become an award winning institution. It is the first institution to receive the shield from Gujarat State Cooperative Sangh. The institution is developing rapidly and has plans to start many other activities for women and children.

HIGHLIGHTS OF THE INSTITUTION

Vikas Jyot offers variety of programmes keeping the campus vibrant with activities and focusing the institution as trend setter in leading needy women to a life of dignity and self respect helping them project their independent identity.

10
BARODA CITIZEN COUNCIL

Year of Establishment

1966

Address

Baroda Citizen Council
Above Health Museum
Sayajibaug, Vadodara–18.
India.
Phone: 0265–2793415, 2328091, 2320944.
Fax: 0265–2339298, 2794596.
Email: bcc.uwb@iwbdq.iwbbs.net

INTRODUCTION

It's a Non Government Organization working for the community development. It is working for the people, with the people and by the people. Its motto is self help–self reliance. The council is recognized as a research body by Department of Science & Technology, Government of India, New Delhi Central & State Governments, National & International Development Agencies.

OBJECTIVES

- To identify socio–economic and civic problems and to encourage various groups, especially the urban poor, in solving them.
- To develop leadership, competence and faith of people in themselves. To activise social organizations and enthuse members to work together. To disseminate correct information and make effective use of available resources.
- To provide a forum through which voluntary organizations at the city level can increase their effectiveness through mutual help.
- To co–operate with local bodies, voluntary and government agencies in tackling city level problems especially of the economically and socially weaker sections of the society.

ACTIVITIES

1. Education Sector

- Programme for School Dropouts.
- Pre–Schooling–Target Group: Children Between 3 to 6 years.
- School Admissions–Target Group: Children of 6 years.
- Non–Formal Education for illiterates.
- Programmes for School Readiness of the Children.
- Recreation Center.

- Providing various facilities such as Uniforms, Shoes, Bus / Railway Passes, School Fees etc. at Nominal Charges.

  Supplementary Education: The volunteers of the Council holds coaching classes in the Central Area of the city and some part of the Slums & supplementary education is provided.

2. ***Economic Sector***

- Skill Development Programme for Youth.
- Short Duration Training Programme for Women.
- Saving and Credit Association.
- Providing Loans for Shelter Improvement, Income Generation, Hospitalization, Low Cost Sanitation, Education etc.

3. ***Environmental Sector***

- Water Supply.
- Solid Waste Management.
- Water Born Disease.
- Gas Project.
- Traffic Education.
- Health Facilities.
- Cleanliness Information.

4. ***Health Sector***

- Health Talks.
- Immunization of Childrens
- Reproductive Health & Sexuality.
- Health Check–Up of Senior Citizen Living in Slums.

5. ***Special Programmes***

For all the special programmes which are listed below, individual approach is used these special programmes are also called project programmes.

- Urban disaster mitigation programmes, towards clean Baroda.
- Community development / personality development training programme.
- Programmes for disabled children.

11
BHASHA RESEARCH & PUBLICATION CENTRE

Year of Establishment

1996.

Address

6, United Avenue, Near Dinesh Mills,
Vadodara – 390007, India.
Telefax: 0265–2331130.

INTRODUCTION

A voluntary organization engaged in documentation, study and promotion of Tribal Arts, Literature and Cultures.

ACTIVITIES

Verrier Elwin Memorial Lectures

An annual Verrier Elwin Memorial Lecture Series has been established in the memory of Elwin, who was the architect of India's national policy on tribal development. The first Elwin Lecture was delivered by the eminent painter and art critic Prof. K.G. Subramanyan, formerly Professor at Santiniketan, Viswabharti. The Lecture was delivered at Vadodara on January 25, 1997. It has been published by Bhasha Centre.

Publications

The Bhasha Centre brings out a bimonthly periodical, "Dhol" in tribal languages of Gujarat and Maharashtra. The first issue of "Dhol" was published in September 1997.

A series of volumes on The Languages of India is also published Prof. D.D. Mahulkar is the General Editor of the Series.

The Scope of Activities Establishment

- Baroda Office
- Tejgadh Office
- Dang Branch
- Shahada Branch
- Computer Units at Chhota Udpur and Pavi–Jetpur

Tejgadh Campus

Library, Auditorium, Workshop Hall, Residency Blocks, Archives.

- Preparation of Directory of Indian Scholars involved in the study of tribal languages and culture.
- Seminar on the Future of Marathi held at Vadodara in January 1996.
- Workshop on Tribal Literature at Saputara, Dist. Dangs, in March 1996.
- Workshop on Understanding Tribal Imagination in collaboration with the department of Art History and Aesthetics, Faculty of Fine Arts at the M. S. University of Baroda on December 20, 21, 22, 1996.
- National Seminar on Interpreting Literature & Oral Traditions at Tejgadh and Chhota Udaipur, January 18, 19, 20, 1997.
- Verrier Elwin Lecture by Prof. K. G. Subramanyan in Vadodara on January 25, 1997.
- Workshop on Documentation of Tribal Culture on March 22, 23, 24, 1997 at Tejgadh.

- Workshop at Saputara, Dist. Dangs, on April 5 & 6, 1997 to finalise the Centre's proposed magazine 'Dhol'. Editorial Committee of 'Dhol' participated in the workshop.

HIGHLIGHTS OF BHASHA

The Bhasha Centre proposes to create a unique Training and Research Institute at Tejgadh, a tribal village situated 90 Km east of Baroda. The centre has acquired, for this purpose, a plot of 10 acres situated in beautiful natural surroundings at the foothills of the Aravallis, the heartland of tribal communities in Gujarat.

The Tejgadh Campus has an open–air auditorium carved into a single rock surface, several small water bodies and a perennial stream flowing down the rocky hill at the back of the campus, seminar and workshop spaces, a settlement of houses built in tribal architectural styles from all parts of India (and even outside), a world–class library, and training cells for tribal artists. In addition to the above, the Tejgadh Campus has residency blocks for visiting and resident scholars.

The extension work at Tejgadh involves a massive plantation drive in nearby villages and beautification of Tejgadh village.

The purpose in creating such an institution is to initiate serious academic interest in the study of indigenous cultures as also to create the supporting infrastructure of archives and documentation cells for the indigenous languages, cultures and the arts.

There are different living languages spoken in India by tribal and linguistic minority communities. These languages, the cultural practices developed through them and the communities themselves are rapidly declining. They are an important component not only of Indian heritage but also of the global heritage. Can we leave them alone to their fate of aphasia?

12
JAMUNA SANSKRUTI KENDRA

Year of Establishment

1995

Address

Sanstha Vasahat,
Raopura,
Vadodara–390001.

INTRODUCTION

For the welfare of women in society and personal development of women this NGO has been working with these following objectives.

OBJECTIVES

- To provide training in nursing, to women for their self independence.

- To provide legal advice to the women.

ACTIVITIES

- They are giving nursing training to the girls.
- Have legal Aid Centre to give guidance and advice to the women for the problems arisen in their life.
- They also give legal advice to the women at their door step in Baroda and out of Baroda.
- They organize legal Aid Shibir twice in a month and their main area covered till now are Waghodia Road, Harni Govind Nagar, etc.
- The key person of the institution Smt. Jamunaben Bhagat is giving training in nursing.

ADMINISTRATIVE STRUCTURE

Key Person/President

↓

General Manager

↓

Manager

↓

Legal Counselor

↓

Social Worker

↓

Helper

13
SHREE SEVA TIRTH

Year of Establishment

1979.

Address

Seva Tirth
Opp. Adarsh Nagar,
Near Swaminarayan Gurukul High School,
Opp. High Way No. 8, Tarsali Bypass,
Vadodara – 390009.
Phone: 0265–2646361.

INTRODUCTION

The foundation of Seva–Tirth was done by Mr. Purshottam Panchal. He is an engineer by profession. He was moved by the conditions of lepers and wanted to do something for them. He was felt for them so from 1969 he set out to work for them as an organisations with support from family and friends. He willingly joined the organisations like Baroda Citizen Council, Shram Mandir Trust and Gujarat Raktpit Nivaran Seva Sangh in 1978–79. To meet the need of lepers and disabled Seva–Tirth was established. Seva–Tirth is a part of Gujarat Raktpit Nivaran Seva–Sangh. It works without government grants and get funds and donation from public.

OBJECTIVES

- Service for Leprosy Patients and Disabled.
- Education of Health, Prevention of Deformity Training.
- Vocational Rehabilitation and Training Center.
- Action for Advancements.
- Treatment of Leprosy Patients.
- Integration of Wealth Services and Training.
- Rehabilitation of Leprosy Patients on Community.
- Takes Care of Leprosy Patients and Their Children.
- Help us for a Smile of Inmates.

ACTIVITIES

- Tailoring
- Agarbati Making
- Chalk Making
- Making Shoes
- Rakhi [in Season]
- Vegetable & Farm Work
- File Making
- Agricultural Activities
- Candle Making
- Quilt Making
- Book Binding
- Nursery & Green House

HIGHLIGHTS

The Sevatirth is very well maintained organisation they have residential blocks for the people who come to take part in different vocational activities can stay in the hostel which is specially made for the disabled.

14
VADODARA DISTRICT AIDS CONTROL SOCIETY

Year of Establishment

1999

Address

Dr. Rajiv Gupta
GF Blue Chip Building,
Opp. Vakal Seva Kendra,
B/h Rajshree Cinema,
Sayajigunj, Vadodara.

INTRODUCTION

This organization helps in arranging blood donation programme, making programmes or seminars on AIDS day and VDACS is involved with Suraktam Blood Bank.

- Street plays are arranged to spread awareness.
- Information regarding what is AIDS, its symptoms, how it spread and why it is serious.
- Different NGO's collaborate with VDACS like Suraktam Society, Women's Club, Semi Government Department, Union of Industrial Unit, etc.
- Facilities like latest equipments for treatment, free treatment provided to HIV persons.
- They encourage young generation for blood donation and provides pure blood which is free from HIV.

15
NYEE ROSHNI DEADDICTION CENTER

Year of Establishment

1990

OBJECTIVES

- Creating awareness and running counseling center for drug addicts.
- To identify risk groups in different parts of Baroda city.
- To counsel and motivate drug addicts to come out of the addiction and also educate their families.
- To prepare pamphlets leaflets and posters to create awareness in the society.
- To motivate people to study and educate themselves with life goals in accordance with Gandhiji's philosophy and teachings.

ACTIVITIES

They organize workshops and campaigns to spread messages for deaddication. Most of the programmes are done in the slums of Baroda like Govind nagar, Kishanwadi, Jalaram Nagar and Kalyan Nagar and some pockets of rural areas like Channi, Dasharath, Dumad, Tarsali. They use different types of counseling like individual, family and group.

They have future plan for:

- Vocational rehabilitation center for the families of drug addicts.
- Day care centers for drug addicts.
- Home for the aged
- Research projects in the field of prevention of drug abuse.

16
OLAKH
(OLAKH MEANS IDENTITY)

Year of Establishment

1996

Address

24 Jalaram Park,
Opp. Lalbahadur Shastry Vidhayala,
Harni Road,
Vadodara.
Phone: 0265–2486487, 2466037.

INTRODUCTION

Its aim is to create physical and emotional spaces for women to share, learn and grow with pride and dignity to assert identities and confidence – Moto is "Together we aspire to reflect and listen to each other non–judgmentally and develop friendship we often dream about".

OBJECTIVES

- Create a safe supportive, confidential and non–judgemental space for women and girls to share information, knowledge and support.
- Challenge the existing discriminatory value systems and practices. They have a good resource base to share, network, interface and create avenues for self assertion, self worth and self dignity.
- Promote feminist literature, which covers social, political cultural and economic spheres.
- Provides feminist counseling to empower women experiencing violence, discrimination, sexual abuse and emotional and mental distress.
- Empower adolescent and women through education and life skill building, conduct issue based capacity building, trainings and workshops to spread feminist consciousness.
- Campaign for lobbying and advocacy at national and regional level initiate the process of social reconciliation, harmony and development by strengthening collective leadership within community with gender perspective.

TARGET GROUP

Children, adolescent girl, women, men and old age.

ACTIVITIES

- Networking and support group and single women.
- Action based research on various issues.
- Workshops, dialogue, seminars and trainings.
- Campaigns in urban and rural areas.
- Advocacy.

Different teaching aids like leaflets, pamphlets, film shows, games are used in conducting different activities.

17
SAHIYAR (STREE SANGTHAN)

Year of Establishment

1984

Address

G–3, Shivanjali Flats,
Near Navjeevan, Ajwa Road,
Baroda–19, Gujarat, India.
Phone: 0265–2513482
Email: sahiyar@softhome.net

INTRODUCTION

Sahiyar, which means STREE NI SAHELI. It is a non–government organization. It was started in 1984 with four members. And now they are having more than 50 members working together. Sahiyar was started by some women, who became aware about the secondary status of women in society by their own experiences as women.

The organization was started by women and for women who felt the need to start a organization for women. It believes that struggle for emancipation (freedom from struggle) is an integral part of struggle from emancipation of human race.

OBJECTIVES

- To work towards a society in which women have equal status and recognition as a human being.
- To create awareness about legal rights and laws given to women.
- To give information about women's health and ways to improve health.
- To create self–employment among women by training them in income generation activities.

- To support women who face violence, sexual exploitation, injustice, etc. by providing counseling, moral and emotional support also.
- To organize discussions, film shows and other cultural activities about issues faced by women.
- For overall development of children, activities centers are established so that child can develop in various field.

THRUST AREAS

- Sahiyar generally deals with women who are from slum areas and women who face discrimination.
- Adolescent girls are given importance, as they need counseling about Reproductive Health.
- Children need special attention, so they are also given help.

ACTIVITIES

1. *Awareness Programmes*

- Street plays, awareness songs, awareness garbas, poster exhibition, film shows are some of the medium they use for people's participation.
- Demonstrations, public meetings, rally, wall paintings, human chain, etc. are organized to attract attention of people on urgent issues of violence or atrocities.
- Students are involved through group discussion, essay writing, workshop, camps, etc.
- Gender sensitization training for various groups like activities of other NGOs, trade unions, etc.
- Publication of leaflets, pamphlets, booklets, newsletters, etc.
- Library and documentations of women's issues.

2. *Campaigns*

- Protest campaigns on issues like rape and particularly custodial rape, female feticide, dowry, etc.
- Other than that Sahiyar participate in and organize communalism, casteism and religious fundamentalism.
- Activities like fact finding during communal riots was undertaken by them..

18
SHRI JALARAM SEVA SAMAJ TRUST

Year of Establishment

1987

Address

Shri Jalaram Mandir
Jalaram Marg,
Karelibaug, Vadodara–18.
Phone: 0265–2462050.

Local Branches

1. Jalaram Seva Sadan, Near Ghelani Petrol Pump, Nizampura, Vadodara–390002.
2. Harni–Varasia Ring Road, Vadodara-390006.

INTRODUCTION

Founder of the organization was Late Shri Chimanbhai Patel.

OBJECTIVES

- To provide basic necessities to the under privileged adults in terms of their health, education, food, social welfare.
- To take care of all the age group members for their health, happiness, welfare, etc. irrespective of the caste / religion.
- To give basic knowledge about physical and mental health problems.

MAIN ACTIVITIES

Health/Medical

- To take care of all the age group members for their health, happiness, welfare, etc. irrespective of their caste / religion.
- To give basic knowledge about physical and mental health problems.
- Blood Pressure camp.
- Regularly they organize Health (Medical) checkup of the members.
- Diabetes detection camps are organized at regular interval.
- Ayurvedic clinic is being run by the trust.
- Trust also provides treatment by a team of renowned specialist doctors to the patients at a very nominal rate under the name of "Shri Jalaram Nidan Kendra".
- In the area of Nizampura, trust has also opened an old age home which is been administered by "Shri Jalaram Seva Sadan".

Food Facility

The trust has followed the motto of Shri Jalaram Bapa that is "Serve food to the hungry".

- With the help of this facility, the trust provides sufficient food to the big hospitals in our city.
- During the most difficult times like flood, draught or any such natural accidents this trust tries to provide food at that time to the poor and needy.

- They help those who are severely poor, who are from helpless families or needy.

19
DISHA

Address

Disha–Information, Guidance and Rehabilitation
320, Race Course Towers, Gotri Road,
Vadodara–390 007.
Phone & Fax: 0265–300059,
Email: dishacentre@india.com

INTRODUCTION

Disha is a Vadodara based voluntary organisation, working for the well–being of people born with disabilities, as well as those who have acquired physical mental and/or sensory impairment.

Disha (meaning Direction in Hindi), was established with a mission to provide a channelised path, primarily for differently abled persons and also to facilitate the process of constructively integrating them in society. It also acts as a support group for parents, siblings and anyone working directly or indirectly with them.

Apart from creating avenues and guiding the disabled onto newer and self–sufficient paths, disha believes in tapping the immense knowledge and experience of like institutions and organisations through several networking programmes.

Disha is a one of a kind institution having initiated a fresh approach to overviewing the whole attitude toward the disabled and formulating better ways of giving them a fulfilling life.

Disha adopts different forums and media to facilitate empowerment of persons with disability. The significant ones are:

- Campaigns
- Workshops
- Seminars
- Discussion
- Publications
- Confereces

Disha looks forward to your support and generosity to keep its activities going. You are welcome to contribute in cash or kind. Your voluntary help will go a long way in bringing a smile to many a face. (Donations are exempt under Section 80 G Income Tax Act 1961).

HIGHLIGHTS

Guidance and Counseling

- Provides psychiatric intervention, psychological evaluation and support.
- Training and counseling for parents and siblings of differently abled persons.

Information/Sensitization

- Acts as a node for disseminating information for differently abled persons, encompassing all aspects of their lives.
- Creates awareness, exposing public and media to rights, needs and capabilities of persons with disabilities.
- Provides referred services.
- Has a detailed databank of all local government and non–government organisations that provide various services to the disabled.

Therapy and Rehabilitation

- Organising recreation and leisure activities using art, music and drama as thereuptic intervention.
- Medical rehabilitation and consultancy.
- Access to assistive devices and corrective surgeries.

Networking

- The thrust of this organisation is on networking, establishing ties and strengthening existing ones with other groups to maximize services for the disabled.
- Involving people with disabilities and their care providers in various aspects to our work.

Vocational Training

- Job placement and/or income generating activities.
- We make sure that all those registered with Disha are provided adequate help and services, based on individual need.

Advocacy

- Facilitating increased self–advocacy by people with disability.
- Working towards bringing about policy changes with active participation of people with disability.

GOALS

- Developing holistic and cost effective services and prevention strategies that are suitable for a developing country like ours.
- Use the abundance of resources and motivated people available in the community to enhance capabilities of the disabled.

MISSION

- Create the possibility for an optimum quality of life for the disabled.
- Facilitate empowerment of persons with disability, their families and care givers by honouring and developing their capabilities rather than focusing on their disabilities.

- Striving to express the highest ideas in service, work ethics, management, interpersonal relations and policy making.

20
ARPAN

Address

"ARPAN"
4, Amaravati Society–1,
Opp. GEB Station,
Gotri Road, Baroda–390 021
Phone: 0265–321758.

INTRODUCTION

Perhaps the only one of its kind in India, "ARPAN" a Diagnostic, & Development Centre for Multiple Handicapped Children was established in Baroda in December, 1993.

"ARPAN" renders a unique Centre and Home based integrated service–oriented programme for children with multiple disability. A multidimensional approach helps the disabled children in their Language, Social, Cognitive and Motor Development.

HIGHLIGHTS

- The child's family is used as the fulcrum of change. Parental participation is encouraged during therapy programmes.
- A multi–disciplinary team is available under one roof for assessment and planning the intervention programme for each child.
- Community awareness programmes for prevention and early detection of childhood disability and intervention are conducted.

STAFF

1. Consultant Pediatrician 2. Physiotherapist 3. Clinical Psychologist 4. Special Educators 5. Pediatric Rehabilitation 6. Speech Therapist 7. Play Therapist 8. Vocational Rehabilitation Supervisor 9. Art Therapist 10. Community Health Workers.

There are also a panel of specialists such as:

- Ophthalmic Surgeon
- Orthopaedic Surgeon
- ENT Surgeon
- Neurologist
- Neurosurgeon
- Orthotitian... all of whom assess and diagnose children sent from ARPAN at concessional rates.

The centre is headed by a Director supported by a Dy. Director and Programme Co–ordinator. The counsel of an Advisor is also available.

WE DREAM OF

- Being able to care for as many handicapped children as possible.
- Expanding our activities and staff.
- Adding more vocational programmes for older handicapped children.
- Having a more systematic transport arrangement.
- A full fledged institute for SPECIAL CHILDREN, who are differently abled.

21
SHROFFS FOUNDATION TRUST

Year of Establishment

1980

Address

SHROFF FOUNDATION TRUST
At & Post Kalali
Taluka & Dist. Vadodara–390 012.
Phone: 0265–2680702, 2680061.

INTRODUCTION

The Shroffs Foundation Trust was instituted in 1980 as a philanthropic endeavor of the Shroff family, a well–known industrial and business group of Gujarat. It is a non–government organization (NGO) with headquarters at Kalali, near Vadodara. It is registered under the Public Charitable Trust Act and the Foreign Contributions Regulation Act (FCRA).

Over the last two decades, the Trust has earned recognition for is result–oriented work in rural development and poverty alleviation by various Departments of the Government of Gujarat such as Rural Development, Social Defense, Women and Children. The Trust receives funds from the Central and State Governments, National and International funding agencies, and private donors.

The project areas of the Trust are the drought–prone and flood–prone sectors in Gujarat state. Such lands are home to the indigenous tribals and rural poor whose lives are a daily struggle for existence. These lands are spread over Vadodara and Kutch districts. As of now, the Trust's activist reach more than 50,000 families (2,52,245 persons) in 164 villages in these districts. These are implemented from project offices in Kalali, Ekalbara, Rangpur and Hodko–Kutch centres.

Shroff Foundation Trust is a Non Government Organisation, work in the areas of extension, Adult and Social Education. Adult Education is one of the area to be served for Shroff Foundation Trust. It plays active role in promoting functional literacy among rural and tribal women.

It has developed the resource center for the tribal learners through which information regarding health and social issues can be imparted.

- Shroff Foundation works for the self independence of women by taking up projects like handicrafts with a view to provide them alternative economic opportunity and prevent migration.
- Trust has also developed anganwadies for children of those women who want to join literacy and economic development programmes.
- Trust open their doors for the schools and universities students to take the advantage of their reading materials, charts, posters, models, games, which are developed by them in the area of education, health and agriculture.
- This NGO tries to imbibe moral and ethical value in the youth of technical institutes located near tribal areas.
- They are playing a very important role in community development and social education.
- Farmers training programmes are also promoted by the Trust to maximize the effective agricultural output.

MISSION

"To assist village populations in improving their productivity, efficiency and creativity through services and goodwill with the support of industries, academic institutions, voluntary and government agencies and with the guidance of competent and committed experts, knowledge inputs and effective management of available resources, such as land, water, energy, livestock and people; to upgrade the quality of life of each villager man, woman, child, youth, aged through their involvement, interest and initiative."

Index